THE DIALECTICS OF SHOPPING

THE LEWIS HENRY MORGAN LECTURES / 1998

presented at
The University of Rochester
Rochester, New York

• DANIEL MILLER

THE DIALECTICS of SHOPPING

Foreword by ANTHONY T. CARTER

THE UNIVERSITY OF CHICAGO PRESS   CHICAGO AND LONDON

DANIEL MILLER is professor of anthropology of University College London. He is the author of *A Theory about Shopping,* coauthor of *The Internet: An Ethnographic Approach,* and editor of *Material Cultures: Why Some Things Matter.*

ANTHONY T. CARTER is professor of anthropology at University of Rochester.

The University of Chicago Press, Chicago 60637
The University of Chicago Press, Ltd., London
© 2001 by The University of Chicago
All rights reserved. Published 2001
Printed in the United States of America
10 09 08 07 06 05 04 03 02 01   1 2 3 4 5

ISBN: 0-226-52646-1 (cloth)
        0-226-52648-8 (paper)

Library of Congress Cataloging-in-Publication Data

Miller, Daniel, 1954–
    The dialectics of shopping / Daniel Miller ; foreword by Anthony Carter.
        p.   cm. — (The Lewis Henry Morgan lectures)
    Includes bibliographical references and index.
    ISBN 0-226-52646-1 (cloth : alk. paper) — ISBN 0-226-52648-8 (pbk. : alk. paper)
    1. Shopping. I. Title. II. Series.
TX335 .M535   2001
306.3′4–dc21   00-011145

⊗ The paper used in this publication meets the minimum requirements of the American National Standard for Information Sciences—Permanence of Paper for Printed Library Materials, ANSI Z39.48-1992.

• To Hannah, Sabrina, Jonathan, and Brandon

CONTENTS

 **FOREWORD**

Daniel Miller delivered the Lewis Henry Morgan Lectures on which this book is based at the University of Rochester in October 1998. They were the thirty-sixth in a series that began in 1963. The thirty-eighth Morgan Lectures will be delivered in November 2000, by Ulf Hannerz.

The lectures honor Lewis Henry Morgan. In addition to his role in the creation of modern anthropology, Morgan was a prominent Rochester attorney. Though he never found it necessary to accept a formal academic position, he was connected with the University of Rochester from its beginning. A major early benefactor, he left the university money for a women's college as well as his manuscripts and library. Until the creation of the Morgan Lectures, however, the only memorial to him at the University was a residence hall wing named in his honor.

Publication of *The Dialectics of Shopping* marks two major changes in the Morgan Lectures. It is the first volume in the series published by the University of Chicago Press in a new arrangement that returns the Morgan Lectures to the United States and ensures a solid financial basis for their future. It also is the first to be published since we have made an adjustment in the focus of the lectures. In recent years we have sought out lecturers whose work is of interest to a broad range of disciplines in the social sciences and/or the humanities. By this we do not mean work that is itself interdisciplinary; it is our intent to remain firmly anchored in anthropology and, more especially, in richly described ethnography. Rather, we are interested in exploring the shape of conversations across disciplinary boundaries and the ways in which anthropology acts as interlocutor in such conversations.

Toward the end of *The Dialectics of Shopping*, Daniel Miller observes that the challenge of anthropology "is to stay onboard a wild roller coaster that plunges theory back into the muddy waters of everyday life and then lunges upward again to gain the perspective of philosophical generalities" (203). Unlike most roller coasters, which start out by slowly climbing to an enormous height, plummet to throat-stopping lows, and then oscillate through ever closer limits before gliding to a stop just where they began, Miller's book gently, oscillates through ever expanding limits before hurtling to a theoretical peak where we are depostited exhilarated and refreshed. It is a good ride. More than worth the price of admission.

The first small decline into the murk of everyday life takes us on a variety of North London shopping expeditions (chapter 2). The landscape of high streets, shopping parades, maisonettes, council housing, and goods "on offer" has the spice of foreign travel for U.S. readers, but the concerns of the shoppers—finding an appropriate outfit for a teenage niece, sensible shoes for oneself, or food for one's pet—are familiar enough. We recognize ourselves in these shoppers. The first small climb toward a philosophical perspective has three major components. Against the conventional view that shopping is about the free choice of autonomous individuals who are alienated from society or, alternatively, fending off its pressures, Miller suggests that it is about the creation and maintenace of relationships. Kinship and the family, here including relationships with the self and with pets, are grounded in and continually recreated through material relations, the consumption of goods used to provision households. But the "labor of love" (53) we put into shopping is caught up in a "dialectical tension" between normative discourses concerning categories of kin and the particularity of the persons in whom our experience of kinship is embodied; everyday shopping is a practice through which people try to resolve these contradictions. If the last of these observations continues themes developed in Miller's earlier publications on shopping, the first indexes Dumont's work on the ideology of individualism and the "sociological apperception," while the second engages the arguments of Leach and Tambiah concerning kinship as a language about property relations.

The second, somewhat larger, drop into the nitty-gritty of everyday life (chapter 3) takes us on a tour of the shops on and in the vicinity of Jay Road, Miller's nondescript North London street, many now owned and/or operated by Asian immigrants; a variety of new supermarkets in the vicinity; and Ibis Pond, a nearby upscale shopping district. The local shops may evoke a sense of cultural and social difference for the U.S. reader, partly because the variety of shops—for example, neighborhood butchers and post offices—are now uncommon in this country and also because so many of us use cars to shop in enormous suburban malls. But those of us who do live or could imagine living in a neighborhood like Brooklyn's Sunset Park and shopping on foot, will find the milieu more familiar. Most of those who buy or read this book will, I imagine, have an Ibis Pond in their shopping routines. And the key issue in chapter 3—the relationship between shops, shopping, and community—will be familiar to anyone who has been concerned with the effects of Barnes & Noble or Amazon.com on her neighborhood bookstore or that of a new Wal-Mart megastore on the Main Street shops of surrounding small towns. The second, larger, but still gentle, climb to a phiosophical perspective addresses issues of community as refracted by class, race and ethnicity. Though the middle class imagines that local shops could and should be sites of convivial experiences of community, both racial antipathies and the quality and prices of goods available in most local shops drive them to the better class of supermarkets or Ibis Pond. And though the working class is imagined by the middle class, falsely as it turns out, to have a tradtional preference for the sociality once available in local shops, they too prefer the prices and quality of goods available in area supermarkets as well as interactions with supermarket employees with whom they share a common class and racial background. Local shopkeepers, who do indeed provide useful services and who are an important component of the urban economy, are trapped among these contradictions.

The third segment of Miller's roller coaster (chapter 4) begins with a drop into an examination of purchases that are informed by the shopper's sense of ethnic identity or her political or ethical positions and, and after leveling off for a moment, delves briefly into practices of product labeling. The American who regularly attempts to grow or, when this fails, purchases fresh sweet corn because it is connected with his Midwestern heartland identity or who now participates in the campaign by the Worker Rights Consortium and United Students Against Sweatshops against sweatshop-produced apparel bearing university logos will recognize these concerns. As in our own circles, there is quite a lot of talk about such shopping standards but remarkably little practice. Those who do consistently shop politically or ethically are thought a bit rigid and obsessed. And our difficulties are compounded by the manner in which government palms off product labeling to all too eager global corporations. The climb back to a philosophical perspective rewards us with the insight that the failure altruistic shopping derives from a contradiction between the inherent morality of shopping in which one practices thrift and sacrifices oneself for the benefit of one's family and discursive claims concerning the potential ethics of shopping in which one would sacrifice thrift in order to benefit others remote from oneself.

The penultimate curves in Miller's roller coaster are much sharper. We plunge through a brief ethnography of a local discount supermarket only to drop into a remarkable account of the twists and turns of corporate relations that takes us to the manuevers of Jardine Matheson Holdings Limited in response to the Chinese takeover of Hong Kong. The fate of the chain of discount supermarkets is disconnected from its relations with and knowledge of local populations of shoppers and is determined instead by the global operations of finance capital. The stomach-churning climb to a high philosophical vantage point offers the suggestion that the last two decades have seen an increasing virtualism in which models that "simulate the real world" have been replaced with models that "have the power to force the real world to change in the direction of the simulation" (168). This virtualism has allowed capital and other "alienating forces" to escape from the social arrangements that "tamed" them and forced them, to some degree, to attend to human welfare in twentieth-century welfare states.

This penultimate rise leads neither to another drop into ethnography nor to a restful glide toward a conventional summary, but instead provides the starting point for a final climb to challenging philosophical heights. In his concluding chapter, Miller turns to Hegel's *The Philosophy of Right*. Indeed, it is Miller's enduring interest in Hegel that generates the energy to propel his remarkable roller coaster. Here he draws on Hegel's dialectics of the activities we live and experience on a daily basis and the culturally specific "real" or ideal versions of those activities that would manifest the human reason, which would legitmate those activities that would make us "at home" in them. He draws as well on Hegel's interest in the several levels through which we go about our lives, here "kinship, community or neighborhood, civil society or . . . citizenship, and political economy" (183). Miller uses these elements of Hegel to tie together the diverse dialectical relations explored in the previous chapters to suggest a way to articulate micro-and macroperspectives and to sketch a way in which anthropology's focus on the particular can be made to speak to a concern with the universal. Perhaps even more interestingly, he uses Hegel to develop the "premise . . . that anthropology aspires to be an ethical profession" (181). This goes well beyond the usual requirements of profesional codes of ethics to do no harm. In addition to offering an analysis of conditions that prevent us from "getting real," Miller actually proposes a set of policies and economic arrangements that would enhance the viability of neighborhood shops and the experience of community that they might provide.

This is a most appropriate launch for the new direction of the Morgan Lectures. Largely as a result of Miller's work, conversations about shopping occupy a growing place in anthropology. They also engage anthropologist with scholars in economics, sociology, cultural studies, and history. Beyond academe, one can hear, too, the voices of political leaders, company officers, citizen activists, and just plain folks.

Anthony T. Carter, Editor
The Lewis Henry Morgan Lectures
19 July 2000

 ACKNOWLEDGMENTS

Comments on draft chapters have been generously contributed by several of my colleagues in my department, Alan Abramson, Mukulika Banerjee, Michael Rowlands, Charles Stewart, and Michael Stewart. I know I am very fortunate for having the Department of Anthropology at UCL as my context of work. I am equally grateful to colleagues in other departments and disciplines who have provided me with often detailed comments and criticisms, including Stephen Frosh, Paul du Gay, Keith Hart, Peter Jackson, Webb Keane, Don Slater, and Nigel Thrift. Meg Abdy helped me find my links with brokers and commented upon the section on retail. Neil Wrigley and Leigh Sparks provided essential criticism and corrections for chapter 5, as did Mark Mullen.

I found the format of the Morgan Lectures most congenial. To have several days of detailed criticism from colleagues who have had to read large amounts of one's work is most academics dream come true. I should also acknowledge the tremendous hospitality of Anthony Carter and all the staff at the Department of Anthropology, University of Rochester, especially Rob Foster. I am grateful for the detailed comments made both by them and the imported critics, Leora Auslander, Henry Rutz, and Brad Weiss. I am also grateful to Anne Pyburn, Rick Wilk, and Webb Keane, who hosted other parts of my U.S. visit. In this case, that cliché about the blame for errors being the author's but much of the credit for the positive aspects of this work going to others is entirely appropriate. Much of chapter 1, for example, was written as a direct response to comments made about lacunae in the subsequent ethnographic sections. I am also grateful to the authors of the reader reports submitted to the University of Chicago Press, and to Maia Melissa Rigas for her patient copyediting.

Most of those to whom I owe a debt cannot be named since they are my informants. I am enormously grateful to the many people who suffered my presence and attention and gave of their time in a manner I cannot feel sure I would have granted if the roles had been reversed. The fieldwork would have been a great deal more difficult (and also far less enjoyable) without the companionship of Alison Clarke. Although this volume was conceived outside of the larger project, the ethnography upon which it is based was funded as part of my contribution to a research study on consumption and identity funded by the Economic and Social Research Council. The writing up of this book was greatly facilitated by my appointment as British Academy Research Reader for the years 1998–2000.

INTRODUCTION

To write a book within the framework of the Morgan Lectures sets a challenge for the author: to be audacious in developing innovations to invigorate the spirit of anthropological inquiry, yet judicious in retaining the inherited strengths of the discipline. The topic of shopping may be viewed as a radical choice, elevating a much denigrated, mundane activity. To choose such a topic is an act of refusal, against the use of anthropology to separate a supposed authenticity of past or of small-scale societies from our own presumed inauthenticity. It opposes an anthropology misused to make us feel alienated by creating a myth of the "other" as the inalienable. But it takes from traditional ethnography a holistic approach, which makes shopping a lens through which we can search for new insights into the nature of our common humanity.

This book's subject is not just shopping, but more specifically, shopping in North London. This choice asserts the continued potential of anthropology for sites where we can have no expectation of homogeneity, community, or even history in any simple sense. It begins, appropriately enough for a Morgan Lectures series volume, with a chapter on kinship as revealed through an ethnography of shopping. But while there have been societies in which the topic of kinship sheds light on the very heart of institutions and even cosmology, in this setting kinship can be only the first level of inquiry. The next chapter confronts us with the street and neighborhood as a place where people live in juxtaposition, rather than in community, and shopping is analyzed as a means by which they tackle the discrepancy between an idealized context and an actual place. The third ethnographic chapter finds shopping deeply implicated in the awareness a North London population must have of its relationship to the larger world: both in relation to its own cosmopolitan nature and to the world itself as the environment for which we may or may not feel responsible. Shopping is also an activity that relates the shopper to the institutions that create the shops. For this reason, chapter 4 is not ethnographic. It is, instead, a study of those institutions that determine the retail facilities, which, because the shoppers have little or no say in their creation, cannot be understood directly from a study of the shoppers themselves.

The structure of these four chapters reveals the wider ambition of this book as a contribution to an agenda for anthropology. Perhaps it is most radical in what it seeks to retain from the history of anthropology. Holism is of value not because there ever was a social group that was bounded and autonomous, but because understanding social life involved attempting to encompass all that bears on society. And the more fragmented and disparate those influences, the more significant a discipline that continues to recognize that none of them lie outside the remit of our inquiries. So this is not a book in economic anthropology or the anthropology of religion. It is a book about shopping that treats commodities in the way Mauss treated the gift, as forms that implicate every aspect of social life, such that kinship and political economy are brought together within the same volume.

If there is one central claim to this book it is precisely that the more complex and unbounded our society becomes, the more we need the traditional holism of anthropology. This holism infuses the spirit of ethnography, which holds out the possibility that its topic of inquiry—in this case, shopping—might turn out to be about anything and everything. But the discipline cannot be reduced to methodology, and a second claim is that if we are not to be mere positivists identifying the world only with that we can observe, then a holistic inquiry must include that which lies outside of ethnography. So the inclusion of a chapter on political economy that is not ethnographic is intended to stake a clear claim that in contemporary anthropology, ethnography must always presuppose a critique of its own limitations. A third claim is evident through the structure of this book, which is that a holistic inquiry may be attempted by setting up gradations from the intimate world of domestic relationships to the impersonal abstractions of political economy.

The title of this book is not the study of shopping but the dialectics of shopping, and the term "dialectic" signifies, first, a fundamental finding and, second, the ultimate ambition behind this work. For chapters 2, 3, 4, and 5, the term "dialectic" stands for the centrality of contradiction in the processes involved in shopping. Within each of the four topics this contradiction takes on a specific form, but there are tensions shared by them all. Above all, there is the irresolvable tension between a growth of particularity that is associated with an equal growth in levels of generality. For example, over the last decade anthropologists have realized that for most people the more they see themselves as global the more we understand ourselves as local. I will reveal an analogous tension to be at the heart of kinship relations, and in the discrepancy between the ideal and practice of community. Shopping comes to be understood as a constant attempt to at least gain a respite from these tensions, which are never, ultimately, resolvable. In the area of political economy, however, where actual shoppers are divested of power, this tension is shown to be increasingly oppressive and dangerous.

While the term "dialectic" remains a relatively modest claim throughout these four chapters as a way of representing contradictions and tensions that make up the context for most shopping, the wider ambitions of this concept are the subject chapter 6. The topics of the four previous chapters are intended to loosely shadow the structure of another book, *The Philosophy of Right,* written by the philosopher most closely associated with the term "dialectics," that is, Hegel. Hegel is invoked as a means by which an enterprise that is older than anthropology itself might still be recognized as vanguard in its potential for recasting and making relevant the holistic tradition within anthropology. It is not just that society was never bounded and autonomous, but also that the task of encompassment, of understanding the influences and forces that bear on social life was never totalizing. The holistic in anthropology is not a goal that is to be finally achieved. Social life is dynamic, and just as shopping takes place within contradictions that are never ultimately resolved and in which it can only provide temporary and partial resolutions, exactly the same strictures apply to the process of anthropological understanding. It was never helpful to pit the discipline between relativism and science—as though understanding society was an aim that either could or couldn't be encompassed. It is precisely because there are never final explanations that the drive toward understanding is so pressing and constant. So the larger ambition of this book is to argue that the proper form of contemporary anthropological inquiry is dialectical. This approach would recognize that generality and particularity are generated by the same process—and see our humanity enhanced by our attempts to understand the myriad forces that give rise to us and that we in turn create. Understanding is heightened, not lessened, by our appreciation that is it constantly being made redundant by the dynamics of our world. That it was rarely seduced by the apparent immortality of scientific explanation is precisely what should give anthropology its maturity and relevance to stand against the immaturity of mere relativism and postmodernism.

A more parochial justification for the juxtaposition of dialectics and shopping comes from the trajectory of my own research. If this volume rests upon a loose connection to Hegel's later work, *The Philosophy of Right,* my first attempt to research consumption (1987) was based on Hegel's earlier work, *The Phenomenology of Spirit.* That book, *Material Culture and Mass Consumption,* had two aims. The first was to construct a vulgarized version of Hegel's concept of objectification as a means to transcend the dualism of subjects and objects. The second aim was to advocate a rethinking of consumption as a process by which people attempt to overcome their sense of alienation from the forces that create commodities. At that time, there was little sympathy for any approach to consumption that refused to regard it as other than merely the final outcome and symptom of capitalism. By contrast, today the problem is to rescue consumption from being seen as a mode for the free expression of the creative subject. Indeed, the reason why the topic of shopping was avoided for a considerable time was that it seemed to focus upon consumption as an act of individual choice from goods supplied by the market. For this reason, my first case study was a London council estate[1] (Miller 1988) in which consumption of state services was at issue, and my second case study was the collective appropriation of goods by Trinidad during the oil boom and recession (Miller 1994), followed by a study of the specificity of Trinidadian business (Miller 1997a). Although the latter study included an extensive analysis of shopping in Trinidad, the point made by these studies is that consumption is much more than individual choice set within a market system.

The ethnography of shopping in North London that provides the basis for this volume has also been the subject of two rather different prior treatments. Miller (1998a) focused upon an extended comparison between the study of shopping and anthropological theories of sacrifice. It approached shopping as a primary technology of love within modern relationships. Miller et al. (1998) was a collaborative research project aimed to study the use of space and place in two large shopping centers. By contrast, in the present volume the topic of shopping is reoriented toward the

---

1. Government-owned housing estate; see p. 6.

problem of articulating microperspectives such as family relationships and macroperspectives such as political economy.

The scope of this inquiry was never limited to any particular discipline, and the bulk of this book consists of a description and analysis of shopping in several contexts. I have tried to avoid obfuscation and disciplinary jargon in the hope that this text will be accessible to readers from a wide interdisciplinary audience. For this reason, my rather more dense points of articulation with discussions within anthropology are given in the form of an appendix to each ethnographic chapter. For the same reason, the more technical discussion of the use of terms such as "discourse" and "normativity" is provided as an appendix to this introductory chapter. It will also be evident that the task of the final chapter as summarized in the following paragraph tackles the topic at a more philosophical level. Chapters 2–5 do not depend upon this, although my hope is that many readers will come see the final chapter as the appropriate conclusion to the whole.

In *The Philosophy of Right* as in several other of his works, Hegel develops his ideas and ideals through a sequence of moments or levels. Each of these has a degree of autonomy but also transcends the previous moment. Those employed in the *The Philosophy of Right* are the family, civil society, and the state. In this volume, the chapters move from kinship to community, citizenship, and political economy. While each chapter, and indeed, each chapter's theoretical final section, has sufficient autonomy to be considered in their own right, there is also a logic to their development. Hegel considered that the fundamental problem of modernity was the increasing distance between particularity and universality and the forms of oppressive abstraction that sundered institutions from their original aim of serving human welfare. Hegel argued that philosophy itself had a major role in forcing us to recognize the ultimate unity within and between these. By analyzing each institution in terms of the forces that would sunder them, and thereby us, from our own humanity, Hegel created a philosophy and the basis also of an anthropology that is ethical precisely by being analytical. It underscores the oppression latent within the institutions we live by and in so doing brings us to consciousness of the threat they pose. On the basis of such an understanding, we may seek to ameliorate the problems of contradiction that are intrinsic to them. So chapter 6 is intended both to transcend the separation into four prior chapters but also to suggest ways of both understanding and intervening that are promoted by the consciousness generated by analysis.

The intention is also thereby to reconnect what have often been separated as macro- and microperspectives. After all, each chapter is concerned with the same people and the same street. Anthropological analysis may first be conducted through such semiautonomous levels and then address the significant connections between them. By insisting upon such ultimate connectedness rather than surrendering to the much easier sense of and representation of contemporary fragmentation, anthropology can, perhaps rather more effectively than philosophy, demonstrate the dangers of allowing micro- and macroperspectives to be imagined as though they were other than different perspectives on the same peoples' lives.

THE FIELDSITE

The street on which lived the bulk of seventy-six households who took part in this study was chosen because it was nondescript. One end of the street (here called Jay Road) includes around twenty shops. One side is dominated by government housing estates, although in Britain these do not have the same implication as do housing projects in the United States in that until a recent decline they represented around one-third of all British housing. Those located in this street would represent more salubrious accommodation than the more notorious "sink" estates that tend to be focused on in the media. The other side of the street includes maisonettes, which would cost a little below average house prices and other terraced housing that would be a little above average house prices. Although for the sake of simplicity I refer to "the street" throughout this volume, some of the side roads (and a couple of households beyond these) provided additional contributors to this research representing more substantial semidetached houses that, while well above average house prices, are not particularly wealthy. In short, the area represented housing that could be found throughout London. The aim was to study households of average incomes including a reasonable spread of both middle- and working-class households. I cannot characterize the street in any absolute sense of income or occupation, since it managed, as intended, to include a very wide variety. It was hard sometimes to see an elderly single person living on state support in a council estate flat where most welfare services have been withdrawn, and a middle-class household of professionals with children at private schools, as living on the same planet, let alone the same street; but they do, both here and on countless other streets in North London. This focus upon the average was intended to reduce any tendency to merely assume the significance of class as a factor in the analysis, although during fieldwork class turned out to be the single most important form of self-classification used by individuals and households to describe themselves in casual conversation.

The street is located in neither the inner city nor the outer suburbs and, as with much of metropolitan London, is not clearly "zoned." It is an area of often quite transient occupation, especially in the maisonettes, which tend to be occupied by families who aspire to a whole house but who are not yet in a position to afford the necessary mortgage. Once again, this is not untypical for a society in which residence in a particular house averages only four years in general. The area is highly cosmopolitan in terms of the number of languages spoken in the local primacy school, and the seventy-six households involved in this project included a wide range of backgrounds from West Indian, through Cypriot, Jewish, and South Asian to South American and West African. There was no dominant "ethnicity" other than the approximately forty English-born Christian households (the precise numbers would depend on quite how these definitions are used). The emphasis in the fieldwork was on shopping with women, although men were the primary or sole informant in fourteen households. The thirty-five households from the council estates were dominated by single-parent or single-person (mainly elderly) households while nuclear families dominated the private housing sector.

This ethnographic project formed part of a larger study of shopping and identity in collaboration with academics from human geography who employed focus groups and quantitative surveys based mainly at two associated shopping centers (see Miller et al. 1998). The ethnography itself was conducted as a joint piece of fieldwork with Alison Clarke (see Clarke 1998, forthcoming a, forthcoming b). My research focused upon formal shopping, while Clarke concentrated on other forms of provisioning such as tupperware parties (see Clarke 1999), car-boot sales, and the exchange of secondhand goods. In most cases we initially approached the households together but much of the subsequent work with these households was conducted separately.

The selection of a street as a unit of study was certainly influenced by a certain localized set of expectations about the nature of sociality. Whether or not the street exists as a community, the ideal that a street is where community naturally resides continues to have considerable resonance in Britain. On the whole, where U.S. soap operas and sitcoms might tend to focus upon relationships in the workplace as their premise, in Britain the dominant television soap operas are about "Coronation Street," "Brookside," or "Albert Square." Even within academic work, sociological community studies tended to focus upon streets (Young and Willmott 1962) as units of inquiry. There is also now considerable historical evidence for the significance of the street as a genuine core to identification with locality in British working-class culture (McKibbin 1998). This issue is discussed in more detail in chapter 3. As ethnographers, however, we never assumed that a street would necessarily be the relevant context for contemporary socialization, and I cannot claim to have been terribly surprised by our lack of evidence for any local community. But this history and ideology gives the field site a certain naturalizing quality such that it seemed quite straightforward to the participating shoppers that the grounds for their being asked to participate was that they lived in the street that had been selected for the research.

This resonance is also important in any attempt to describe the street in more experiential terms. If asked, most of the shoppers would probably reaffirm an image of the street that supported rather than detracted from the ideal street that "looked," at least superficially, like a key locus in their sociality and identity. For example, I suspect that they tend to picture it in summer rather than in winter. On a warm summer's day on the street, people are washing their cars, kids are playing in front of the estates, householders are working proudly on their front gardens. It may not be that there is any considerable social communication. The greetings and "how are you's" may be as tokenistic as ever. But the way they are said, the smiles that accompany them, would suggest that people are exchanging their common delight in and observation of the fact that, they are together in the public sphere of the street rather than at work or inside watching television. The ethnographer might well be tempted to report a thriving street community. Walking in a residential street in the United States without encountering another pedestrian reveals to me how much I take a certain level of street sociality in London for granted.

On the other hand, in the depths of winter the street seems largely empty even though it is not. Most people probably walk to work or at least to the local node of public transport rather than drive, which, along with the custom generated by the shops, means that one is rarely alone when walking along the street. Even in winter some kids still play around outside the estates. Still, in the experience of winter the depressed ethnographer would probably report on urban wastelands and the decay of street society. English people on the whole avoid any kind of eye contact that may appear aggressive or flirtatious. Apart from those summer days where friendliness is itself being exchanged, people often walk past at the same moment that they are giving out a greeting such that nothing could possibly follow other than a token return of "and how are you," although some more substantial gossip may be observed on occasion.

There are a number of other places where the inhabitants of this street can be found socializing. Indeed, a focus on the street has its obvious costs in excising other ways of telling stories about the experience of living in cities. For example, it misses the richly documented narratives of town life that may be found in Finnegan (1998). Of immense importance is the local primary school, which is not only where parents meet, but also where children create relationships that end up with negotiating who is coming over to visit or stay with whom. New middle-class mothers meet through the local National Childbirth Trust or similar groups and forge relationships, many of which may last. On the main estate some of the long-term inhabitants check that each other are well and whether they need help. At the same time, much of the socialization is negative. One estate is dominated by the conflict between single parents with teenage children and the other major presence, the elderly, who feel persecuted and often are persecuted by these teenagers. By contrast, another smaller estate occupied largely by migrants is distinctive in its atmosphere of shared sociality and friendly relationships between the tenants. Both Clarke and I tended to retreat there with some relief after hours spent trying to be friendly in a manner that often felt like franticly swimming against a rather cold tide.

From the point of view of the topic of this book the single most important location of interaction (and its conspicuous lack) is the parade of shops that occupies one end of the street. The use of these shops is described in detail in chapter 3. In terms of my field experience I was less likely to be involved with people just popping out to the local corner shop for some milk or sugar where the shop is more or less just an extension of the fridge or stock of provisions within the home. On occasion, this may involve chatting to a storekeeper or fellow shopper, especially where the shoppers have in part been driven there by boredom and isolation. Most often such shopping is carried out as quickly as possible, or vicariously through sending children whose swift return is often carefully monitored. I observed local shopping more often when it was part of a longer or larger shopping expedition that I accompanied. Quite often I would be walking with a pensioner who stopped by the local post office in order to pay some bill or obtain their weekly benefit, from where we would walk on to some larger shopping area where some of this benefit might be spent immediately. In the queue we might meet an elderly man with a walking frame. His string of medals pinned to his lapel and the fact that everyone else in the queue is studiously avoiding looking at him suggests that he is something of a "character." There are a few others who hang around the shops for company, even when shopkeepers try various ways to hint that they are not really wanted. A shop door being opened is more likely to expose one to a blast of conversation if one happens to be passing the hairdresser, or the betting shop, while the pub is more often mournfully quiet. One of the aims of chapter 3 is to provide a much fuller sense of this localized shopping, while Miller et al. (1998) traces the experience of the same peo-ple at a larger shopping center and a mall.

The methodology was ethnographic, that is, a year or more of research at a specific field site with a commitment to adapting oneself to the situa-tion and developing sensitivity to the people one is learning from. So methodology does not arise as something taken from textbooks, striving to be systematic and consistent as in most disciplines. Rather, it is a process that arises from the same task of learning about one's context. Ethnography, at least in our case, is a reflexive pursuit, which changes with the knowledge one gains. I started my research according to my prior expectations as a native-born North Londoner. We began "cold calling" households with only a leaflet that preceeded us to prepare them. Intro-ducing ourselves as a team provided Alison Clarke, my cofieldworker, with security and also a sense of security for the women whom I needed to per-suade to work with me. In many ways I subsequently learned to change my methods of research. For example, I came to realize how disconcerted English people became when an ethnographer appears on their doorstep in the morning. I would therefore drive my car to the street, and on a mo-bile phone I would then call householders from my car. As long as I had telephoned first and confirmed that it was all right for me to come around that morning, then the few minutes between my call and my arrival in which informants could "prepare themselves" seemed to make a consid-erable difference in the relationship that developed.

Similarly, if I felt there was a sense of distance created by a male accom-panying a female shopper, I may have discussed problems of parenting or cake decoration (my hobby) as a way of dissolving any latent sense of threat. Or if it was more appropriate to the woman concerned, the topic might have been their undergraduate degree in psychology and how it re-flected on trying to write an academic book about shopping. While shop-ping, my manner attempted to match that which was expected of me. If my companion seemed to prefer to shop uninterrupted, with me as mere observer a few paces behind, then that is what I did. More often shoppers preferred for me to come with them as the friend I tried to be, especially when we had already met on other occasions. In this case, I acted as I would normally act, sometimes helping people to choose the goods they would buy through giving an opinion when asked, as well as pushing trol-leys or baby buggies or stopping for cups of tea. Overall, the aim was to be good company and not particularly irritating. So rather than act consis-tently I tried to act specifically sensitive to the particular character of each individual or household. At the most extreme it might, for example, seem that getting fed up with an informant's indecision and interfering in what they chose to buy, would be an appalling lapse of fieldwork observation. This hardly ever happened, but if and when it did, I would argue it simply confirmed me as a natural shopping companion—that is, it occurred at a stage when just about any coshopper would have gotten fed up and interfered. I believe that this ultimately helped people to relax, to be forthcoming, and return more readily to their habitual forms of shopping.

Working in North London obviates some, though by no means all, of the problems raised by both Clifford (1997) and Gupta and Ferguson (1997) about the presuppositions that underlie the concept of a field site in anthropology. First, this site clearly includes many of the conditions of migration, travel, and diasporic life that have been excluded by some parochial field sites. For example, in chapter 4 the relevant context is often North London as a diaspora setting, where shoppers identify goods with their place of birth. Second, this population can hardly be regarded as constituting the same claims to community and homogeneity found in more traditional ethnographic settings. Working with such an extremely mixed population may have also helped us avoid assuming some simple social parameters and instead allowed our description of the population to emerge from the ethnography. The study of shopping provides more insights into topics such as the reproduction of class (Carrier and Heyman 1997), when class emerges as the result rather than the presumption of such research.

Discussing and accompanying shopping as part of an ethnography is an extended encounter that brings within the frame of inquiry friends and relations from other places and situations such as work. It is probably a positive sign that I feel I could more easily now write a book about the problems of parents trying to decide about schools for the children in this area than one on shopping, even though the former was never a topic of inquiry. The ethnography of shopping was undertaken as part of a larger project that included both quantitative questionnaires and focus groups (see Miller et al. 1998). But I will not pretend other than a bias toward the qualitative information gained from those ethnography. My results could also be directly compared with those of Alison Clarke, since we undertook our research mainly with the same families (see Miller et al. 1998; Clarke 1998, forthcoming a, forthcoming b).

Although the British ideology of the street as a proper unit of sociality was helpful in legitimating our fieldwork, this idealization did not reflect any actual community. In most such areas of North London, neighbors, often of many years' standing, may be found who have never exchanged more than a few words with one another and for whom the main relationship is one of hostility (a currently popular television series is called

Neighbours from Hell!). I have used the term "North London" somewhat tongue in cheek. No such place exists (except perhaps as a term of abuse from people living in South London!), and it, therefore, establishes the arbitrary nature of the field site as a representative group. This worked against any attempt to characterize the population by initially emphasizing a particular trait, such as ethnicity, age, or income. Instead, the ideal was to encounter whoever happened to live behind the closed doors. As fieldworkers, our commitment was to persuade as many people on the street to take part, so that households that might otherwise be excluded, for example, people who shun public representation or, conversely, who we don't particularly like to be with, would be included, as much as those who thrive on sociability and whose company we enjoyed.

The absence of any "categories" of households means that some of what can and cannot be said from the ethnography is fortuitous. There may be generalizations that may be made about gay shoppers as suggested in recent work by Mort (1996) and Humphery (1998, 191–92), but since no individuals represented themselves to us as such, I have nothing to say on such a topic. Our aim was never to treat individuals or households as token representations of prior categories. Although we worked with only 30 percent of the households in the street, this included 80 percent of those we approached to take part and who could have made themselves available. There was a bias in my work toward households that included people at home in the daytime, though this was partly redressed by Clarke, who spent more research time in evenings and weekends. The corollary was that we should take the effort to make the experience as pleasant as possible to all those taking part, often by trying to change our behavior and opinions to make ourselves more acceptable companions. Our aim was to learn from, not to challenge, our informants.

The ethnography is presented as a series of levels of generalization. I do not assume that either the diversity of the population was such that generalizations cannot be made, or the opposite, that the process of generalization can be assumed. In this project generalization is always in itself a finding of the study itself. In practice, the degree to which this is warranted varied enormously. Many households display highly idiosyncratic aspects of their experience and behavior, which therefore appear in anecdotal and exceptional form. The account given in Miller et al. (1998) tends to analyze this material in terms of certain core differences, for example, class, gender, and age. On the other hand, almost the entire content of Miller (1998a) consists of very high levels of generalization made about the population as a whole. This is defended within that volume on the grounds that, notwithstanding the diversity of origins, there were many discourses and practices in relation to shopping that were found to be extraordinarily common to the population of the street (see the discussion of discourse in the appendix to chapter 1). I presume that the more a finding may be generalized within the street the more likely it applies much more widely, but at present there is precious little additional ethnography available on shopping to make such extended generalizations (though see Falk and Campbell 1997; Humphery 1998; Miller et al. 1998, chapter 1, for literature reviews). One thing that may be said with some confidence is that the eventual unit of significance for such generalizations is unlikely to be that of North London!

Every choice made in fieldwork will have implications for the conclusions of the research, and I am sure I am only aware of some of these. Where I can acknowledge them they constitute a series of caveats to the volume as a whole. The bias toward daytime and weekday shopping has already been mentioned. Several other such instances are commented upon in the relevant chapters. For example, I note in chapter 2 that the concentration on shopping as the daily provisioning of everyday goods produces a different perspective on kinship than would have been the case if the focus had been on what in the United States are called "big-ticket" items such as the purchase of the house or car. Shopping as a topic tended to emphasize intrahousehold relations and especially couples and parent-child relations, while informal provisioning tended to focus more on women's networks beyond the home and the more extended family, which will therefore be a more significant focus of Clarke's publications than of this volume. No doubt there should be further caveats, but as with any academic study, I hope the following chapters will present the material with sufficient clarity that readers may draw conclusions that will complement and challenge mine.

Appendix

A DISCOURSE ON DISCOURSE

This book employs a number of terms and distinctions that have been used in diverse other contexts and are, therefore, subject to overlapping and inconsistent meanings. The primary dichotomies are those between discourse and practice, what is said and what is done, the universal and the particular, and the abstract and the concrete. The terms "discourse," "contradiction," and "normative" are also much to the fore. It might be helpful at this stage to provide some guide to what is intended and what is not intended by the use of these terms, since sometimes I wish to evoke colloquial as against academic literatures, while in other contexts it is a particular academic rather than colloquial meaning that is employed.

Overall, the best guide to the meaning of a term is the context and the consistency with which it is used. The meaning of a term is developed through the elaboration of its appropriate context of use. A good example of this may be found in the use of the term discourse within Seale's book *Constructing Death* (1998). Seale makes reference to many approaches to discourse but ultimately creates his own through the attempt to understand the experience of death in societies such as ours. Seale argues that at least for forms of dying that are often more extended, such as cancer, we call upon several developing discourses in order to make sense of our own and others' experiences. Some psychological discourses typically help people create narratives of the self they feel secure in and allow people, in effect, to become the key mourners within their own process of dying. Medicalized discourses, by contrast, are based more on routine practices that make less use of narrative structures but also present themselves as realms of meaning within which the experience being undergone makes sense and we can consider the options open to us. This logic of alternative discourses is then applied to other institutional representations, which can also become appropriated in certain cases. For example, Seale suggests that "the media discourses analysed in the present chapter can be understood as further emanations of dominant cultural scripts, which offer dying people and those facing loss ritualised opportunities to imagine that their experience belongs to a wide, indeed universal, community of care" (144).

My usage of the term discourse will differ from that of Seale in large part because my context differs. The discourses that appear in these chapters are less liable to be creations of heavily institutionalized formations, often derived from the state. In my case, they are as likely to be linked to commerce as to the state, or more often they may emerge from popular culture itself. But this does not in any way suggest they are forms of resistance to institutions, simply that, as I will come to suggest, institutions do not supply nearly enough discourses to satisfy the desire of the population for them. The meaning of the term "discourse" is, therefore, given by its usage within the book. For this reason, the term "discourse" needs to be free of its evocation of particular theories. I have no intention when using the term of invoking either the perspective associated with the work of Foucault or with recent work on "discourse analysis" (e.g., Burman and Parker 1993), although there may be times when my use overlaps with either or both of these.

In general, the term "discourse" is used here for the manner in which language and practice become routinized and externalized beyond the expressions of particular individuals and become, therefore, a common location for the standard generation of normative ideals and sentiments. So in chapter 3 the discourse on the corner shop is that set of general statements that people tend to bring forth, often without much reflection, since they have become the standard repertoire of comments on corner shops and may be found in media other than those of the voice of informants. Discourse tends to privilege language, although it may also be found manifested in a set of practices. Almost any relationship between these two may be encountered. In some cases, what people say about their actions is much more diverse and critical than the actions themselves. In another arena it is what people say that is conservative and almost automatic with little diversity or critical acumen, but their actions seem barely constrained by the discourse that is used to legitimate them. In some cases, the said and the done are entirely consistent and, in effect, continuous expressions of the same set of values, while in another arena they are entirely contradictory. Keane (1997) has provided a profound description of the similarities between material culture and language both in terms of the rituals of formalization that are applied to them and the way their materiality subverts attempts to control them by ritualization.

Where discourse creates the basis for the normative (which is by no means always the case), and if as has just been suggested, the normative is often something created by and sought for by subjects, then there is no clear relationship between discourse and power. Sometimes discourse and often the normative is an expression of or the form taken by power, but instances will be found in this book where this is clearly not the case. Sometimes discourse is constitutive, but while some theorists such as Thrift (see Leyshon and Thrift 1997, chapter 8; also Thrift 1996, 79–91, 126–34) see this as a definitional aspect of the term, there are instances in this volume of discourses that are constitutive of little other than themselves. An example of this is the environmentalist discourse described in chapter 4. Everyone knows about "Green" arguments and can reiterate them at suitable moments of legitimization, but hardly anyone internalizes them or acts upon them.

This may become clearer when the term "normative" is included in the argument. Here, as in its colloquial use, this implies much more than normal or typical. It implicates a pressure, most often a moral or consensual pressure, to behave according to the precepts being described. So a particular family structure or an ethic of consumption will often be normative. However, one of the main conclusions drawn from the ethnography flies in the face of the typical academic response to uncovering evidence for the normative, which is to assume that this represents an external pressure, often attributed to some massive power such as the state or capitalism, which is then assumed to act as a force pressurizing individuals toward conformity. By contrast, in this book the argument is made that the shoppers themselves are "normative seeking," that is, they consider that they have insufficient access to normative pressures, which they seek to either develop themselves or accrue from the media and from other people. So as in the case of Seale's book, there will be many instances of phenomena that can usefully be termed discourse or normative within this book, but both their form and consequences will vary and have to be accounted for within the terms of their context. A tight and prior definition of terms such as discourse, abstract, and normative can therefore constrain a potential contribution to the creative nuancing given to a crucial distinction.

THE DIALECTICS
OF KINSHIP

SHOPPING FOR RELATIONSHIPS

Susan[1] had planned to take me on a more "typical" shopping trip with her own two children, but as it turned out we had company in the form of two of her brother's seven children, who had been staying with her and wanted to stay on an extra week since they were enjoying the opportunity of being in London rather than at their rural home. For their part, they would have preferred to go to the more prestigious West End of London but settled for the large shopping complex around nearby Wood Green. The trip would be dominated by Susan's self-appointed task of buying clothes for one of the visitors—sixteen-year-old Joanna. Susan had decided that she might be best placed to intervene within the different desires and demands of her relatives. The two visitors had recently been staying with Susan's mother, who had complained to Susan regarding Joanna's clothes. These were castigated as being either too "ethnic" or too revealing (short skirts or see-through shirts). Susan could see trouble ahead, as they were all going to be together for a family holiday in Italy.

1. All names in this text have been changed to preserve the anonymity of the informants.

Susan was also concerned that Joanna should have some clothing that would not attract too much attention from Italian men, who she assumed were more predatory than English men. On the other hand, she did not see herself as particularly prurient and felt that there was little point buying clothing without some attention to her niece's sense of fashion. If the latter didn't approve the garment, it probably wouldn't be worn anyway. Joanna herself was not especially clothes conscious for a sixteen-year-old girl. To go shopping she wore a midthigh, black, fairly unpretentious dress.

Overall, Susan seemed pretty harassed throughout the shopping trip. This was due to a combination of factors: having to self-consciously mediate in an area in which she was inexperienced (her children being of a different age), not seeing herself as having any particular flair for fashion, even with respect to herself, and the constant demands of her own small children (not to mention an accompanying anthropologist). Nevertheless, her approach to the problem was skilled and effective. She came up with the idea of bicycling shorts as sufficiently fashionable and sexy to please her niece while from her point of view safer than a short summer dress or skirt. The top, however, was more of a problem. We were looking for a white blouse, but these seemed to vary between teenage shops that sold ones too much like crop tops and the rather dowdy blouses found in older women's clothes shops. We found a blouse with "tails" intended to be knotted together at the front which looked suitable for a holiday, but the material was of poor quality and the size was wrong. Later we considered several others including one with shoulder pads but rejected them on various grounds. After half a dozen more shops we found another shirt designed to be knotted around the midriff, and made of better material, the right size, and on sale. Although she did not particularly like the buttons on the sleeves, Joanna was as happy with this as was Susan. In this case the result of a concerted effort has probably been a success. The choices made will hopefully prevent the development of those tensions that threatened to arise from various family members fears of the effects of a sixteen year old's sexuality on a family holiday in Italy. This was helped by the fact that this particular sixteen year old was rather acquiescent compared with many, although it is quite possible that this was because she was not on this occasion shopping within her own nuclear family and therefore less concerned to use the expedition as a chance to assert her growing autonomy as a teenager.

Against this success, however, were all sorts of little shopping details that constantly spoke to the frustrations individuals had in meeting their goals for the shopping trip. For example, Susan purchased a card for her own tenth wedding anniversary that was to be celebrated the next day. She found most of the cards utterly tasteless, but in the end settled for one of two cows nuzzling with pink mouths that had been made to look like hearts. She noted that the formal present for a tenth anniversary should be something made of pewter, but she and her husband Charles could not think of anything of pewter they wanted. Last year they had bought a coffee grinder, something that seemed a luxury compared with their current spending, as they were saving against the envisaged costs of moving. This anniversary they might buy some china. In general, she noted that Charles was not very good at celebrating such events, although she tried to reconcile herself to this on the grounds that "that is typical of men." It was clear that shopping for both card and present was imagined by her as something that should have been a positive aspect of a developing relationship (especially if he had gone out and bought them for her). But given Charles's failure to live up to her desire to use this as an opportunity for a romantic gesture, the actual buying of a card and gift were in practice last-minute embodiments of the emptiness of the purchases as a ritual and an obligation.

She had also planned to make the shopping attractive as an expedition based on a model she had developed from earlier shopping trips. Lunch at McDonald's served as the treat to compensate for her toddler having to spend the day shopping. But the toddler in question fell asleep in the buggy at just the wrong time and so missed this highlight of the outing. Her older son Jean was interested in a competition sponsored by Coca-Cola but since the token that told you whether you had won was inside the folded lid of the cup, he spilled the drink four times on his clothes while trying to look for it, and so overall this part of her plan for shopping was not a success.

Similarly, she was sensitive to her nephew James having had to spend so much time looking for clothes for his sister and was determined to get something for him as well. But she found that at thirteen years of age, he was too small to fit anything from the men's shops while he rejected the idea of clothes at the children's shops that might have fitted him. Anyway, by this time she was too tired to do anything but admit defeat and hope she could buy him something another day. James's sister Joanna was none too happy with him since they had decided to buy a card for Susan and her husband, but he had forgotten to keep this a secret from Susan.

The biggest failure of the expedition was Susan's attempt to involve her three-year-old son, Tommy. Before we started out, Tommy said that he enjoys shopping; Susan feels that he ought to be more involved in creating his own taste and choices. So when an opportunity arises at the supermarket she asks him to select something to eat. By this time Tommy is bored by shopping and by the idea of choosing. He simply says "yes" to a whole row of things in a manner that clearly shows he doesn't really mean it. Frustrated by this, she takes the last of his selections (some fish fillets) and buys them, choosing to thereby ignore the fact that they both know he didn't mean it. She notes to him that "I hope you will like it now you have chosen it," to which he replies that he doesn't like shopping with her since she always buys food he doesn't like. Her response to this accusation is, "There isn't much you do like, is there!" At this point he flings himself in tears half at the shop floor and half at his mother.

Another problem involved the family cat Suli, whose food has run out. Susan notes that Suli is the most fussy eater of all. This presents a problem, as Susan really can't be bothered at the moment with the long lines at Sainsbury's (a large supermarket) just to buy a special brand of cat food. She settles for a different cat food in what she herself probably regards as a victory of hope over experience.

Finally, in order to keep her own children happy, she spends some time in a toy shop, allowing them to run around and try things out. She does not actually want to buy anything but feels some token purchase is needed in order to compensate the shop for her having, in effect, used it as a zone of entertainment. But in the end she can't find anything cheap enough to count as the token purchase she had in mind.

There was nothing particularly special about this shopping expedition—quite the contrary. The problem it poses is how to draw some insights into the nature of contemporary relationships from such ethnographic encounters with shopping. The first problem is that generalizations are best made with respect to specific sets of relationships, but in the actual shopping trip a whole variety of relationships become tangled up. Then there is the complexity involved in shopping choices as an objectification of relationships. Often, as in the case of the food for Tommy, the question is not so much what is purchased as how the purchase reflects her desires for and expectations of a relationship. The particular choice of fish fillets is irrelevant. While the mother wanted her son to participate in the choice of his meal, he at this point wanted his mother to continue to take this responsibility but also to buy things he "liked." Here we see the contrast in projected ideals of the relationship. For a three year old, a mother by virtue of being a mother should simply "know" what he liked, while the mother, having experienced her own failure in this regard, feels that if a three year old can be so choosy then he should jolly well also express that autonomy through participation in the choice.

The situations that arose were far too complex to allow us to place the choices made within some clear grid of difference. Perhaps this works with aggregate statistics in the manner suggested by Bourdieu in his book *Distinction* (1984). If there is a gradation of difference that can be drawn from upper- to lower-class fractions then perhaps some tastes and some choices can find their niche along this line, but viewed ethnographically the issue is far more nuanced. Taste here is less a representation of difference than a process in the creation of relationships—that is, the choice of Joanna's blouse is constructed in the space between her own, her aunt's, and her grandmother's ideas.

There are also other players in this game of choice. At one point Susan has quite a long discussion with a woman about how a particular blouse looks on Joanna before she realized, shocked, that the woman talking so animatedly was not actually a shop assistant as she supposed but simply another shopper. This woman had an accent that suggested she comes from a country where fellow shoppers would be much less reticent about engaging in such a discussion with strangers than Susan felt appropriate in England. Susan and her family were visibly shocked by this culturally inappropriate scene.

Another unusual encounter was the presence of the anthropologist. I had paid for lunch, as part of the compensation for suffering my company, having asked to be allowed to do this before we ever agreed to go shopping. Nevertheless, Susan found this uncomfortable and was never quite at ease with me until toward the end of the shopping trip when she decided to buy me some sweets (which I had noted a fondness for) in the shape of some pink pigs.

The other major player on this outing is, of course, commerce. The commercial imperative is to foresee and fulfill the demands made by the shoppers. In practice, it is impossible for anyone to predict the precise configuration of desires constituted by the choices that had to be made. Indeed, we can start to see why, despite the vast number of goods available, it may be such a struggle to find anything that is just "right." In particular, there was no shop that catered to the niche occupied by young teenage males such as James, still wearing "child" size clothing but having the desire to be seen by others as an adult. Certainly any attempt to understand this shopping expedition solely from the perspective of commerce would include little of what seemed to matter to the participants.

The ethnography lends itself to a book that consists mainly of the "thick description" of such shopping expeditions. This would certainly help to develop an empathetic appreciation of the way relationships are involved in shopping, which was one of the primary aims of my previous

book on this topic (Miller 1998a). In this book, however, the aim is to situate this particular ethnography within several more academic dilemmas
that face contemporary anthropology. For this reason, the account now
moves up to a higher level of generalization based on abstracting particular examples of relationships and considering them in turn, before turning to their contribution to the larger project of anthropological studies of
kinship. But I hope that throughout this chapter and indeed, throughout
the book as a whole, an impression is retained of Susan's shopping expedition such that it remains a testimony to the kinds of experience upon
which any generalization must be grounded. The focus of the chapter will
be on the two most important relationships that permeated this ethnography of shopping, that between partners and that between parents and
children. From that foundation the account moves on to an attempt to in-
corporate more problematic examples of relationships, such the construction of the self as a "relationship" and various forms of pseudorelationships.
At that point the account will have reached a level of generality through
which it can be situated within the more general trajectory of kinship
studies.

PARTNERS

One conclusion that may be drawn from the initial example of a shopping
expedition is that a great deal of shopping consists of one person envisaging a situation in which the act of shopping would resolve a tension between some normative model and what the actual person one is shopping
for appears to want. Susan and her relatives are dealing simultaneously
with "norms" about what sixteen-year-old girls, and her niece in particular, should and should not wear. Sometimes this works, as in the blouse
purchase. Other times, it fails. Another moment in this expedition
demonstrates how well this applied also to the particular relationship between partners. In the relationship between Susan and her husband
Charles, we have two irreconcilable norms. On the one hand, there is the
potential purchase that would live up to a normative ideal of how couples
should celebrate their tenth anniversary. Since, however, Charles fails to
live up to this ideal of romance, Susan falls back upon another normative
model, this time a model of how men are in general. Men in general are
viewed as rarely living up to romantic expectations, so that in failing to
achieve one norm at least Charles manages to appear typical of Susan's notion of what men are like. There are other such normative models avail-

able, for example, one that suggests that men have a tendency to buy things for wives and partners precisely to compensate for their lack of involvement in those aspects of the partnership desired by the woman.

Shopping thus highlights the way relationships in question are posed between a series of normative models and the particular relationship of concern. The plethora of items in the shops would allow any particular shopping decision to demonstrate a modern form of love that is based on a refusal of any given "norm." In modern love, affection is often thought to be "in the details." People are touched by a partner who is knowledgeable and sensitive enough to be able to select precisely the right garment for them; equally, a thoughtless choice is evidence that love has not been translated into the detailed effort demanded of it. To understand such individual choices demands paying considerable attention to the particular relationship at that particular moment. But shopping is equally often an expression of the many highly explicit norms of relationships that make the purchase an example of a genre rather than of the particular. Commerce finds it easier to provide for such normative genres, and the shops are full of suggestions as to how to shop for male or female partners in general.

It is this relationship between the general and the particular, as it relates to shopping, that I want to focus on. However, in practice this is mediated by many other factors such as the type of relationship people want to have and whether the relationship is in formation, stable, or in decline. Both the selection of goods and the act of shopping itself may be involved. As a starting point, we might expect that during the period of courtship the act of shopping would be used to create a movement toward greater similarity (or at least complementarity) of taste and practice (e.g., Young and Willmott 1973). Changes in retail have also in themselves tended to promote the ideal of couples shopping together (Humphery 1998, 190). The following example is one of many in which couples do attempt to dissolve their differences in the hope that this will produce a relationship of high congruence. Living together becomes in part an expectation that each will develop as a result of learning about the other. This couple met in art school, routinely shops together, and rationalizes any differences, because for them sameness also has strong connotations of equality.

 We both like cooking but Henry does most of the cooking at the moment because usually he'll cook dinner while I'm giving Timothy a bath. We used to sort of do more a 50–50. We would take turns cooking dinner, but at the moment he does most of it.

(Q)   Are you both equally interested in cooking?

(A)   Yeah, we're both very good cooks.

(Q)   Was it your husband's house before you?

(A)   Yeah, he lived here for about four years before I met him, and
      it's all changed since then. He's gotten a lot better because
      you know what guys are like on their own—really scruffy. . . .
      Since I've been around, I think the look of the house has
      changed a whole lot more. Because he used to have more eth-
      nic-y things—like the skirting boards were sort of terracotta
      colour, and the walls were cream, and he had these big Turkish
      carpets. I hated the Turkish carpets. So it has changed quite a
      lot, but I think his taste has changed genuinely. I mean, even
      his paintings have started to use bright colours where they
      didn't used to. I mean, these are my paintings—bright
      colours. Now his are starting to get bright colours.

Many people tend to focus on this process of congruence while making
it respectful of the relationship as one between individuals. These would
equate with what Giddens (1992) has claimed to be an increasingly contractual form of relationship of mutual respect for each partner's individuality. But at least in this ethnography, few cases of this kind of unmediated
dissolving of difference could be observed. Rather, the relationship between the partners is mediated by a further relationship that is based on
the normative projection of the individual as an exemplification of the
generic category of spouse/partner. As well as learning about her, in particular, the male partner is often much influenced by ideas about female
partners in general and by how they are expected to behave. Most of these
models seek to develop complementary difference rather than similarity
between the partners. When set alongside each other these two expectations of congruence, on the one hand, and difference, on the other, create
a potential gradation of relations between partners that seems close to
what was observed.

It is not hard to find material to illustrate complementarity based on difference as in the following account of a range of wives' attitudes to the
purchase of their husband's clothing. This varied from complete control
by the wife over the uninterested husband to complete autonomy of the
husband.

Eleana, a Cypriot, provides a good example of one end of this spectrum. She states that her husband never buys clothes, all of which come
to him from her or her two daughters in the form of birthday, Christmas, or Father's Day presents. Almost all of these clothes come from the

same shop—Mark and Spencer, which is viewed as completely neutral in terms of style in men's clothes but highly efficient in terms of quality and size such that it is hard to go wrong when buying for a man. All of this is set against his lack of interest. At one point she notes:

> Well, he tends to—I think like all men, really—he tends to wear the same thing all the time. Unless you change them around in the wardrobe! A friend of mine came round one evening and I said to her, "Did you have a power cut?" And she looked at me and she looked at her husband and she said, "Oh, he dressed himself tonight!" She knew exactly what I meant. And my husband and her husband, they just looked at each other, but she knew exactly what I meant.

Clearly, within such a conversation the discussion of her husband cannot be separated out from her ideas about men in general. In many ways, his lack of concern simply supports her view of him as a "proper" man, and his inactivity is entirely explicable in relation to this sense of the normative. A lack of interest in clothing was certainly the most common norm for men in well-established relationships, as these two examples indicate:

> It's years and years since he's had a new suit. That's why he's finally got to the stage. I mean, how I've ironed some of his shirts I don't know.

> I buy his clothes. If he needs a suit, he'll come with me. Clothes are not a priority in his life. He doesn't choose and match; he needs to achieve a certain look, but he's not that interested.

In some cases there is an expectation that the man will at least participate in buying his clothes. Indeed, in some cases women throw away clothes to force the husband to come with them and choose some new ones. As one wife noted:

> I have to nag him to buy clothes. . . . like with a lot of men, but I don't think he's even bought a pair of underpants on his own for God knows how many years.

While these statements exemplify a general norm of women dominating clothes purchasing for their spouses, they do not necessarily tell us very much about the nature of the relationships themselves. Indeed, it proved to be of considerable importance that the same descriptions of practice may hide very different expectations about the relationships and therefore may have very different consequences. In the Cypriot household, with which the examples began, the husband and wife share what they regard as a traditional division of labor and interests, and he fully appreciates her labor on his behalf. Each becomes a "real" man and woman in the eyes of the other. In another case, however, the female partner is intensely frustrated because she feels her partner completely disregards her labor and takes being clothed for granted. In a third case, a wife is extremely interested in both his and her own clothes, and after a while it becomes clear that his complete lack of interest is more an expression of his sense of resistance within a relationship in which he is by and large the dominated partner. She acknowledges her own pressure:

> It's me saying, "You need some trousers"; "Don't be so silly, you've got to buy some more"; "Let us go shopping"; "You must take a day off to go." It's really me pushing him to buy it and go together.

Superficially, with respect to who does what, all three cases look the same, but the effects on the internal dynamics of the family are quite different. This is due in part to differences in expectations, of which one's sense of the normative in gender relations is a factor. This confirms the importance of viewing relationships as a triad in which the normative is as much a key agent as the two partners themselves.

Just as there is diversity in expectation, there can also be diversity in practice. In many households, male and female partners buy their clothes separately. But in one case this may be representative of a relationship in which the partners are trying to express their growing sameness in the sense of symmetry, while in another case this mutual autonomy may represent a strong sense of complementarity between genders actively defining themselves through opposition. For example, one wife remarks at length on the differences in the way she and her husband shop for clothes. She hates going with him since his practice of quickly establishing what he wants and buying it upsets all that she feels is achieved be her own leisurely browsing before determining her purchase. Yet because she explains both of their styles of shopping in terms of norms about men and women, it become clear that she would be even more unhappy if he were not behaving in accordance with her expectations of men in general.

A husband's autonomy in buying his own clothes may be a sign that he is concerned about his own appearance and wishes to assert his own taste. But this is not necessarily the case, as in the following example:

Q You buy clothes for your husband?

A No, I did once! I did it as a present. And he got really angry, and he said he wouldn't dream of buying clothes for me, and how dare I buy clothes for him. He very rarely buys clothes. I have to say, "Look, I think you need to get something new," or "This is getting very threadbare." And I think this is what he's conscious of himself. I think that's probably why he ordered the Next catalogue just to have a look rather than going round. He does tend to just go into the saver center and just buy things from the saver center. He's not a very dressy person. He's Australian—he just tends to wear sweaters and jeans and very casual clothes.

The other extreme of this spectrum is where the husband would not agree to his wife's involvement in buying clothes for himself because he is the dominant partner with respect to taste in clothes more generally:

A Benjamin is very much more stylish than I am about clothes, quite unusual. His father was a tailor, so he's into beautiful fabrics and he hates the fact that I wear a lot of black and, you know, very boring, and he has a kind of influence on my clothes. I would never take him to a shop and show him an outfit. I bought something in Marks and Spencer last year, a bit daring for me, a kind of orange and red suit, and I thought, "Oh, my God, I'm going to take this back, this is ridiculous. I'll never wear this." And I showed him, and he raved about it so. He was so angry at the thought of me taking it back that I had to say, OK, I would keep it, and then he had to say, "You've got a presentation tomorrow. Why don't you wear that suit?" And everyone, when I wore it, every situation I was in, someone would comment on how wonderful it was. So I am influenced by him, but I wouldn't take him.

Q Does he buy all of his own clothes?

A Yes, I don't think I've ever dared buy him an item of clothing because he's got more confidence in his style than I have in my choice.

Q What about the other way round?

A Yes, and I've always liked what he's bought.

Q Is that like birthday presents?

(A)   Yes. When he goes on conferences abroad occasionally he will buy me things.

(Q)   More daring than you would buy for yourself?

(A)   It's only daring in terms of colours, yes. He would never buy me a black item.

Even in this case, she starts the discussion by noting that he is "unusual."

The question arises, can the impact of the feminist movement, filtering through society over the last twenty years, be observed in these exchanges? While the influence of feminism is apparent in discussions concerning more general aspects of gender relations, when it comes to the concrete arena of assigning who does what in the house even the growth of a diversity in practice seems to have made little dent upon the normative expectations of gender roles in the area of male clothing (see Beardsworth and Keil [1997, 77–86] for gender conservatism in provisioning more generally in the United States and Europe). Instead of a prefeminist norm being replaced by a feminist norm, we see diversity both in normative discourse and in shopping practice. The lack of congruence between these varies considerably in significance according to the sense of power and dominance, according to the degree of understanding between the partners of where they should be along this gradation of possibility, and according to the degree to which each overtly demonstrates their appreciation of what the other is doing or not doing.

Pauline, born in Ireland and married to Dan, born in the United States, may serve as an example. As for most families, it is easy to discern in their shopping a tension between the contradictory imperatives of thrift and spending. When they visit Ireland their child is given an abundance of presents by Pauline's large extended family. This irritates Dan since he is concerned about the contrast to their own pattern of giving gifts, which is to give gifts on an infrequent basis and which are useful, in order to not "spoil" the child. Pauline notes that she could intervene to prevent her parents from giving so many gifts; indeed, she is also upset by this practice for another reason. She remembers that as a child she received almost no presents since the family was too poor to afford them. But this is precisely what accounts for the extravagance of the extended family who happily pour out their pension cheques upon their grandchildren in explicit compensation for the fact that they were unable to do this for their children. For this reason, notwithstanding their resentment, she feels unable to curb their generosity. As in the case of Susan, any particular relationship is much effected by the broader context of other relationships.

With respect to their everyday shopping, the roles are reversed. As a housewife Pauline tends to buy the more pragmatic things that are largely essential to the household. Dan, on the other hand, shops more rarely and therefore wants to make his shopping into a more special occasion where he purchases the kinds of things they do not normally buy—on this occasion chocolate éclairs and "kettle" chips. Pauline's response to this is quite contradictory. On the one hand, she relies on this difference, which preserves her own role as the pragmatic one, while allowing herself to feel rewarded by the "treats" he purchases. Pauline admits she would be disappointed if Dan did not come back with something special. On the other hand, there are aspects of the way he goes about his shopping that Pauline resents. First, she notes that when he brings back something for their daughter he tends to present it to the child as a gift from him alone rather than as a gift from both of them, which contradicts her own scrupulous avoidance of individualizing gifts to the child. Her resentment becomes evident also in a discussion of the difference between homemade and commercially produced soup. On the whole she favors homemade soups or, at most, packets of soup that are then used merely as a base for her own concoction. At one point she notes the following:

(A)   Do you mean the soup in the cartons now? Well, I don't usually ever buy those, 'cause I think they're too expensive and that I could make one just as good myself. My husband buys them, you know, 'cause every Sunday he drives over to Hampstead and buys bagels and on the way back he'll often stop in at Tesco's and if I haven't made soup. I think he buys them because he likes the taste of them and he thinks it's a lot of trouble for me to go and make soup for him. So that's the reason why he buys them.

(Q)   So it suggests he's trying to save you time?

(A)   Yeah. Or he'll just feel like soup on the spur of the moment and rather than say to me, "Would you mind making some soup?" he'll buy a carton of it. But it tends to annoy me a bit when he does that because I would prefer to make it myself.

(Q)   But you would still see it as something where he's trying to be supportive?

(A)   Yeah.

What is not mentioned here is another facet of their relationship that turns on his U.S. origins. One of the things he clearly misses from the United States is certain soups, in particular, clam chowder and chicken broth. She has tried to make both, but neither live up to his memory, and they have tried to purchase commercial versions, which also proved disappointing. So here in the case of soups, just as in the case of present buying, the couple's relationship rests also on the relationship between her Irish and his U.S. origins as elements that are, in a sense, lost in return for what they regard as the gain in coming together as partners. She would wish to demonstrate her inheritance of the mantle of motherhood by providing him with homemade soups and therefore resents a gesture of store-bought soups that she admits is made on her behalf. As in the case of clothes buying, the complementarity of what each partner does only makes sense when considered in the light of this projection of expectations.

This case also exemplifies one of the most common effects of normative gender practice in the English household. In those cases where women cover more pragmatic areas of expenditure and create their expressive relationship with their children through their longer interaction with them, often the men, who may have greater responsibility for generating household income, also want to use their own shopping to develop an expressive relationship to their children through gifts. In the case just illustrated and perhaps in many other households, this creates some resentment as the wife sees the husband trying to individualize his gift-giving relationship to the child. In their case, the problem is perhaps a slight one, but it can be greatly exacerbated when circumstances change, as has been discussed recently by Simpson (1997) in some observations on the effects of divorce in a Northern English town. Simpson notes that after divorce the woman who often has a shrunken income but still responsibility for the child has to increase her pragmatism in purchasing for her household. The situation for the father is rather different. His interaction with his child is severely curtailed, and he may wish to compensate for this by increasing the expressive nature of the gifts he buys directly for his children. His ex-wife, however, requires maintenance funds from him for her own ordinary domestic purchasing and becomes much more resentful that the money he is reluctant to give her toward household bills is being spent on extravagant presents given directly to the child. The husband, in turn, resents the evidence that his ex-wife seems only to want to deal on a marketlike business transaction of funds and denies him the desire to make a relationship of affection out of his gift buying for his children.

The situation described by Simpson is one that often begins as positive complementarity in which gender is used to promote creative difference. Notwithstanding the modernist version of feminism as the elimination of difference, the ethnography suggests that the partners still tend to find each other attractive through the development of gender as difference. But this provides fuel for imminent contradiction. Simpson enters this story at what be called an advanced stage in schismogenesis (Bateson 1936), where this initial difference has become the foundation for the exacerbation of conflict and contradiction.

Even within relatively cohesive partnerships, the construction of differences around gender remains as powerful as it is problematic and is constantly reiterated in discussion of shopping. The conservative discussion of how "husbands" are expected to act will not have caused much surprise in the case of my early example of an older Cypriot couple who might be termed "traditional." But the most recent example or the Irish and U.S. partners, their neighbors, and many similar households mainly work in professions, have university degrees, and are well versed in critiques of conservative gender relations. Nevertheless, many similar quotations could be taken from their dialogues. For example, in the case of their neighbor, the husband is working in another town owing to the lack of local employment. His wife discusses her shopping for microwaveable meals to keep him supplied during the week, and if anything seeks to exaggerate his helplessness in food preparation, it is discussed in terms of the way husbands as a generic category are expected to be. Not only does she show some pride in disparaging his masculine hopelessness, but in this case it is clear that such a statement has the effect of asserting his dependency upon her, in circumstances where his absence is keenly felt. As one comes to know the practices of such households better, what becomes striking is that one can observe more equality and symmetry than would be evident in conversation. Though far from equal, men are undertaking more domestic activities such as shopping. What is curious, then, is that so far from taking credit for this "modernization" both partners find ways to distance themselves from the activities conventionally associated with the other gender. Although the male goes shopping he may conspicuously be sent with a list, which reduces his role to that of a kind of mechanical contrivance where he becomes merely the means by which she secures her shopping choices.

The importance of the generic "men," "husbands," and so forth increases still further when the context moves from discussion or observation of any particular relationship to overheard discussions among one gender. For women in mothers' groups or neighbors on a housing estate, the singularity of their spouse becomes secondary to their use as an exemplification of these categories. Here the reference points are as likely to be the behavior of a husband in that week's television soap opera or some other figure prominent in the public sphere. Much of the conversation that may be overheard at the local hairdresser's has this quality. Women constantly move between discussing the promise and problems of the particular relationship of boyfriend or partner to general comments that (partly in order to include the person they are talking with), move to the general level of the nature of male partners or, more particularly, their deficiencies. The particular problem is related to the gender expectation of *Men Behaving Badly* (the title of a popular current television sitcom). Men's conversations in the absence of women, for example, in the pub, similarly tend to the generic and stereotypical though with rather less reference to "wives" and rather more to "women."

This abstraction in discourse from intimate knowledge of the specificity of one's actual partner becomes central to understanding the act of shopping itself, since most shopping is usually undertaken without the physical presence of the partner. It is the partner as internalized representation that comes to the fore in actually making shopping choices. This was evident in the previous discussion about buying clothes for the husband, and indeed, the use of Marks and Spencer as a kind of retail symbol of generic "husband wear." It is also clear in the discussions about why wives don't want husbands to shop with them and the denigration of males' lack of abilities in browsing and finding bargains. As noted in Miller (1998a), wives constantly attempt to buy goods that will move their actual husbands in the direction they would like to see them go. A common example is in buying them slightly more adventurous garments than they would have chosen for themselves, such as the last couple to be mentioned in this section, where the wife brought her partner bright orange underpants in an assertive gesture against the drabness of husbands in general and her husband in particular (much to the disgust of her daughter who was accompanying her at the time!).

The same substitution of actual partners by "introjected" (to implicate the psychoanalytical jargon) partners is even more evident when it is the husband's projection onto a generic category of wives. There is the "classic" case of the gift of "sexy" underwear by the husband to the wife that is returned the week after Christmas and exchanged by the wife for something more suitable. Since such sexy lingerie is an example beloved of television sitcoms, I was quite surprised to see how often this scenario actually occurred. Wives also reported gifts that from their point of view simply reflected the husband's desire for them to share an interest that they manifestly did not care for, such as tickets to a sports game. In some cases it is clear that the husband simply cannot bring himself to believe that this is not something that his wife would desire for herself. In most gift giving between partners, the purchase is not usually so extremely discrepant from expectations. Rather, the gift is merely a little push in the particular direction desired, such that there is a good chance that it will be accepted and will be instrumental in changing the other.

To conclude from this initial case of partnership relations, what has emerged is a triangle drawn between

- the actual partner as they are experienced in day-to-day life,
- the model of the category of partner that is derived from the day-to-day encounter with discourses about partnership and about gender both in the media and in conversation with others, and
- the commodity that is purchased in the shop.

My argument has been that in many cases the act of shopping is an attempt to resolve a tension between the objectified representation of the partner as discourse and the experience of the actual spouse. This is the reason why shoppers are so keen on finding yet further discussion and commentary upon such generic discourses, for example, through watching television or buying magazines. These provide the basis for considering the particular individual with whom one lives. Finally, the mediation of discourse creates a variety of effects dependent upon the diversity of relations of power or expectation in particular contexts. These conclusions will be reinforced and clarified when examined with respect to other relationships in the household.

PARENT-CHILD RELATIONS

The processes of projection and introjection that emerged toward the end of the discussion of partnership relations are immediately evident when we turn to the relationship of parent to child since they are central to both the development of the parent's conception of the child, but also (as psychoanalysis has constantly asserted) to the development of the child's understanding of the parent. Indeed, Freud attributes the development of a conscience and more general moral concerns to the introjection of the infant's model of the parent as superego, arising itself out of conflicts between the ego and the ideal ego (1984, 373–79). This in turn becomes the model for later introjections of authority and presumably discourses that represent morality and authority. I do not myself ascribe to psychoanalytical theory, but this does not prevent me from acknowledging that Freud provides a rich model of the type of processes that I would argue are evident in these kin relations. In particular, I would affirm the importance of projective identification as analyzed by Klein (1975, 141–75; also, Miller 1987, 90–93) and evoke Klein's work also because it was instrumental in allowing us to acknowledge the importance of rage, jealousy, and complex forms of splitting and inversion in the normal development of relations of love within the family.

It is also within the psychoanalytical literature that one can find evidence for the increasing importance of discourse itself as the third point in the triad of relationships that was described at the end of the last section. In a book called *Torn in Two* (1995), Parker strives for an empathetic approach to the minutia of family dynamics that help mothers deal with the sense of guilt and anxiety that she argues emerges from a fundamental ambivalence that they feel toward their infants. She suggests that what has been ignored is the inevitable concomitant to the love mothers feel for infants, that is, their hatred and jealousy of the infant. By acknowledging the centrality of ambivalence she creates a much more constructive approach to the problems experienced by many parents.

So far from seeing mothers as controlled by the institutionalized representations foisted onto them, Parker argues that mothers are driven to seek out more examples of such discourses in their desire to establish a normative base against which they can conceptualize their own actions as mothers. In this search they look for as many models as they can find; advice from health care workers, watching television programs, buying magazines about mothering, and also mothering "guide books." One problem is that many of these guidebooks take a very different view of mothering. Most seem to employ a vulgarized version of a position attributed to the British psychoanalyst Winnicott (Winnicott 1971—although he himself had much to say about ambivalence) that tend to imply that whenever mothers experience rage against their infants they may attribute this or indeed any problem for the infant to their own failings as a mother. The infant appears natural and perfect and never cries without good reason; crying is then almost always attributed to some failing of the mother. Mothers therefore idealize the concept of motherhood, which they constantly see themselves as failing to live up to.

It is not surprising that mothers therefore also look to each other as a source of normative discourse, as Parker suggests:

> Sometimes mothers use other mothers as mirrors. Each mother scrutinizes the other in pursuit of a reflection of her own mothering. They look for differences from their own style of mothering and they look for sameness. But above all they look

for confirmation that they are getting it right, in the face of
fears that they are getting it hopelessly wrong. To the outsider, especially to the child-free observer, exchanges between
mothers seem to be carried out in a language of measurement
and invidious competition, but the desired outcome in not so
much a victory as a search for deep-needed reassurance.
(1995, 1)

The evidence is not that mothers all want to be like one another, but
that particularity is developed largely through a constant reference to normativity. In a similar vein, when children are old enough to create their
own peer groups, one of the first things such groups share is a discourse
about "parents." Later on, the experience of a new boyfriend is first taken
back to the "girls" for dissection and consideration. The mistake has been
to treat the normativity of discourse as something that must develop top-
down, having been first generated by institutional forces. At first it seems
absurd that pop stars and actresses should be constantly asked their opinion on politics and social problems; opinions for which they have no
qualifications, or that we buy newspapers that consist far more of moralis-
tic gossip than what might otherwise be called news, or we watch soap operas that focus on endless replaying of the internal dynamics of family
relations. These discourses are generated by our desire for them. There is,
quite simply, a vast "market" demanding even more sitcoms, soap operas,
gossip, and celebrity opinion that can be reflected back on the moralities
and practice of relationships. This becomes evident in the ethnography of
shopping since the dominant concern of shoppers is anxiety not only
over reconciling discourses with individual persons but also in developing
some self-confidence in determining for themselves what such persons
are supposed to be like in the first place. The constant hope is that there is
a convincing discourse somewhere that will tell them.

In the ethnography, parents could be seen to be usually more aware of
the degree to which they project desires onto children than was the case of
partners. Indeed, there is a curious discourse about the "vicarious" gift.
This is where a parent suggests that another parent (e.g., a woman in full-
time work) who is unable to express their love for their child to the degree
to which they would wish, will compensate for this by buying the child a
profusion of gifts that are merely attempts to assuage the parent's own
guilt. The vicarious gift was often mentioned in discussion, and one can
often see it portrayed in the media. But it was very rarely observed in the
ethnography. I suspect it forms part of a larger discourse about the evils
of materialism where it is said that people are replacing real relations to

people with relations to goods. So ubiquitous is this assertion that it may be one reason why the vicarious gift is rare. In practice, people are working hard to refute any possibility of being categorized within this quite explicit model.

More common than the vicarious gift are mothers who constantly refer to their conception of what the infant should or would like, but where there is a crucial slippage between statements that suggest they are imposing their desires on the infant and claims that imply that the infant has selected such items for themselves. Olivier, for example, in talking about her two children aged four and two, goes through the following sequence:

(A)　Her clothes? My children are all designer children, and I've always been like that as far as my children's clothing is concerned.

(Q)　How do you mean?

(A)　I've always liked—there's different places: Benetton, Patricia Wigan's in Hampstead, and Selfridge's. I pick things out, you know, from certain designers rather than from just any shop. Also, I find that I shop because of things I always had when I was little—my mother. And also, what other things influence me? The children, definitely.

In shopping with Olivier one can observe this tension in practice. She often tries to involve the children in making choices, taking their opinion on around a third of all objects purchased, partly with a view to "educating" them in shopping and expressing their own taste. But she does this in such a manner as to ensure that they choose what she had already decided that she wants to buy. On another shopping expedition, she first informs the children that they will not be buying anything, and then takes them into a shop with a toy section in order to discuss the various toys on display. She explicitly establishes a distance between abstract consideration and actual purchase. In an action remarkably close to Bourdieu's (1984) analysis of middle-class taste in *Distinction,* she appeared to be systematically trying to ensure a Kantian division between the immediacy of desire and the making of judgments. Another mother has clearly mapped out her plan for what her child will want at each age based on what she wants to relive from her own childhood. She admits she simply can't wait until the infant is old enough to read this or that of her own favorite children's books or play with a particular doll or toy that she loved in her time.

As the children develop their own desires, these are at first often assimilated into a general discourse about the inheritance of traits. As in the above case, it is very important to the mother that the children have "designer taste" as a natural inheritance from her. Parents commonly discuss which of their interests and predilections the child has inherited, an analogy with the inheritance of physical properties. So a child is said to have inherited her "sweet tooth" from the father and her love of watching cartoons from the mother. Sometimes the mother can be observed revising her opinion of herself in her reflection upon the infant. She may decide that she really does like Disney films, having previously told people she loathed them, because she wants to remain consistent with the child's preferences. In a more complex case, the ambivalence the mother feels toward food is explicated in her representation of the opposition between her two children, one of which is said to be like a "dustbin," eating just about anything and constantly on the prowl for edibles, and the other being extremely fastidious and abstemious. Of course, it is quite possible that these represent actual differences between the children, but they certainly follow her own powerful ambivalence toward food and the two opposed representations that she has of herself. Indeed, it is quite likely that here maternal ambivalence has become introjected into the opposed characters of the children.

These cases show the intimate nature of the relationship between normativity and the particular, since the very creation of a child and their personality is infused with the same tensions that were described in the analysis of shopping by partners. As in the case of partners, however, these can also be manifested in the larger social environment of shopping. For example, there are the problems that the relationship between children pose to the relationship between households. In two cases noted during the fieldwork, there was such a close relationship between households that the respective children also saw each other frequently. In both these cases, the households were quite different in terms of income and what might loosely be termed class position and expectation. In one, the middle-class parents held to a common stereotype that working-class parents are too indulgent to their children, and notwithstanding their smaller income, spend with a lavishness that is bad for (i.e., spoils) the child. The idea that their own children's expectations were influenced by comparison with their peers, and the children's growing awareness that this inverted rather than reflected their relative wealth, put quite some strains upon the relationship. In the other case, the poorer household was dominated by and condescended to by the wealthier. During one shopping trip, when the former was buying shoes for their infant in Ibis Pond (an upmarket local shopping center), they met the latter doing the same thing, and the immediate result was that the subordinate mother was no longer satisfied with the choice she had begun to settle on but felt constrained to emulate the more expensive choice of her wealthier friend, though with the added problem of not wishing to be seen as directly copying her by buying exactly the same shoe.

The most important evidence, however, for the extent to which shopping is based upon a projection onto the child as opposed to researching the desires of the child is the constant reiteration of the problems involved and differences created by having the child actually accompanying the mother as against the mother shopping on her own. There are plenty of pragmatic reasons why women do not want to have their young children with them when shopping, but it soon became clear that the antipathy to their company on this as against most other occasions was based on more than simply the logistical nightmares and potential for embarrassing scenes. When I was shopping without the presence of the child, mothers would often explain to me the choices they were making in terms that idealized the child as the deserving and appropriate recipient of these purchases. This was much harder to maintain in the light of the actual greed and materiality of an accompanying child. The extent to which mothers sensed a contradiction posed by the manifest desires of the child depends upon the age of the child in question. The first signs of independent choices almost all revolve around food. Again and again, mothers note the desire of children for particular breakfast cereals being promoted on television and fostered by some special gift within the cereal packet. This is the start of a general attribution of the child's desires to the malevolent effects of television, and commerce more generally. The next stage revolves mainly around issues to do with sweets and biscuits. Later on the focus shifts to burgers and chips, until by the time the child becomes a teenager the conflicts have largely moved onto to issues of clothing and appearance, and the bad effects of commerce are compounded by the impact of "peer group pressure." It seems probable, then, that the constant attack on the evil impact of commerce is in part an attempt to reconfigure the role of mothers as preserving the natural link that the infant is seen as inheriting from her from the corruption of these external influences.

The problem, then, of the presence of the child is the degree to which they deviate in actuality from the model of the child that the mother has projected, which consists in part of her idealization of the infant but equally derives from what she takes to be her responsibility to the child as given by general discourses on proper mothering. These are discourses that are constantly referred to by mothers, though depending upon class and context they vary in practice from highly influential books about mothering, the advice of other kin and, most especially, their own mother, and conversations with other mothers either individually or as part of formalized groups such as the National Childbirth Trust (see Miller 1997b for more details of the argument of these last two paragraphs).

One effect of this ambivalence, evident in some shopping expeditions, was a certain coldness of the mother to the actual child that would not have been expected given the animated way the same mothers talks about their children in the abstract. Although the numbers of families that could be used to exemplify a particular relationship or tension were often small within this particular ethnography, I would hazard a general observation that this particular style of coldness—where the mother seems to almost systematically disregard the child as a shopping companion—was associated only with parents of English descent. It seemed to be a local exemplification of something that certainly occurs in stereotypes by many of those who took part in the ethnography (but are not of English descent) about an "English" reserve or coldness toward children in general and sometimes toward their own children in particular. If my observation that this is not consistent with the way these parents discuss their children in the abstract is included, then it may hint at the possibility that this coldness derives from the same contradiction between the child as the projected imagination of "a child" and the actual presence of the particular child. In short, it suggests that English parents, in particular, tend to have difficulty coping with their being embarrassed by the behavior and the materialism of their children in that it confronts them with the constructed nature of their own projected ideals about the infants in question.

With older children the ambivalence between identification and opposition to the child's taste continues. One common result at this stage is that where the mother (or at this stage, more often either parent) perceives a commonality of desire, they will go to quite extraordinary lengths to secure the object of desire. Two cases illustrate this, though to very different degrees. One mother is concerned with the particular kind of sausages that her son enjoys. This variety is found in Sainsbury's, but only in their larger supermarkets. She had passed one of these a couple of days before but could not be bothered to queue for the sake of this one item. But she then found that her local Sainsbury's didn't stock them. She tried the delicatessen, but they had no grilling sausages. We then tried Marks and Spencer, which has six kinds of sausage including some named after counties such as Lincolnshire and Lancashire, but she decided that the only ones that would come close to those she desired would have been Cumberland, which they didn't have in stock. We then went in search of another delicatessen at which point we were exchanging jokes about "hunting the sausages." We failed to find the shop and finally returned to the local branch of Sainsbury's to buy the ordinary English type, which they did have in stock. The reason for spending so much of a morning in "hunting the sausage" is not simply the sense of having to get something the child will actually eat, (although long expeditions were often caused by fastidious kids), but also because being with the child it was an expression of the mother's concern to cultivate and respect the child's choice in an area where she felt that—for a change—it was not one of those occasions where a child is claiming independence of choice simply in order to cross their parent's desires.

In another case, a mother on a low income had a teenage son who was highly proficient in a particular sport and a considerable proportion of the household income was spent in obtaining the best-quality goods that were required for undertaking this sport at an international competitive level. On the whole, this mother was clearly finding a sense of fulfillment in the degree to which almost all other concerns of the household were sacrificed to this one aim of keeping her son in these competitions. But this triumphant negation of family poverty did not prevent some of his specific requests for, for example, various kinds of body-building foods finally and visibly exasperating her. Once again, there is the additional factor that the drive to accommodate the difficulties of such shopping is best understood when held against the sense of a constantly growing battle in which the child's autonomous choices seem willfully constructed in order to frustrate and negate the evident desires of the parent. In short, parents will go to considerable lengths to retain a relationship with teenagers that they fostered when the children were younger and where the labor of shopping is an expression of their love, but with teenagers the limits they may have to go to may defeat them.

What these two examples of shopping for teenagers also shows is that in this trajectory of the development of parental relations the balance has moved from a tremendous reliance upon normative discourses in the manner described by Parker (1995), which provide the model for both parental and child behavior, to a much more specific and individualized representation of the child as an actively desiring subject. By the stage of teenage life the object bought is less a reflection of any normative discourse and more a desperate attempt to find something that resolves a tension that grows with the evidence of the child's autonomy (for further elaboration of this argument, see Miller 1997b).

THE OBJECTIFIED SELF

In both the examples of kin relations examined so far, the study of shopping has generated an approach to kinship that centers upon the contradictions between the use of normative discourses about the kin category in question—what wives in general or sons in general are supposed to be like—and the particular individual one lives with. The two examples of partners and of parent-child relations will serve to stand for many other similar relationships, such as that between siblings or that between grandparents and children or between in-laws. In each case, there are clear normative discourses about how such relationships should be, and shopping is used to resolve the tension between these and the specific person who occupies that kin position.

But I want to turn now to a more surprising advantage of such a perspective on kinship. When conducting the ethnography and coming to the conclusion that shopping could best be understood as being about relationships and not about individuals, one of the critical comments most commonly made was that this ignored the rise of the single-person household. Yet when this question was viewed from the point of view of the ethnographic observations, it was quite clear that the single-person household was not exceptional. Rather, such households seem to have developed an understanding of their shopping that separated the recipients into two categories. The first was shopping for oneself as a household, which included most provisioning, and the second was the exceptional items one purchased for the "self." This followed the same logic by which other households also divided purchases between general provisioning such as food for meals and clothes for work, and special "treats" for the selves that made up the household.

In this section, I want to use the perspective being developed to take this argument one stage further. It seems quite clear that the individual is best understood today as an example of kinship, indeed, quite likely the single most important kin relationship in our contemporary society. This is especially significant since in most accounts of Western kinship, the rise of individualism is viewed as something opposed to that of kinship or a symptom of a supposed decline of kinship. So instead of seeing kinship in decline at the expense of individualism, I will make the opposite argument that individualism has become increasingly incorporated within kinship to form a category of kinship. So far it has been argued that a major player in relationships is the externalized discourses about kin roles and their normative form. But the example of such normative models that has flourished as a discourse in recent years is the literature on the self and the proper nature of the self. That is to say that we are constantly offered models in the media, in conversation, and in moral and other debates about how we should or could relate to the self. These discussions are not especially different from the way we encounter discourses about the other key kin relationships such as those that dwell upon how a mother, child, partner, or sibling should be.

The advantages of this perspective may best be illustrated by first presenting some ethnographic details based around three individuals. Not surprisingly, because these three focus on the individual rather than a relationship to another, my presence as the ethnographer was a more pertinent element in the shopping itself.

The first case is an expedition by Carla specifically to buy a new pair of shoes. At the time, Carla possessed four pairs of shoes and two pairs of boots. She was undertaking an M.A. having been outside of academic life for some time and was, therefore, in a position where what she would regard as her relative "dressiness" and concern with appearance was confronted by the tendency to "dress down" and play down appearance, which was typical of the student body she now had to relate to. This was reflected in her initial intention, which was to buy "sensible shoes that can be used in everyday settings." As she said with reference to this ethos, "not summer shoes since summer lasts for such a short time." Such shoes would not be sensible and not suitable for student life. Students are not her only reference points, however. The week before, her husband had gone out and purchased for himself a pair of shoes of an informal "Italianesque" variety. He had spent hardly any time on this purchase, and she generally espoused what she saw as a feminine virtue of proper extensive and considered shopping, to oppose her husband's minimal shopping practice, which she disparaged (although also admired as confirmatorily male in him). So we were not going to be in any hurry—notwithstanding the fact that her daughter was accompanying us.

We started with the shoes on special sale within a department store. Here, after some browsing, she picked two pairs, the first black, made up of interwoven strips, the other a cream-colored closed-toe style with a ribbon. She preferred the cream shoes but decided that they would soon become scruffy and that therefore did not really count as sensible. She wanted these put on one side, but the shop assistant refused to do this, as they were sale goods. We continue through several other high-street[2] shoe shops, in each of which she tried on at least two pairs, with one foot bare and the other with pop socks so she can see both backgrounds at once.

2. "Main street" in U.S. usage.

Then comes a more serious encounter with three pairs in a further shop. One is a black equivalent to the cream shoe first seen, since it also has a ribbon, though it is slightly less elegant. Next to this, she tries a blue suede shoe with a heel higher than any of the previous ones. It has a back strap and is probably the "sexiest" of all the shoes tried on that day. Here she confronts her dilemma at its most explicit, since the black is clearly sensible, the blue is clearly not, both however are comfortable and she claims that from the outset she had stated that this was her most important criterion. At this stage she makes a point that she will later repeat as she develops a growing interest in shoes that are similar to this blue suede style. She says, "the problem is that I am really just frivolous." We break for lunch and are then distracted by other shops at which she buys a bra and some sun cream before returning to the main task at hand.

We go to two further shops, one of these, Shoe Express, is probably the cheapest on the high street. She admits that the shoe tried on there is comfortable, but then says she will probably feel crippled after ten minutes. There is no evidence that this should be the case, but it is typical of the kind of statement shoppers make when justifying their distance from various forms of bargain shops, a distaste that is much more likely (as here) to relate to class prejudice that is defensive since her income is rather low at this point of time. In the next shop, she tries on four pairs, including a black patent shoe with heels and front straps that continues the line started by the blue suede shoe, and then a closed shoe with single curved strap tied with a "pearl" that comes in various colors. This has clear potential but she says it is not comfortable, and surprisingly, the shop assistant agrees, pulling up one trouser leg to reveal blisters she had received from wearing the same style! At this point she has tried on sixteen pairs of shoes over a period within which three hours has been devoted specifically to shoe shopping. She then says she is bored—not by the shoes—but by her own indecision. She finally selects a cream-colored pair, without a ribbon but otherwise not unlike the sensible pair she had first seen in the department store sale.

The story does not end here, however, since several days later we met again, and she tells me how much she regretted her choice, which has proved not to be comfortable. She tells me she really should have gone for the high-heeled shoes, which were really much more her kind of thing. Indeed, as so often in post-shopping reflection, this becomes a kind of moral fable, in which she has made her failure into a kind of justified punishment for not having been true to herself when making the decision. A whole swathe of issues has been raised in this expedition. Her sense of herself is challenged by her current role as student. On the one hand, this is a return to younger company, which makes her self-conscious about her age, and yet these others are dressed down, which is something she would normally associate with older people. She has a strong sense of dressing as the cultivation of aspects of her own self as woman, and although she is not flirtatious, my presence as a male reminds her of this project. More important, she knows this is a project she is "good at," being both good-looking and dressing to enhance her looks to a degree beyond that of most of the other housewives on the street. All of this can be remolded in this context to a sense of authenticity, that is, her real self as against the project of the self that it opened up to her by her fellow students. As a result, she starts the shopping trip with the intention of buying something that suits the new ethos of her academic work, but gradually finds that this is undermined by her exposure to shoes that are of the type she would previously have opted for as her style. This gradual transformation in her intentions was not enough to make her change her mind at the moment of purchase (despite her ploy to make "comfort" replace the previous criteria of "sensible") but was quite enough to make her regret that action within a few days.

The point, of course, is that it could so easily have been different. Other women who had been less successful within one particular normative model of dressing as a woman within this highly gendered terrain of shoe shopping, could be seen to leap at the opportunity given by the rather different ethos of the students, with evident relief. What the act of shopping did in this case as for others is reveal the alternatives and contradictions around these possibilities of the self, because the shoes themselves are designed to objectify these various aspirations and potential versions of being a woman. The shoe here is not just a commodity that intervenes in the relationship between person and discourse, but it reveals itself equally as discourse, that is, as the commercial semiotic of difference that feeds into the imagination of different possibilities for the self that were raised by the very idea of shopping for shoes. A parallel may be drawn with the various writings by O'Hanlon (1989) and Strathern (1979) on self-decoration in highland Papua New Guinea. In direct opposition to the common Western feminist statements about appearance being a covering up of the true self, they suggest that for the New Guinea highlander it is not the "natural" physiognomy that one merely happens to be born with that reveals the self, but the self that is constructed through the labor of self-decoration. For them it is obvious that the true self is what one constructs not merely fortuitously starts with. Similarly here we can see shopping for shoes as the labor involved in creating the particularity of self out of a field of possibilities, exploiting the discourses of potential selves that commerce provides in its range of shoes.

The second example—Margaret—is a housewife whose shopping reveals the extent to which she is unable to resolve discrepancies within her own self-conception. As a housewife whose only work has been in a minor supportive role to her husband, she is clearly lacking in confidence. The word "clearly" needs to be highlighted. In fact, at first meeting she comes over as one of the most self-confident informants, talking at some length about her aspirations and sense of herself. It is only when this discussion about shopping is turned to the actual practice of shopping that the problems of her self-image and lack of confidence arise. When examined in the light of the shopping, however, the earlier conversation does reveal the importance she attributes to the values and ideals of those around her as constituting her own ambitions. When we start shopping she is quite clear that she wishes to use the vast stock of the supermarket to demonstrate her creative and unusual qualities. She talks of interesting wines and being "inspired" by exotic and unusual goods. Yet at the end of the shop she has bought a most mundane and clearly uninspired lists of goods, at least when seen against that of her peers within this middle-class milieu. Not a single one of the goods purchased suggests the slightest "inspiration," and this is equally evident in that her whole manner, which was enthusiastic and positive at the start of the trip but ended as dispirited and lackluster.

The reasons behind this failure may lie in the way her relationship to goods is modeled upon that of her dependence upon the others she would strive to emulate. This was one of the surprisingly few cases when the presence of the anthropologist may well have been critical to the development of the shopping expedition. It was already evident in earlier conversations with Margaret that she relied heavily on others views about who she might be. She had married a man whose friends seemed much more sophisticated and knowledgeable about questions of food and drink, and she aspired to emulate them. For this reason she felt the need to demonstrate her creative skill as a shopper to me as her companion. So her marked shift in spirits would also have reflected the public nature of her failure to appear as the kind of shopper she aspired to be. The problem appeared to be her lack of confidence in her knowledge with respect to any particular area of grocery purchase as against those such as her husband and friends, who were the models for these aspirations. For example, while trying to emulate the "wine conversationalists" (Lehrer 1983) that she had clearly encountered, she had little knowledge of her own and was afraid to make the wrong selection. She therefore retreated back to the only type of wine that her actual lack of confidence would permit her to select as safe. The same applies to her aspirations to purchase exotic foods, which were never realized despite the fact that the supermarket is packed with potential choices. Here, then, is someone who is trying to cultivate a self-image under the pressure of a husband who works in a creative job and brings home many people who are probably impressively opinionated. She uses this and other media to create a powerful image of who she would like to appear as in shopping and makes explicit claims to her skills and abilities. But the actual act of shopping in company that she wishes to impress forces her to confront the discrepancy between the fantasy and her actual lack of skill and knowledge in this quest to be the proficient cosmopolitan. In other words, she is intimidated be her own projections of who she needs to be. The discourses that counted were the discussions that her husband and his peers carry on in her presence.

This retreat into the safety of familiar brands might seem to parallel a very common perspective that has arisen in the last few years in marketing research, based mainly on the work of Fournier and her research into American women's relationship to brands (Fournier 1998). It has become quite fashionable in marketing to talk about people having relationships to brands much as they do to people. So people are seen in marketing as betraying a long-term loyalty to one brand and going out for a "one-night stand" with a competing brand. On the basis of my ethnography, I would suggest that most of this discussion is misguided. Relationships to brands certainly matter, but they are important because of the way they express and mediate the relationship to the other people that is the foundation of most shopping.

The third case relates to a man who I have given the nom de plume of Casaubon in this account. When we meet and he is appraised of our interests, Casaubon responds with the classic husbandly sentiment, "Oh, you should talk to my wife. She has a degree in shopping." Casaubon has some affiliation with academic work, though the exact nature is unclear, but what emerges very soon is his passion for books and the purchase of books. Indeed, he is the only shopper encountered in the project who travels into central London for shopping as often as four or five times a week in his search for books. As well as shopping, he is using a newspaper service that puts readers in touch with each other in order to find books that might be more difficult to obtain in the shops, in this case anthropological works:

 What's the other one? Spencer and Gillen, the Australian one. I got that from someone in Hampstead. She was interested in why I wanted that book. Typical of these sort of academics, you know, they worry about who's working on what and

> whether it's going to be plagiarizing their area, their patch.
> You know, they own it. It's a very famous book. I mean people
> like Fraser were involved at that time, Morgan. I mean, Morgan
> was the best one I read.

The discussion was again influenced by my presence, especially in as much as after a while he was unpleasantly aware that from my perspective his passion for books was being integrated by my research into precisely that activity of "shopping" that he found so distasteful and he had been so keen to delegate to his wife's interests. But on the other hand, he proposed the passionate nature of his book shopping.

> (A)   Oh yeah, it turns you on, because don't forget, books are very
> sexual. You smell the cover; it's like a young female, isn't it?
> For a male, isn't it? If he's being honest with himself. I mean
> also it's got an argument in it that you haven't yet fathomed
> out, so you haven't mastered somebody else's thought. I mean
> invariably you're disappointed because a lot of them are mar-
> keted rather than having any sort of substance in, but yes, it's
> tactile, smells good, it's new, and you might just change your
> level of thought by looking into it.

Later on he defends his preference for new books on the same grounds: "It's a sexual thing, I prefer it that way."

My impression was that this relationship to books hinged in large part on his ambiguous relationship to academic work, which is evident again in the many references to himself as an "outsider" both to academia proper and to the world at large. His discussion was replete with representations of government, media, and various establishments in some kind of conspiracy against people in general and him in particular. Here, then, the books themselves have a pristine integrity (virginity?) that transcends their relationship to these polluted establishment contexts that have rejected him, and it is the books that provide his objectified authenticity (virility?) as a man and a scholar.

Although these represent three quite distinct cases, they make a common point with respect to the main theme of this chapter. As long as we are prepared to accept that the self is itself taken as an example of kinship rather than an alternative to kinship, they provide further evidence that the act of shopping is most frequently an attempt to resolve contradictions between the discourse of a kin relation and the relation itself. They also help extend the evidence that this does not mean that shopping is always a successful resolution. On the contrary, although each shopping activity—the search for shoes, food, and books—has the potential to resolve such contradictions, in each of the three cases described here this fails, largely because of the objective conditions that separate out the self-image (or self-discourse) of the person from their practice in the world. This proves too wide a gap to bridge through this activity of shopping alone. Nevertheless, in the case of shoes and books the activity is not without what the shopper would see as positive consequences for both elaborating and helping determine the objectified self (by which I mean a self that is constructed through its own practice of externalization and then introjection in the act of purchase [Miller 1987, 19–32, 86–93]), even though in the case of shoe shopping the positive result is ultimately a clear rejection of the potential for the self that had become objectified in that particular purchase.

ON THE BOUNDARIES OF KINSHIP

The ethnographic presentation started with a single shopping expedition, which demonstrated that in practice many different relationships are interwoven in any given shopping event and then went on to separate out three particular relationships, those of the spouse, the parent, and the self. It would be redundant to try and explicate every category of relationship that is found in the ethnography. Quite apart from the other relationships that will not be discussed here, there is the concept of the family itself, which is one of the most significant areas in which people confront the relationship between normative discourse and the specificity of their family—a set of contradictions that is particularly evident when shopping for family festivals such as Christmas (e.g., Löfgren 1993). Nevertheless, the general conclusion in each case would largely follow that which has been drawn from the three examples used so far. Instead, I want to conclude the presentation by considering the wider field of relationships, beyond that of close kindred, that also enter into the general dialectic between particularity and discourse. Because these are less constrained by the actual presence of the kin in question, such cases reveal various forms of projection and fantasy to be a part of the objectification process and thereby shed light upon the dialectical nature of kinship as a process.

With an increase in both the numbers of divorces and of children born out of wedlock, there has been a proliferation in the number and variety of step-, half-, and other more complex variants of relationship. At the same time, long-lasting friendships may acquire kinlike attributes. Particularly within ethnic minority families, children experience a wide range of persons who they are told fall under the generic English term "aunties" and "uncles." In such cases there is creativity at the level of constructing a normative discourse as to what such a relationship is "supposed to be" as well as dealing with its day-to-day particularities. This process may also be extended to fictive figures or media figures to whom people feel particularly close. The clearest example came in the response to the death of Diana, princess of Wales, where individuals throughout the country made the claim that the death was experienced as though that of a family member.

Taken from the perspective of this chapter, the case is highly illustrative. Diana came close in appearance to the idealized princess that along with wicked stepmothers play a powerful role in infant socialization. But unlike the fairy tale princess, Diana also revealed many common human frailties. She thereby reflected the problem of kinship in reconciling idealized norms with particular instances. Though in this case, her tragic and premature death catapulted her back into the realm of mythic figures who stand for such resolutions of social contradictions in a transcendent manner (Lévi-Strauss 1985). More particularly, she also stood for the contradictions between materialistic hedonism and philanthropic sensitivity that is highly pertinent to the role of shopping in steering a route within a sea of contradiction.

Closer to the home, a category that makes itself very evident to the visiting anthropologist is shopping for pets. When viewed on the boundaries of kinship the perspective clarifies the importance of processes of projection found in core examples of kinship. It clarifies this in the sense that there is little to prevent the owner projecting onto the pet those attributes that one desires the pet to have. What is striking is that when people have this "free range" to project qualities onto those that they are shopping for, they do not make them appear as compliant and simple recipients of one's shopping. Quite the contrary: pets are typically viewed as obdurate and obstinate forces that would distance themselves from the relationship unless one strives to overcome that distance through acts such as shopping with sensitivity to their particular characters. When informants talked about their pets in relation to shopping, it was with a strong emphasis on the recalcitrant nature of their pet as refusing to conform to the wishes of the owner. Cats in particular are seen as very similar to young children in being highly fastidious in their choices of food. For example, one owner noted that her cat was very fussy. It was not just that it would not eat fish and various other foods, but there was a specific ritual by which she would not eat at the time the food was put out, only when she returned and then only if it could see that the food was within a new tin. So lots of food had to be discarded. The same, however, could apply to a dog as in the following conversation in which it is clear that the needs of the dog dominate the organization of the shopping for the week:

(A)   Actually, he is quite expensive, because he won't eat dog food out of tins. So we buy him heart, pig's heart and chicken. We have to cook those for him. We buy fish for the cats, so actually, they cost me the earth.

(Q)   Is this why you need to go shopping three times a week?

(A)   Yes, mainly.

(Q)   That is the main reason?

(A)   Yes. We want to get chopped heart for the dog, frozen. Fresh is quite expensive from the butcher, but it seems Sainsbury's have stopped doing it. I made some journeys to other supermarkets to find it, but now I can't find it anywhere. It had been very convenient and a good size, but now I'm not sure. So [*she adds apologetically*] I bought some lamb mince.

The logic of the dialectic of shopping is particular clear in these cases. First, the pet is projected upon as constituting a significant gap between the ideal unproblematic relation and the actual pet itself, which is thought to be "full of character" precisely to the degree that they do not conform to the bland expectations of animals. So the obdurate stance of the pet is viewed as their endearing quality. The owner then puts themselves through all sorts of difficulties in obtaining the perfect food for their pet, which is represented as the only food acceptable to the pet, and thus their labor in shopping becomes itself the resolution of this distance between the pet as constituted in discourse and the pet as constituted by its individual character. The whole phrasing of the relationship can be strikingly reminiscent of discussions about the food preferences of infants and their consequences for shopping. The pet is easier only in as much as the shopper can more easily convince themselves that they genuinely appreciate the labor of love that has gone into the labor of shopping for their particular dish.

The point of contrast would be the set of more distant relatives that make up the core of the more classificatory anthropological studies of kinship in other societies, but here are relegated to quite formal gestures of gift giving at such holidays and events as Christmas, children's birthday parties, or weddings. These cousins and in-laws differ from the example of pets precisely because they do not undergo this dialectical process of relationship formation. Distant relatives that one does not care about are "easy" to shop for, since on the whole people merely follow rather formulaic procedures, and buy goods that are determined by knowledge of the "genre" of appropriate gifts. Although they have the potential to thereby become "real" relationships, such as that one has with pets, only in particular cases does this occur.

The final example of how shopping contributes to the dialectical process by which kinship is generated as relationships is taken not from my own ethnography but from some recent work by Layne (1999a, 1999b) on the anthropology and material culture of pregnancy loss. This is used as the concluding example because again it brings out with particular clarity some of the general points that have been made here. Her work and those of her colleagues (e.g., in Layne 1999c) is of particular importance because it raises a foundational question in anthropology in general and material culture studies in particular. In analyzing shopping, we have to appreciate the degree to which objects are an integral part of the process by which relationships are formed and maintained. This means dissolving our usual dualist perspectives in which objects and subjects are defined in opposition to each other. But it has been evident at least since the work of Mauss (1954) that the other side of this coin is that persons are also treated in ways that we would normally understand as suitable only for objects and not for subjects. When we look to the kinds of society that anthropologists traditionally have studied, we find that people are often understood in terms of exchange, gifting, and other processes that we see as only fit for commodities. This is not because those societies are more "materialistic" than we, it is because understanding the object nature of persons is the other side of the coin to understanding the subject nature of things.

I have posed this question is academic terms, but the importance of Layne's study is that the question is posed with considerable poignancy for the subjects of her research. For them, the critical question is precisely how do they dissolve away a subject-object divide that threatens the way their loss will be perceived by others. Embryos, fetuses, and neonates are liminal forms, but Layne argues that they are best understood by avoiding a dichotomy of person-thing or real-unreal and instead examining the processual nature by which social beings are constantly created but also only gradually lost. The key to this extended temporality is the use of material culture to both create and then to dissipate the sense of the person.

Most of the contributors to Layne (1999) are concerned with the concept of the gift as used in areas such as fostering and surrogate parenting. Layne, however, examines the complex means by which the developing embryo and fetus are constructed socially. Shopping is often an important aspect of this development. The fetus becomes a person as they become the object of a shopping expedition and the gifting of goods. This is especially evident at the time of miscarriage or stillbirth, which is experienced as a disruption in this process. But typically the parents who have suffered this loss may wish to continue this process or at least terminate it in a form that is more acceptable to them. They may, therefore, continue to buy or collect things for the deceased, or on behalf of them. They find complex ways of maintaining them as part of gift exchanges, being memorialized at events such as Christmas or "would-have-been" birthdays. So, for example, a family member may be given a gift of the kind that would have been purchased on behalf of the baby if they had lived. As in Melanesian ethnography we see the centrality of gift relations both in the imagination of the deceased as gift from God or gift/sacrifice to God, and the importance of the social acceptance of the loss as a gift to the bereaved along with several other strategies for the incorporation of the event within a discourse of gifting. The evidence suggests that central to the process of creating the person is their creation as kindred with the social obligations and benefits of kin (cf. Strathern 1988; also Miller 1997b).

The particular material culture is also significant here. The continued reality of the deceased is experienced in terms of their specificity such as the gendered or tiny size of the clothing purchased for them, evoking with additional poignancy the objects used by adult persons. Here we see the same strategies that are found in shopping for kin more generally, that is, the creating of specificity as sensitivity to the other. Layne makes clear that what drives this process above all is the general sense that other people might doubt the "reality" of the being that has been lost and its subsequent social identity. In other words, just because there is the danger that this will be regarded as the loss of a thing rather than the loss of a person, there is all the more need to continue with those processes that establish that what has been lost is a relationship to a person. Shopping is not, therefore, tokenistic, as for distant kin, but uses the specificity of particular goods chosen out of the diversity of the market to create a sense of the specificity (if possible, even the personality) of the deceased.

The same material practice that gives acknowledgement to and the substance of social identity in the first stage of loss can be subsequently used to allow the sense of loss to shift from the uncontrolled event of death to the controlled, as it were "reasoned" dissipation of its presence through the gradual loss of associated objects and exchange relationships. Again, one can see a parallel in Melanesian literature with Kuechler's (1988) work on the memorialization of death in Malangan sculpture, where it is the gradual dissolving of the object put up in memory of the dead that creates the social experience of the loss of the person. Instead of simply accepting a death as an act of fate taking place at a time not chosen, people will reenact the death as a gradual and controlled dissipation of their social efficacy. Similarly in the U.S. case, the death is reenacted through a gradual separation from the commodities used as gifts which would have led to the social construction of the new baby as a relationship.

CONCLUSION — ETHNOGRAPHY AND KINSHIP THEORY

There is no reason why anthropologists should not approach kinship within their own communities with the same questions they have traditional posed to others, for example, determining the rules and principles by which kinship categories are generated and organized. But if, as here, the topic arises from an ethnography and seeks the light this might throw upon kinship as experienced, then we should start by asking whether there may not be more pertinent perspectives that more closely mirror the nature of that experience. The material presented here is not intended as a critique of Schneider's (1968) work on kinship in the United States or any other particular approach. It is rather intended to complement such perspectives. Cultural anthropology tended to focus upon the study of kinship as a system of meaning. It explored the semantics of the categories used and the principles and ideologies that generate the sense of relationality. But the term "relationship" has connotations today much closer to the word "meaningful" than to the word "meaning." Indeed, the most common question people ask themselves today of relationships is precisely whether they are meaningful. The argument of this chapter is that what makes a relationship meaningful, as opposed to merely having meaning, is almost always a process of objectification (for definition of this term, see Miller [1987]). We hope to make our close relations desire that which we can provide for them and thereby appreciative of our labor of love in shopping. But within this expression of our care and concern, what is constantly to the fore is a dialectical tension between specificity in the form of the actual person one is shopping for and universality in the form of the discourse about the category of kin to which they belong. Shopping and similar practices are viewed as (among other things) attempts to resolve these dialectical contradictions. Although such resolutions are always temporary, the process itself is what is understood as giving a relationship depth.

This is why in some cases favorite pets seem more like relatives than distant relations. They come to form part of what constitutes the field of meaningful relationships, being seen as both obdurate and demanding of our labor on their behalf. This shift from meaning to meaningful also means a shift from kinship as a *system* of categories of the kind normally studied as kinship to a *set* of categories. The reason for this emerges out of the approach taken here. It has been argued that today we see a proliferation of discourses about the normativity of particular kin and other roles. We are constantly talking about actual friends and relatives but also interpreting television soap operas or newspaper stories about celebrities in terms of normative models of kinship. How partners, parents, or siblings ought to be (see discussion of Parker [1995] above). These have developed to such a degree that any particular role has become relatively autonomous from its definition within an internal "system" of kinship, to become its own point of reference against which the particularity of the person who embodies that relationship is constantly viewed. So we can relate an actual grandparent to the discourse on grandparents not to the grandparent as a position in a classification of kin. In the appendix to chapter 2 an attempt is made to follow through this trajectory by tracing the history and current developments in anthropological theories and approaches to kinship. A point made there is that my approach is similar to one that is being developed in the study of kinship in other areas. For example, in a rare case in which a study of kinship has focused upon the topic of love, Trawik (1990) also argues for the kinship of the South Indian Tamil people that the actions of individuals are constantly set against what each individual represents in terms of categories of identity. These may include not only kin relations but also nationality, gender, and family history, although in that case, kinship remains quite clearly a system of classification.

I am not making the claim in this chapter that the study of shopping has revealed the true or authentic nature of kinship in our society. Rather, the conclusion is more parochial in that it has merely tried to understand and theorize those aspects of kinship that pertains to shopping. This may be significant, but it does not constitute kinship per se, which includes many other facets and forces. Even with respect to shopping, some caveats may be noted. By selecting this topic some relationships are brought into focus, and others are underemphasized. For example, the relationship between siblings are much less evident in household shopping than they would be in a study of eating together (e.g., DeVault 1991). Shopping, for "big ticket" purchases such as a new house or car might well have emphasized the more extended family than the daily shopping that is focused upon here, and topics such as caring would turn us still further in that direction (e.g., Finch 1989, 1997).

A popular misrepresentation takes us to be individuals desperately trying to create our individuality in the teeth of sanctioned norms and constraints. This is hard to square with the overwhelming evidence that shoppers ignore most of the diversity of goods that already exist and emphasize the standard purchases such as yet more pasta dishes, little black dresses, or seaside holidays. Although consumption as specificity may be used to negate the alienating experience of the market and other massive institutional forms (Miller 1987), this need not be through an idiom of individual free choice. What makes people feel secure from such forces of alienation is not the development of the self but the development of relationships (although higher status groups may feel the need to live up to the dominant ideology of individualism—see Holt 1998). It has been argued that the individual is becoming subsumed as a relationship, a position quite different from the argument that the individual is increasing a goal in its own right as suggested by most contemporary sociology (e.g., Giddens 1991). The importance of relationships may not have declined. Assumptions about the contemporary or narcissistic self may also have romanticized a contrast with the scale and solidarity of the nineteenth- and early-twentieth-century century family. Gillis (1997) has recently pointed out, for example, that the experience of transgenerational elements often now extended to three generations has enormously increased with the decline in early mortality. He also shows how family life has been reinvented through a complex growth of rituals and myths, that refer to, but owe relatively little to, a past where the family was a much more fragile beast (see also Miller 1993 for the specific case of Christmas). Although engaged in the quite different task of documenting the history of the normative family we live by, Gillis's conclusion is close to that of this ethnography. He starts his work as follows: "We not only live with families but depend on them to do the symbolic work that was once assigned to religious and communal institutions: representing ourselves to ourselves as we would like to think we are. To put it another way, we all have two families, one that we live *with* and another we live *by*. We would like the two to be the same, but they are not" (xv).

The same conclusion arises from an analysis of the ethnography of shopping. This is because they are exactly what shopping as a daily routine of provisioning is about. From the very first extended illustration of Susan's shopping expedition through the case studies of partners and parent-child relations there have been myriad examples given of how shoppers struggle to make specific purchases that will not just reflect but act directly upon the contradictions they constantly face between the normative discourse that tells them who they and their family members should be, and how they find them in their specificity as individuals. Through the study of shopping, therefore, we can reveal a great deal about the core relationships we live with and live by.

Appendix

THE DEVELOPMENT OF KINSHIP STUDIES FROM MORGAN

In chapter 2, a particular approach to the study of kinship was developed out of the ethnographic study of shopping. In this appendix, my aim is to complement that material by attempting to reach a similar point but by a very different route—one that I admit in advance may be of more interest to anthropologists than to other readers. If I now try to situate the advocated approach within some comments on the history of kinship studies in anthropology it is not to suggest that my approach is an advance on, or culmination of, that history. On the contrary, the history of kinship studies should be seen more as an accretion of important perspectives that together create a field, since although this history clearly includes an element of fashion suggesting the successive replacement of genres of analysis, closer inspection would show that each stage has in the longer term held its ground to become one within an eclectic but productive field. We might hope that this does not merely reflect academic history but represents also the gradual adaptation of academic endeavor to the diversity of contexts within which kinship as a phenomenon of human practice reveals itself. The evolutionary metaphor is Darwinian in that the claim is not that kinship analysis is getting better so much as it has become richer in its exploitation of the diversity of human social habitats that it has to colonize.

Nevertheless, the approach that has been applied here has its own phylogenic trajectory, being more precisely related to some branches of kinship studies than others, so that it may be historically situated without implying that that history has a direction. The implication is that the perspectives on kinship developed by Lewis Henry Morgan are not so much redundant as more relevant to particular social and historical contexts. I would hope this is obvious enough, except that one of the faults of prior kinship analysis has been to project to an unwarranted degree models developed in one region onto another. In North London it is possible to inquire as to the meaning of the concept of second cousin once removed, but my evidence would suggest that hardly any North Londoner uses or cares in the least about such categories and that this lack of salience should bear on our choice of approach. This does not gainsay the importance of both accurately translating and identifying the fundamental underlying structures behind kinship when working in a society where kinship categories are salient since they are constantly being invoked in determining who has rights over the performance of a ritual or who can speak freely to whom in everyday life.

While acknowledging their centrality to kinship studies, the approach I develop in this work owes little to what may be described as the three main branches of such studies within the discipline; that is, the study of structure, of function, and of culture. I take Morgan to be a foundational figure in the study of kinship structure, while I recognize that the context of that interest changed markedly from his evolutionary speculations to the redevelopment of an interest in the basic patterning of kinship that arose following Lévi-Strauss. What they have in common is an interest in both the formulaic element of kinship—that is, the logic that underlies and generates it as a system and also in seeing this as the source of insight into larger anthropological issues than simply what kinship does in organizing the relationship between people.

By contrast, the question as to what kinship does within society is precisely the common element within that mundane use of kinship as part of the larger ethnographic inquiry that is characterized as functionalism and structural-functionalism. This question is implied in the presentation of kinship in most standard ethnographic accounts, though potentially leading to wider questions about function that has roots ranging from Durkheim to Freud through Malinowski and Radcliffe-Brown. It may be suggested that a variety of articulations between a concern with kinship as classification or structure, on the one hand, and its role in organizing social action, on the other, dominated the mainstream of anthropological enquiry up until the 1960s. Particular schools concerned with topics such as alliance and descent developed, and with them an emphasis on particular underlying principles such as exchange or reciprocity, which often involved as much work on structure as on function. Kinship studies also expanded through various forms of comparative analysis and the growing sophistication of historical studies. Such mainstream approaches did not entirely neglect the region in which my work is situated, most famously through Firth, Hubert, and Forge's (1969) study of kinship in North London, although this was decidedly "exotic" with respect to kinship studies as a whole.

The third approach, which today may be regarded as one of a dominant triumvirate, is kinship as part of the study of culture. This is most closely associated with the influence of David Schneider. It coexisted with American developments such as componential analysis that in some ways paralleled French structural studies, but it clearly contributed something original. It emphasized the symbolic rather than the classificatory elements within structuralism and blended these with a North American mainstream cultural anthropology. This is particularly significant from the point of view of a North London study in as much as prior traditions were largely developed through the study of other societies, while the influential examples of cultural analysis were applied to one's own society, Schneider (1968) to American kinship and later Strathern (1992) to English kinship. They focused upon the principles and ideological values that underlie the general use of kinship terms, principles such as blood or individualism. The cultural approach then took root as a point of articulation between kinship and a rising interest in gender studies, which also fostered a focus on symbolic spheres, and in particular, on symbolic power and which was also oriented as much to the societies of the anthropologist as to comparative studies.

This simple tale neglects many other powerful movements within kinship studies, such as the relationship to class or the state, and I defer to a succinct summary of the wide brief of kinship studies given by Peletz (1995) in *Annual Review of Anthropology*. Although the titles of his sections are somewhat different, focusing upon topics such as structure, power and difference, I don't think his outline contradicts the few remarks I have made here. In his article, however, there is a slightly odd entry, odd in that it does not fit particularly well in the section where it is placed, which otherwise would have moved relatively seamlessly from a discussion of kinship and inequality to the particular issues of gender and reproduction that have been highly influential in recent years. This section is titled "Contradiction, Paradox and Ambivalence." It contains a discussion of studies that the author clearly admires, such as Wikan (1990) and Trawick (1990), but is introduced simply as a category of new interests rather than being related back to the history of kinship as a whole. Why does it appear at this time as a class of kinship studies? I suspect that one cause lies in the desire for a different kind of ethnographic experience, one that bridges the study of the "other" and one's own society by a profound desire to relate to one's informant's experience through the same form of empathy used within our own experience, while recognizing the differences founded in cultural norms. We want to feel that we can, as it were, get under the skin of this particular informant/friend and her experience of that particular brother. This desire returns us to one of the foundational antimonies of anthropology, that between objectivist and subjectivist approaches, since we both want to see the world from this individual's experience but also retain the ambition to utilize this empathy in order to represent more generally the nature of the sibling relationship in that society.

Trawick is one of those used to illustrate this new style of kinship studies, and her work is particularly impressive. At one stage (128–54), she presents her perspective on kinship through a similar history to that given here, though grounded in South Asian regional anthropology. She examines the differences between the structuralist emphasis on affinity exemplified by Dumont (1983) and the work of David and Barnett who become her local equivalent to the culturalist perspective (e.g., David 1983). In trying to bridge the gap between both of these and the desire to present kinship as lived experience, she employs the theory of practice developed by Bourdieu (1977). But this still stops short of the sense she has of the diversities and ambiguities that arise in practice as ethnographic encounter and she concludes with post-Freudian approaches, most especially, the influence of Lacan. In any event, her ethnography is much better read as her own original contribution rather than simply a rendition of any of these theorists as models. Through effective ethnographic illustration she examines particular relationships within a society in which the type of highly elaborated kinship system that has dominated anthropological work is clearly evident (e.g.,155–86). This allows her to argue that the forms of love or bonding that arise in some relationships may be the model for others. To some degree, sibling, marital, and generational relations are understood as playing with a general arena of love whose foundation is ambivalence expressed as fully in argument and cruelty as in tenderness and affection. This complex concept of love becomes the pivot around which the book is constructed.

What writers such as Wikan and Trawick have in common, then, is that they discern a congruence between the ambivalence that inevitably arises in the development of their own relationship as ethnographers to the field and the ambivalence they observe in the relationships between the people they live among. The sister we encounter as informant is just as concerned as an anthropologist would be with the problem of how far her experience of a particular brother relates to her understanding of the cultural norms of sibling relationships. Both the Tamil and the Balinese contexts are ones in which the exigencies and informalities of events are grounded in a powerful consciousness of the moralities and constraints imposed by the normative. These can become fundamental antinomies as where Trawik discusses the contradiction between identity and separation within Tamil ideals of love, which she argues is central to the maintenance of engagement (1990, 246).

This is different from the perspective developed in the "culturist" approach since it is not the underlying ideological principles that are of concern except inasmuch as they set up problems for the practice of kinship. If there is a well-established theoretical agenda that would provide the underlying trajectory behind such developments it might well, as Trawick suggests, pass through practice theory, but then lead to areas outside of conventional anthropology, in particular, to psychoanalysis. To conclude—notwithstanding the dominance of three main approaches to kinship, some of what may regarded as the best recent studies have created a focus upon ambivalence and contradiction that may owe more to new sensitivities to anthropological experiences in the field than to any logic in the history of kinship studies per se.

Having remarked that the most obvious theoretical grounding of this development might be practice theory, I now want to come to the same point by way of a rather different route, which starts with the application of practice theory to the study of kinship by its most influential exponent—Pierre Bourdieu. In this case, the discussion starts with the category that often stands for kinship when applied back within our own societies—that is, the "family." In an article called "On the Family as a Realized Category" (1996), Bourdieu recognizes that the concept of family (as employed in France) overlaps with many different fields— juridical, residential, alliance, and so forth. As often in Bourdieu's work, he tries to reconcile subjectivist and objectivist appraisals of the category. He fully acknowledges a perspective that says the family is created by its discourse as a classificatory term subject to a process of naturalization. This would render it as a social constructionism made real. At the same time he recognizes that the term is descriptive as well as prescriptive, and against the ethnomethodologists, he argues that it is a constituent part of habitus and thereby of the reality we all perceive as members of families. That is, the family is both immanent in individuals and transcendent in the Kantian sense of a priori. The match between the objectivist and subjectivist creates the circle (he does not here use dialectical language) that makes our social reality appear as "natural."

Bourdieu then turns to the forms by which the term is institutionalized as a site of social reproduction. Again he recognizes the affective dimension of "family feeling" maintained especially by women as a principle of cohesion. But his emphasis is on the family as a privileged category supported by state principles governing areas such as the transmission of names and properties, where some "great" families have more power over the designated individuals than others. In effect, then, Bourdieu at this point confirms the culturalist approach to kinship by noting that what he has done is serve to make explicit that which tends to remain implicit as the underlying principles of organization. But then he asks, "who constructed the instruments of construction that are thereby brought to light?" (21). This leads him to claim that

> It is indeed clear that in modern societies the main agent of the construction of the official categories through which both populations and minds are structured is the state, which through a whole labour of codification accompanied by economic and social effects (family allowances, for example), aims to favour a certain kind of family organization and to strengthen those who are in a position to conform to this form of organization.

This final section is called "The State and the Statisticians."

I think Bourdieu fairly summarizes the state of current play in the academic analysis of the family. He is supported by the more sociologically orientated work that dominates the empirical studies of families in Europe, for example, Gullestad and Segalan (1997). To take a typical textbook on the American family, *Gender Roles* by Lindsey (1997), the book starts by looking at the mechanisms of socialization, the comparative study of gender roles, and the implications of the history of Western gender. Most of the book then consists of an analysis of a series of domains within which gender roles may be understood to be constructed, these include the home, the workplace, education, religion, the media, politics, and the law. This perspective particularly dominates "critical" studies ranging from Donzelot (1980) to Barrett and McIntosh (1982) where the concern is to locate the forms of power that generate the family as a realized category.

The study of the Western family that leads up to practice theory is then rather different from the study of non-Western kinship in that the overwhelming influence is on the institutional forces that construct and reproduce normativity, while in traditional anthropology, although the concern is equally with the normative, the forces of reproduction are held to be more systemic within the kinship system itself. Most recently, these have come together in feminist anthropological work on kinship and the family. Much of this has attempted to complement Schneider's cultural approach through a focus on power and class. The particular route taken has been to emphasize the role of kinship and the family in naturalizing power as discourse, which returns us to Bourdieu's emphasis on the state and the institutions of power (e.g., Yanagisako and Delaney 1995; Collier, Rosaldo, and Yanagisako 1992). Does practice/feminist theory, thus applied, fulfill the potential of a dialectical approach to kinship? Although Bourdieu does not use dialectical terminology here, he does elsewhere, and its influence upon his work is evident. The subject and the subjective are properly identified as products in a history codified as law and practiced as governance, but are also understood as the agents that realize and manifest this historical legacy as discourse and as practice.

I want to argue, however, that Bourdieu's analysis of the category of the family remains an unsatisfactory realization of the potential of dialectical thought in the same way that Trawick had to go beyond conventional practice theory. I do not wish to deny that the state and its codified discourse on the family is immensely powerful, or that it creates problems and constraints for those who attempt to defy it at the point at which they require the state, for example, in inheritance disputes or strategies for payment of taxes. But I submit that the overwhelming evidence is against his conclusion that the state is a prime or even a particularly important mover when it comes to the dynamics of family and kinship.

In his first page, Bourdieu recognizes the extraordinary dynamics of the present family form. All sorts of new arrangements are being made in practice, such as married couples living apart, various kinds of stepfamily systems, etcetera. Yet he uses this only to suggest that our normative category is more recent and more friable than we usually admit. He does not address the implications of this evidence for his own conclusion. This century has seen an unprecedented radicalism in the dissolution of customary norms of family life, but I know of no argument that this is the direct result of a radical state or that it is the state that desired this dissolution. There are many forces that may be responsible, including feminism and new ideals of contractual or consensual love (Beck and Beck

1995; Giddens 1992), but all of these have in effect caused problems for the state, which suddenly finds itself quite unsure of its own stance. The state in Britain and probably in many other places is clearly genuinely confused as to whether, for example, single mothers should be encouraged back to work or encouraged to stay at home to reproduce family values. The rise of single parents is hardly what a tax-raising, increasingly anti-welfare state would have encouraged.

Bourdieu's analysis is consistent with the historical expectations of dialectical thought. Abstractions tend to become institutional categories that then oppress us. For example, a recent study suggested that the advice given by divorce lawyers in Britain, which leans strongly toward the maintenance of two-parent contact for children, may have been detrimental in many cases because of its inflexibility in holding up what has been turned into a conventional morality despite the diversity of the circumstances encountered (Neale and Smart 1997). There are, no doubt, many similar examples of the controlling and constraining authority of formal institutions and their interpretation in practice. But there is much more to the potential of dialectical thought than this contradiction between the state and the population. There are many other areas of life that generate normative expectations other than those that emanate from authority and power.

Writers such as Trawick have taken their work beyond practice theory by focusing upon ambivalence and contradiction in their ethnographies of the lived experience of kinship. The same route is as yet rare in the ethnographic study of the Western family. The literature here is dominated by work on the institutionalized forces that are assumed to dominate the form and social reproduction of family life. Even the cultural studies associated with anthropologists such as Schneider (1968) and Strathern (1992) have so far tended to eschew ethnographic involvement in kinship as a form of practice (though see Strathern 1981 for an exception much closer to the approach advocated here). By contrast, Parker's (1995) book, with its close attention to mother-infant relations described in chapter 2, argues that discourse is something that mothers go in search of and try to generate rather than seeing it as something that descends down to them from institutionalized forces.

The other advantage of Parker is that she shows how in the study of the Western family as in that of non-Western kinship there has arisen a new literature that focuses directly on the experience of kinship relationships and its central affective dimension, and seems to imply that central to understanding relationships at this level is the problem of ambivalence and contradiction. It contrasts with most current studies in which Bourdieu's original desire for a dialectical path between subjectivism and objectivism has been abandoned. Instead, we find the subjective is relegated to a reified ideal of authentic "experience" while it is the objective representations that bear the brunt of critical analysis. This is the problem with the increasing body of studies influenced by poststructuralist theorists such as Foucault and Barthes and, most especially, Baudrillard, which have become prevalent in some forms of sociology and cultural studies. These have tended to work on institutions and their representations. The danger of this focus is that it preserves a romantic notion of the individual struggling for free expression but unable to surface as authentic agency thanks to the weight of discourse generated by forces such as state power and capitalism, which merely employ the individual as legitimization for their project. Within this volume there is considerable attention to the forces that constitute power and the way it both constrains and creates subjectivity, but the starting point was that of ethnography. From this perspective the world looks very different. The emphasis in chapter 2 was upon ambivalence and contradiction in kinship and especially that between universality exemplified in discourse and the particularity of practice. But a key finding is that discourse is not something we seek to confront but something we constantly strive to develop.

To conclude—a new approach (though one with many precedents of which the clearest may be Leach [1954]) is being developed within anthropological studies of kinship that focuses upon ambivalence and contradiction. Furthermore, this approach provides a means to reintegrate what otherwise would be a rather one-sided focus of abundant new studies that are mainly a critique of normative discourses. The approach is justified in that for us as much as among the Tamils, people struggle with the discrepancy between their specific experience of particular kin and what they are socialized to view as the normative model of that kin relation. The effect is a dialectical tension between the objectification of the relationship in discourse as expressing a universal and the experience of the specific individual as kin. Bourdieu fails to achieve the dynamic implied by dialectical thought, since while his concept of habitus draws attention to the generation of specificity and strategy out of normativity, it avoids the contribution that arises from the creative uses of ambivalence and the contribution of the particular and subjective to the generation of normativity, something that is recovered through the approach taken here.

This conclusion takes us a long way from the trajectory that starts with the work of Morgan. Anthropological studies of kinship have continued to draw on Morgan's original classificatory perspective. Even the most vanguard forms of "culturalist" study emphasizes principles of relationality as the core to kinship, that is, the criteria by which people understand there to exist a pertinent relationship. But the approach advocated here is based neither on classification nor on relationality. I would argue that for us the rise of normative discourses around particular relationships can become largely autonomous of the network of relationships as a whole. That is to say, our main concern today has become how our particular brother matched our introjected and projected images of how a generic brother might be, rather than the sibling relationship being one exemplification of principles that permeate kinship as a whole. Articulation between different kinship roles continues mainly through the extent to which one genre of relationship may become a metaphor or model for another. To put this bluntly—with respect to the topic being studied here—we have no kinship system. Instead, as I argued in chapter 2, these principles may be applied to any relationship including those with a friend, a pet, with oneself, with a fictive figure, or with any other for whom there exists a discourse generating the normativity of that relationship, irrespective of whether they are defined by blood or marriage or some more ad hoc legitimization. In effect, relations of marriage and certain close relations that are ideally of blood (such as siblings, which may now also be stepsiblings and ad hoc fictive siblings) are not the foundation but simply the primary exemplification of a stock of relationships.

THE DIALECTICS
OF COMMUNITY

THE CONTEXT — A STREET, NOT A COMMUNITY

This chapter will start with a largely descriptive ethnography of the local shops from the perspective of both the shopkeepers and the shoppers. My analysis of the basic contradictions that emerge in the relationship between the shoppers and the shops emerges gradually from a comparison of middle-class and working-class attitudes and practices. In the conclusion to the chapter, I argue that the power of the dominant ideologies that fashion both the discourse and the attitude of shoppers is such that these do not appear to be much affected by the actual experience of shoppers of the shops themselves. As the final case study demonstrates, shoppers are simply unwilling to allow their assumptions about corner shops to be contradicted by their shopping practice. This conclusion adds to my disquiet over the current dominance of phenomenological approaches to the anthropology of landscape, and in the appendix to this chapter, I combine my own ethnography with work on Australian aboriginal societies to suggest that in many cases the senses may be the last place, rather than the first place, from where we encounter the world around us.

One cannot presuppose that local shops will be central to the normative discourses that surround the notions of community and sociality for any particular people, but there are grounds for expecting that they occupy such a position within British ideology. Where a U.S. soap opera or sitcom might privilege the workplace and the home as the two key localities of sociality, in Britain these are complemented by the ideal of street life based around the pubs and shops that remain paramount sites for the imagination of sociality and community. People are expected to meet at corner shops, which function as the hub of news. They also expect to retain a sense of the street as a place where, at least in the summer, there will be an active public presence—of children playing, people washing their cars, gossip at street corners, places decorated by front gardens cultivated with considerable care and attention. Many of the poorer people on this particular street do not have cars, and therefore constantly occupy the street as pedestrians.

These expectations conform in part to historical evidence that suggests the street really was the hub of sociality at least for the working class (Allen 1998; McKibbin 1998). Also important in the European as against the U.S. experience is the relative lack of clear zoning. Especially in North London, the real estate value of a property can change markedly from one street to another or even within the same street. Class is of paramount significance, but it is so localized as to be highly fragmented. As a result, council estates and quite wealthy middle-class housing are often found, as here, in the same street, and the street lends itself to considerable potential for mixing between people of quite contrasting social backgrounds.

One of the problems with choosing a single street and its periphery as the spatial unit for our work was that it implied an anthropological unit corresponding to community or neighborhood. Indeed, the street had served as an important unit of study in early sociological community studies. Unlike most of these studies, we had no expectation of community. Rather, our aim was to ascertain through fieldwork the dimensions and degree of sociality that might reflect a typical London street in the 1990s. The difference between the reality of this street and the kind of fictive street enshrined in soap operas such as *Coronation Street* (the most popular television program in Britain) was very evident when a crime occurred in one of the shops on the street during the course of our fieldwork that was sufficiently important (involving a celebrity) as to be reported in a national newspaper. Yet two months after this event occurred, many of our informants were unaware that it had taken place. We found this astonishing, but it certainly put to rest any remnant expectation that this was a community. On the contrary, it clearly demonstrated that most people did not exchange sufficient communication with their neighbors for "news" to travel in this street. The evidence was, however, quite compatible with observations made by others. For example, a bartender who was working in a new pub that was trying to establish itself remarked that, apart from people who came in by themselves, there was much less conversation between the customers within this pub than in other areas where he had worked. Likewise, many households reported that their relationship with their neighbors was cordial but minimized to formal gestures of greeting.

If this street was particularly lacking in sociality then the reason given by most people who dwelt there lay in the nature of the housing. One side of the street was dominated by maisonettes seen as most suitable for transitional families that could not yet afford a whole house but believed that a mortgage was more efficient than renting. On the other side of the street were council estates, of which the largest, the Lark Estate, was dominated by an uneasy mixture of the elderly and single mothers with children and where the general atmosphere along the dismal concrete corridors was anything but friendly. There are clear exceptions to this generality, pockets of intense sociality, lasting groups and long-term fond neighborliness, but these were based on smaller networks rather than on the street itself. So our field unit consisted of the juxtaposition of households and crosscutting networks, but there was no whole that transcended the parts. The street was definitely not a community.

Piecing together the oral history of the area it is clear that forms of sociality come and go. At one stage there was a relatively stable Irish community in the area. When the Lark Estate was first settled, its occupants saw themselves as relatively privileged in terms of state housing, and there was more confidence and community within that estate. One of the smaller estates inhabited largely by immigrant households was highly convivial and had come to exist as a genuine social unit, including most (though not all) its occupants. New groups to emerge include the National Childbirth Trust, which organizes meetings for new mothers, and other groups that provide new facilities for the elderly. Several of the informal provisioning and exchange activities studied by Alison Clarke (forthcoming a) produce at least temporary networks among mothers. Locations such as the church and a luncheon club are important for the very small numbers that actually attend but hardly impinge any more on the street as a whole. For the elderly there is a day center not far from the street that hosts events such as bingo. Indeed, the more active among the elderly know of a number of such centers in the vicinity and may have a regular set of five, one for each weekday, which they tour in the style of the old weekly markets, keeping themselves fully occupied. In some cases their weekly shopping routines could only be understood when it became clear that accessibility to these particular day centers was the key underlying factor explaining their choices. The single most important locations other than the shops are probably the two local primary schools where many householders meet as parents.

As the ethnography progressed it became evident that sociality tended to divide into two distinct modes, with class the central variable in understanding the neighborhood. The literature on this subject and the history of these modes will be discussed in the conclusion of this chapter, but roughly speaking, the working class (and, most especially, the English-born working class) living predominantly on the estates tended to be wary of their neighbors and rarely invite them in their flats. For them domestic sociality was largely synonymous with kinship. On the other hand, they were friendly and cognizant of others in the public domain, which varied from inside shops to the street itself. Middle-class families, who dominated the private housing, tended to invite people back to their homes, but these were from a diverse range of contacts including work or friends from previous areas they have lived in. Their contacts grew to include others of this area either through mother and baby groups or through friendships among children in the local primary school.

As will be shown below, the shops themselves fluctuate in terms of their integrative role.[1] The street appears to have included a shopping parade (a row of stores) from the time it was built. Memories go back several decades, and past shops included a pet shop, a needlework shop, a chemist's, various varieties of greengrocers, a butcher shop, a delicatessen, a video shop, a real estate agent, a minicab office, and shops selling cut flowers, children's clothes, sweets, car parts, electric repairs, among others. There was a high degree of consensus that it is the chemist's that is most missed today. There are several current shops that have been in the same hands for a dozen or so years, and one for twenty-five years. One side of the street has suffered from structural problems. On the whole, the parade does not look prosperous but is it not especially rundown. Like the street itself, it is best described as nondescript.

---

1. There is a certain fictive element to my description of the shops in order to protect their anonymity but not such as should influence the academic consideration of them as evidence for the points made.

SECTION ONE: THE SHOPKEEPER'S PERSPECTIVE

Neighborhood Shops and Functional Shops

As well as being home to most of the households that participated in this study, Jay Road contained twenty or so shops (with some closing and opening during the year's fieldwork) that formed part of our study. Two shops stood out clearly from the mass as key focal points for people living in this area. One was a hairdresser's, and the other, a hardware store. The hairdresser's was run by a fashionable-looking male with several young female assistants in a modern, largely white, small salon that was constantly full. The salon was highly suited to one of the main groups that lived in this area, the young–to–middle-aged female aspiring professionals who tended to want to work in careers such as media or journalism. The most successful lived closer to Ibis Pond, and residence in Jay Road itself would suggest aspiration rather than any great measure of success. Many of those who frequented this salon, however, came from other, more affluent streets than Jay Road. Although this group dominated the salon, elderly women and some men and families could also be found there (cf. Furman 1997). Many customers come to this salon in the expectation of chatting, often at considerable length. As trust and continuity has developed, so has the depth of content of these conversations to the extent that the hairdresser's has become something of a local confessional. Since it is sometimes whole families who use the hairdresser, a number of particular functions of this conversational space have opened up. These are best described through examples.

On my first session, sitting and listening within the shop, a man having his haircut was talking avidly to the hairdresser about the other members of his family, Both his wife and two daughters had their hair cut there, and it was soon evident that he was fishing for information about them that he had not been able to obtain at home. Asked if this was common, the owner, Frank, replied,

> Oh, very much so, and very much so with married couples. Very much so. That very often happens. It's quite interesting, really, because it's amazing what they want to tell each other, but don't have the time. Or they're too self-conscious or inhibited to tell each other, which is quite as interesting. There is this really stupid example: Two people wanted to go on holiday, wanted to go to the same place on holiday, but didn't tell each other that they wanted to go there. And I just happened to say, "Oh, I hear you want to go to such and such a place," and, "Yes, but how did you know?" And I said, "Well, I gather

> that the wife was talking about it," and he was quite taken
> aback because he said, "Oh, I didn't think she really wanted to
> go." You know, there's that kind of thing. Then there is a com-
> mon case of them talking about kids, and private education
> and state education—one who is terribly for it, and one who
> is terribly against it, but again for political reasons. But then
> they had to talk around it, insofar as what is best for their
> child rather than how they felt about it politically—I mean,
> that's quite (when I say a common one) you get that quite
> often. Yes, they'd each sort of talk to me about it and what
> have you. It's almost like they're sounding me out before they
> confront the partner, and I try and stay as neutral as possible.
> I mean, otherwise, you get taking sides. We do also have ex-
> amples of marital difficulties, when we know there's a third
> party involved, that I find difficult because then I am involved
> in that.

Other situations arose when he had become party to information such
that he felt in a genuine quandary as to whether he should respect the
confidence of the person telling him, since the implications were potentially harmful to others. Overall, Frank clearly recognizes that he has become a kind of amateur counselor. As he notes,

> a lot more people are having counseling than ever, which I
> think is wonderful, Yeah, there's a lot more people reliant on
> me, but that builds up over a period of time, before they real-
> ize that I can be quite discreet and not get emotionally in-
> volved in the whole situation.

Most of the chitchat of the day is less personal and revolves around in-
nocuous topics such as the theater, beliefs, and things people have been
doing. But he admits to encouraging certain kind of counselor-related
topics such as mourning:

> I'm quite open to that kind of thing—death [I do] not enjoy,
> but I know I can help people and that is something that I am
> good at. That's the kind of counseling that I am good at. I
> mean, I don't call myself a counselor but, I mean, that's some-
> thing that I enjoy.

One of the main topics of conversation is related to the particular concentration of young single professional women in this area. The classic
topic has become that of the woman who is dissatisfied with men but

equally fearful that as an aspiring professional she "frightens off" men. The fieldwork took place before the novel *Bridget Jones Diary* was published. The extraordinary sales of that work in Britain over an extended period are instructive given the close parallel between its content and ethos with the dominant concerns expressed in this hairdresser's salon. Both suggest a core quest for a relationship with a man, undiminished by a simultaneously avowed feminism, and the problem of keeping this compatible with other desires such as retaining female friendships and a career. The female assistants cutting hair can discuss such concerns with depth and empathy, but even the male hairdresser manages to be an effective confidant. Men, by contrast, sometimes talk of their implied sex lives, although more often in relation to problems than simply to boast about "conquests." They also converse rather more about how they have achieved their current position and status in life. Another core topic is schooling, which is the one genre where the constant and profound concern observed in the salon was also evident in conversations within the more general ethnographic context of the shopping study.

In general, the middle-class clientele prefer to talk about such things only to Frank instead of discussing such issues among themselves within the shop. Evidently, Frank has become a kind of conduit, not only within families but even more between people whose friendship is constituted by their common use of his salon. Quite often those who use the salon on a weekly basis do so in recognition of the others for whom this is their regular "slot" and who they therefore expect to meet again. Regulars will often ask Frank about how a particular person is getting on these days, since they may have lost direct contact. This is very different from the public sphere constructed by the less-well-off elderly population that also frequents the salon. They are much more prone to create a general collective chat or to sit together in twos and talk for considerable periods of time. As Frank remarked to me about two elderly ladies sitting in the corner, "Oh those two, they chat like a couple of old birds, like budgies they are. They'll talk to anybody, which is lovely." He acknowledges a certain responsibility to his elderly regulars and will initiate inquiries if they do not turn up when expected. During the general fieldwork the cut-price scheme for pensioners run by the hairdresser was one of the most common facilities remarked upon by the elderly on the street.

Frank's reputation also extends to the other end of the age scale, as one of his customers noted:

> Yes, he's always very chatty, and he knows every child in the area. He's the one you should talk to about everything. I

> should think he knows everything about this area. I mean,
> we've left Michael's mac in there, or coat or something, and
> somebody brought it round for us because she recognized it as
> being Michael's. It's such a community that he can say to us,
> "Well, would you like Michael's hair cut like Jack? I expect you
> know Jack, don't you?"—you know, this sort of thing.

Even those who don't go there know of his reputation, through the re-
porting back of those who have been, as one person remarked of her partner:

> Because the last time he came back and said, "Linda said
> you shouldn't use fabric conditioner because that might
> make her eczema worse." So they were obviously discussing
> the children, because Linda has a young child, too, and
> Linda's always tells my husband and his brother how much
> hair they're losing. I don't think that's the best thing for a
> hairdresser to be telling people, but yes, he does, he often
> reports back.

The hairdresser's salon is complemented by Sonia, who lives in Jay Road
but works exclusively in the homes of her clients. Unlike her rival, Sonia
does not serve the pensioners, but works almost entirely through the
"thirty-somethings"—mothers with children. Only about five or six of
her list of over two hundred clients comes from Jay Road. Most of them
live in the better-off areas, such as Owl Crescent. Her original recruitment
came through advertising with the National Childbirth Trust as well as
cards in mailboxes. The overwhelming emphasis in her conversations
(once beyond the initial chitchat of everyday events, or topics such as
clothing and recipes) is concerned with problems in relationships, sometimes with clients in tears as they tell of being deserted by their partner or
some similar concern. Almost all have long-term partners at work. One
difference is that there are more "natural" networks within this group
since it was by word of mouth that most people came to know of her.
Sonia is also willing to pass on suggestions made by her clients to others of
various kinds of services, for example, the use of Colour Me Beautiful, a
firm which gives advice on clothing. The nature of these networks became
clear to her when around a quarter of her clients sent her a card for her
birthday although Sonia could only recall mentioning the date to very
few people.

There are two or three other shops on the street in addition to the hairdresser's salon and the hardware store (discussed below) that also promote
considerable sociality among their clients, but this is a smaller clientele, so

that while the shops may have considerable significance for their clients, they are mentioned but rarely in the ethnography as a whole.

One of these is the local café. In particular, there are four or five groups of women with children that tend to come in on a regular basis, most commonly after school. With its wooden floors and plastic tablecloths, the café is very suitable for young toddlers and their frequent spills. The waitress said that she would introduce one mother with children on her own to another mother with children the same age that she knows about and who they might want to meet, because she knows that people wouldn't talk to each other otherwise. It is also a major meeting point for widows and widowers who come in regularly and feel comfortable there. Here also the waitresses can oblige, for example, a particular widower who is a bit deaf and doesn't like sweet corn and peas. Like other regulars, he no longer needs to order and is still assured of receiving his "usual." There is not the same level of community involvement here as in the hairdresser or the hardware shop, but the café provides a valuable service to those who most need a public space for socializing.

Another example would be the betting shop. Of those who use this facility, around 60 percent simply come in to place a bet and then leave. Most clients are from within a three-street distance of the shop but also include construction workers who are there just for the duration of a particular job. Even for those who only use the shop to bet, this may be an important feature in their lives, as one strongly suspects for the elderly woman who arrives as the shop opens and seems to feel it is her ritual duty to be the first customer of the day. Another elderly woman commented in typical fashion:

> I done a little bet today, because my name's Loopy, it's not my real name—a nickname and there's a little horse running today called Loopy. It is a coincidence bet. I only have a 10p to win. It's something to look forward to in the paper tomorrow or on television. I might go in once a week, sometimes twice.

On the other hand, around 40 percent of customers hang around in the shop itself. These are a close-knit group. Unlike larger betting shops that supply tea and coffee, there is no such facility here, but this does not seem to prevent quite long stays by the regulars. The conversation is essentially sports, sports, and more sports, dominated by horse racing but also dog racing and football. There is very little reference back to domestic and other matters. Nevertheless, for a group of around forty people, mainly men, this shop serves as a community. Unfortunately, this is not sufficient to make the shop commercially viable, and the chain that runs it is con-

stantly threatening to close it down, in which case it is unlikely that an independent will find the capital to keep it going.

There are several shops that once would have occupied a position in the
sociality of the street that would put them on a par with the hairdresser or
the hardware store, but today have been relegated to a position closer to
that of the betting shop. An example of this is the local pub. Oral history
shows that there was a period in which a particular female manager made
the pub into a thriving community center patronized by many locals. Today, however, very few people talk of using this particular pub, and while
it is important for the few that do use it, it certainly does not occupy the
kind of focus for local identity that pubs in other districts clearly maintain. For oral histories that go back several decades, there were others in
this category, as one elderly resident recalled, "Mrs. Jones, a greengrocer,
she was a lady who had, you know, she liked to gossip, so people used to
congregate there and listen to all the general gossip."

A similar history could be told of the launderette. Of particular interest
here was the role of this establishment in integrating the Asian owner who
was one of the first Asian retailers in the parade. At that time the family
was strongly involved in the local community, supporting their children
through the local school, and the launderette itself seems to have occupied a position close to that of the current hairdresser's as a place where
people talked not only among themselves but also to and through the
owners. People would put their clothes in, get a cup of tea from the bakery,
and then come back and chitchat until the clothes were finished if not
longer. The atmosphere was full of fun and gossip. Today, however, the
launderette is a rather sad and empty place where I do not recall ever seeing people engaged in conversations with others they had not come with,
except on strict functional matters such as how to use the machines. The
main users are home-helps, students, and a few other, mainly elderly, persons who have been using it for decades. Almost all of these (apart from
home-helps) would be single-person households. There are two main reasons for this. First, the shop itself is becoming redundant, as washing machines are now ubiquitous among the middle class and prevalent among
the working class. But equally the current owner has none of the interest
in creating the sense of community around the shop that was characteristic of the previous owner so that there is no one to occupy the kind of role
played by the hairdresser.

A similar fate appears to have befallen the post office; despite the fact
that it is the single most common shop mentioned by householders when
considering the functional requirements that they have for the local parade. Again, there was a time when it had a strong factor in the sociality of

the street, particularly for the elderly, since the main assistant was herself an elderly person living on the Lark Estate who knew just about everybody who came in there, but also for others in that it ran a toy shop as well as the usual stationery and related goods. The owners were known as chatty (and the man, in particular, as cuddly) and they were said to often give back too much in change. Today the sociality of the post office has been replaced by the functionality of a counter service where the only concern is the degree to which it carries out its duties well and the complaints are largely to do with the length of queues or the lack of some facility. One shopper who previously worked as an assistant pointed out that there is now only one person behind the counter even on days when people come in to collect their pensions. Despite these long queues, customers come in without any expectation of further social relations.

The shops discussed so far already provide the basis for a firm conclusion, which is that the relationship between sociality and the functionality of the shop is relatively fluid. It does not follow from these stories that there was once a time when all the shops were friendly and sociable, something they have almost all lost. Rather, the oral histories suggest that within the twenty or so shops there were always a couple where the personalities of the owners or assistants turned them into key sites for neighborhood sociability. Any one of these categories might serve as a core contributor to local social life. Today it might be the hardware store and hairdresser, but another time these may have played a minor, largely functional role while the newsagent, or the pub, or the electrical repair shop functioned as the key sites. Much depends upon contingent factors such as personalities and particular histories; racism also plays a role (see below). In conclusion, shop functionality proves to be relatively unimportant in determining its place within street social life. Overall, what is striking is how few shops on the parade operate in the manner of the corner shops nostalgically invoked when shoppers describe "the old days."

The eating establishments are used largely on class-specific lines. The working class tends to use them as rather anonymous fast-food outlets. The middle-class customers are much more likely to come inside for a sit-down meal, usually as either families or couples. Both classes are intent upon using the facilities to develop their own conversation with no interest in engaging either the work staff or other diners.

Dilip, one of the newsagent corner shops is conspicuously friendly to customers, but he has not been particularly successful in establishing the kind of social integration that he would have desired. Indeed, he notes that there is much less chat than when he used to run a post office in another district. On a typical morning, some older people stay for up to fifteen minutes talking. The conversation is almost always dominated by whatever is in the news that day. One customer, a Labour Party supporter, airs his grievances about the government as he buys his *Guardian* (a national newspaper); two others discuss the recent budget—for example, the effects of taxation on smoking. Another chats about *Eastenders* and third about *Neighbours,* both assuming that Dilip has seen the relevant episodes of these soap operas. Several talk about their own or their partner's illnesses or, in one case, about a friend who has died of cancer and how they were going to give up smoking. Another held a long conversation about budgie seed!

These conversations are, however, few and far between and do little to alleviate the general sense that people are coming and going as quickly as possible. A noticeable trend is that, apart from illness, they do not discuss things near and dear to them. They hardly ever discuss their own children and parents, although they will discuss grandchildren. Very occasionally something more emerges from these discussions, for example, the shopkeeper has had a carpet fitted and some electrical work done by customers he has come to know well enough to employ. The fact that his children go to local schools has not, however, in any way overlapped with his role as shopkeeper.

Garib, a grocer, by contrast, finds that his children's presence in the local schools is one of the few things that does impinge on his work, in that he is commonly being asked to give help toward various fundraising for school events. On the other hand, the fact that he lives on the Lark Estate only makes his neighbors conspicuous by their absence as customers in his shop; as Garib notes ruefully, most have never even stepped inside. As with the previous corner shop owner he would like to have closer social relations, but these do not emerge. Even the desire for sociality cannot be assumed. Several of the other shopkeepers who run either groceries or sell specialist goods clearly have no interest in going beyond the strict functionality of selling goods and are quite happy that their customers make no attempt to breach the distance between buyer and seller. The post office maintains a fairly cold and formal relationship between those serving and the queue of those being served; similarly, the fish and chips shop owner recalls few if any social encounters and restricts their work to something as close to a fast-food system as possible.

The Travails of Local Retailing

One of the advantages of the long-term involvement of ethnographic enquiry is that it allows the unpalatable to sink in gently. During the yearlong fieldwork, I used to frequent one of the several corner shop newsagents. To be honest, I needed a local refuge during the many pauses of fieldwork (when no one would spend time with me!), and the owner was a particular friendly, Asian shopkeeper. I also chatted to him about his business as part of my own study. He had been working there for nearly two years, and one of his statements in particular could not fail to impress and worry the listener. He noted that he had never taken a single day off since the day he opened his shop, not even a Sunday, Divali (a Hindu holiday), or Christmas (a Christian holiday). Parts of days, yes, when his wife would take over, but never a full day, and never had he therefore been able to take a holiday. He made a very small sum on the occasional use of photocopying facilities. He ran a newspaper delivery service to one hundred homes in the area. He had so far been refused a license for the national lottery, while the big supermarkets had been operating the lottery for nearly a year. The magazines that used to be sold on a sale-or-return basis are increasingly having to be purchased on a firm sale basis, but customers who make firm orders do not necessarily turn up for and buy the magazine requested.

Around a year after I had completed my fieldwork I chanced to return to visit an informant/friend and wanted to pay a visit to the shopkeeper. I found the shop closed and boarded up, and the only information I could obtain was that the shopkeeper had had some kind of nervous breakdown and the shop had subsequently closed. My work was not focused upon the lives of the shopkeepers themselves. A fine example of how such lives might be portrayed has recently appeared from Shachtman (1997). Taking a single block within contemporary New York City, he narrates the story of shopkeeping, the sheer diversity of hopes, fears, and fates that they reflect as well as insights into the structures they must inhabit. It is clear from this work that an outsider looking in on the activity would have many other factors to consider, such as the values that are being expressed in the activity, the enjoyment as well as need of risk. But the New York block remains a larger and perhaps more optimistic setting than Jay Road, and the relationship between values and entrepreneurship differ between the United States and Britain. On Jay Road the situation of the shopkeepers was also quite varied. The hairdresser represents the other extreme from this corner shop, but his plight was the more characteristic of the shops taken as a group than was the hairdresser.

There were several specific problems affecting this neighborhood, but mostly the problems are those faced by small shops more or less throughout Britain today. One very local issue concerned a rerouting of transport that made it easier for people to travel to the main local high street, which meant that they were less likely to walk past this shopping parade on their way back from work. This had occurred three years before, and estimates of the effect on income ranged from a drop of 10 to 40 percent in trade. In other respects the street reflects the more general decline of small shops unable to compete with high street stores. The supermarkets' dominance of groceries is well established, but every year the supermarket seems to add another genre of goods that impinge on local shopping, such as newspapers or underwear. Specialist shops such as fishmongers and bakeries have been particularly hard hit, and the number of village shops almost halved in recent years.

The main resistance to this trend are the so called c-shop symbol groups such as Londis and Spar, which help independent shops come together under a single "brand" name or symbol pool their resources and thus remain viable, and also the growth of petrol-station forecourt shops.

This decline is hardly news. If there is one great monument to perspicacity in considering the future of shopping this remains Emile Zola's work *The Ladies' Paradise* ([1883] 1992). If told with greater eloquence and ability, my stories of the small shop would vary little in implication from those Zola described for the Paris of the 1860s. One could not hope for a more carefully observed account of the struggle between the largest and smallest shops than what is found in the Zola novel, or one that so evenly tempers empathy with realism.

The shopkeepers in Jay Road are well aware of their problems and the implications for the attitude of local people to them. Margins are driven down to below 20 percent but that still bears no comparison to the kinds of margins the major supermarkets can work on. Meanwhile, there are many costs involved locally. A newsagent that makes much of its money from the sale of cigarettes can't afford the capital to buy bulk goods at low prices and so has to obtain cigarette stocks from a cash-and-carry. The shop owner's wife visits this once a week in tandem with their neighboring shop that goes on a different weekly cycle so that they can help each other with goods that run short. The grocer has to be up at four o'clock in the morning to travel to buy fresh goods, many of which go bad and have to be thrown away if they do not sell.

All of this translates into conversations with customers that shopkeepers would rather not have:

> I know the locals will be complaining about me, they must be. Even if I cut margins this would not bring in more people to compensate for it. Some customers say, "Mr. Banerjee, why are you selling 79p bread you know Tesco is only 45p?" I say, "Look, dear, it's not my price." They recommend the price 79p. So I can maybe match with 70p, but Tesco is a different story. They can squeeze manufacturers and do whatever they like.

Meanwhile, fixed costs continue to rise. Most of the shops are owned by two landlords—one for each side of the street. One is a large property firm, the other, a private owner living abroad. Both seem willing to allow shops to fail and remain empty rather than refrain from raising rents on a regular basis. Both seem quite isolated from the drama and trauma of shop-keeping at the present time.

The impossibility of earning a decent living was only one of the problems incurred by shopkeepers on the street. One shop was also having a running battle with one of the tenants on the Lark Estate. This particular drunkard had managed to obtain some short-term credit from the shop but when this was refused he became angry. At this stage there were some five other regularly drunken males living within his flat. They came over and smashed the shop window. The police came but more or less told the shopkeeper there was nothing he or they could do. As they pointed out, the assailant would get state-funded legal aid while the shopkeeper wouldn't, and the assailant was on social security and no compensation could be obtained so there was no point in prosecuting. In effect, the shopkeeper is impotent. At least with the other problem of the occasional kids' stealing, he can threaten to inform their parents since they are mainly local. Violence on the street had traditionally been low, but recently there had been a more serious incident, including armed robbery with guns pointed at customers. However, as the shopkeeper of the particular property (which is estimated to have lost £2,000 in the raid) noted with a shrug of his shoulder, this is just "part of the job." If the pub seems to have little problem with drunkenness, this may be because hardly anyone goes to drink there! It should be said that trouble is not always simply visited on the heads of innocent shopkeepers. The street also included several recent cases of accusations made against shopkeepers, including one of the attempted rape of a customer.

Other services on the street are also in decline. The postman and milkmen are both local figures that are said to be important to householders. But the postman notes that no one wants to do this round since there are one to two people in the area who attract very heavy postbags. The milk round is now barely viable. As a result, there has been considerable change in the personnel occupying these positions, and this in turn decreases the scope for developing social relations. The current postman greets everyone but noted that he would be cautious about exchanging anything more than a greeting even if people wanted to—which they don't seem to. His social connections come much more through the betting shop where he is a regular visitor. Meanwhile, he has plenty of little problems to negotiate. Is it all right that at one house the dog always takes the letters from him? Is it all right to leave with a neighbor a card marked Do Not Bend but is too big for the small mailbox? Should he leave alone a front door that has clearly been left open? As I accompany him on his rounds, people are very friendly in their greetings, but the greeting never turns into conversation as he hurries on to the next door.

My concern in this chapter is only with formal shops and services. It should be noted that there is a vast range of more informal services and trading that are being studied by my ethnographic coworker Alison Clarke (e.g., Clarke 1998). In her work, the situation is much healthier with respect to the development of social intimacy.

As individual shops have declined, so too have the relationships between them. According to local accounts there used to be much more reciprocal help between them and many informal agreements to avoid overlap in the selling of merchandise. A newsagent owner noted:

> (A)   Yeah, there was unwritten rules. I wouldn't sell Coke because they sell Coke—I wouldn't take away their business. They wouldn't sell washing powder because they knew I would sell it or he would sell it, they wouldn't sell newspapers because they were selling newspapers—it was just all these unwritten rules about how we would do in business.
>
> (Q)   How is it now?
>
> (A)   It's just everyone out for themselves now?

Certainly such oral histories are generally nostalgic and unreliable on such matters, but it is clear today that apart from a few acts of cooperation between neighboring shops and some local supply (such as the café by the grocer), many of the retailers are competing directly in the same areas, and there are several examples of fights in the courts over licensing issues and other rivalries. There is, then, good reason for thinking that the external pressures on survival have led to a spate of self-destructive competition that will eventually only enhance the negative effects of these pressures.

SECTION TWO: THE SHOPPER'S PERSPECTIVE

Racism

The ethnographic evidence presented thus far suggests a parade in which at any given time a few shops stand out in their close relationship to the people of the street as against those shops that see themselves and are seen by their customers in largely functional terms. It seemed that both in the past and in the present it is the particular personalities of the shopkeepers and assistants that determined this difference. Before reaching such a conclusion, however, there is a rather obvious additional factor on the street that needs careful analysis. The hairdresser and hardware retailer happen to be the only two shopkeepers on the parade today who are white and English and whose shops have been there for several years. All the other longer-term shopkeepers are either Asian or Mediterranean in family origin.

The hairdresser himself seems quite clear as to the importance of this factor:

> That's the reason they choose to come over here. It's very sad, and they're bigoted about everything—sexuality, absolutely everything. That does influence who I employ. I had a Black girl for three days who was a lovely girl, and I didn't sack her—she just didn't come in. But I mean the amount of people—"Why are you employing . . . ?" To me, it is disgusting that this is happening in this day and age but, I mean, it is happening. And the children's clothes shop was Black, and you've got the launderette, and the Londis, and the take-away, and the Indian. They're all Asian [-owned], which isn't any problem from my point of view, but it is a problem from the other people's point of view because they won't use them. The only two shops that they actually swear by are Bob (the hardware) and here, "That's the only ones I use." It's true Bob's very helpful and he's very nice, and I'm going to say a totally racist thing now: We're both English and we're both White, I mean you can put that in your report but it's true.

The overwhelming evidence of the ethnography on the street backed up this statement. The main difference was between the explicit way this was treated as a topic on the Lark Estate and the more subtle expression of the issue in the private-housing sector.

Two comments would be typical of the estate:

> (A) Oh, no. We haven't had English people down there for a long, long time. And it has changed, you know, it has made a lot of difference really.
>
> (Q) They try to be friendly, the people (shopkeepers)?
>
> (A) Oh, yes. They are friendly, but you don't get the same relationship as we did with the other owners. You see, they were White people and, I don't know, we just have our own way of communicating.

(Q)   So, that has made a big difference?

(A)   Yes, yes. There's a ghastly woman that I met by accident be-
      cause she was collecting books, and I was, she was talking as
      sweetly as you like to him over there. And when she came out
      she said, "I hate those fucking Pakis." I said, "You know if I
      hated them, I wouldn't give them my business."

By contrast, middle-class racism is said in knowledge of its unaccept-
ability, which is either made explicit or avoided through joking, and usually with some ulterior justification for the sentiment expressed.

> It's something that I would rather cut my tongue off than say,
> really, to be honest with you, but you know it's . . . We have
> the very same thing down there with the supermarket, you
> know. And it's all these shops round here who depend on local
> families whose children go to local schools and when it comes
> to things like, "Could you possibly contribute to our fun day?"
> or whatever, you know, if you're lucky you get a packet of
> broken biscuits. And I tend to think that it's a form of (and I
> don't like to put it too strongly) sort of racism in reverse,
> really, yes.

> Well, I don't think the one at this corner is particularly clean,
> so I try not to buy things like bread. Actually, we have a joke
> about it because sometimes in the morning if you go in there's
> often a smell of something gone off. You know, if, for example,
> the fridge has been turned off during the night or you smell
> bad eggs or something. And whenever you do that they have
> incense burning. So whenever we smell the incense burning
> you think something must have gone off in the shop.

Racism is not universal; there are a number of examples of people who
either do not care about such matters or act to discriminate positively. For
example, one middle-aged woman on an estate noted the following:

> I know them very well . . . They're Hindus, you see, and I
> thought it was a real honor because he came up here and said,
> "We're holding a party down at the Asian center down behind
> the shopping city, you know the Asian center?" and he said,
> "We're holding a birthday party." And I saw them in a com-
> pletely different light. And the one thing I was a bit worried
> about, I said to Paul, "I hope they don't bloody go on in Pun-
> jabi or whatever they speak in." And they didn't. You know as

> soon as I was in earshot they'd roll off English which I thought
> was lovely. He works so hard.

According to oral histories of the shops on the street, it appears that the first shopkeepers from a nonlocal background were highly integrated into street culture. The case of the launderette has already been mentioned:

> When I was at work I used to go Saturday morning, and I still
> see one of the chaps, the other chap who was away. And it was
> like a little club, and there was another lady who unfortu-
> nately died. And it was a real sort of chatting club.

The owner's son, who went to the local primary school, remarked on the degree of solidarity he felt then with white youths who united to see off any racists from other areas. Similarly, a Turkish woman established a very positive relationship with her customers. Today, however, one is faced with an exact correlation between race and lack of affection for individual shops, which locals will justify as a resentment that has grown with the degree of control by immigrant shopkeepers.

One of the possible causes of this correlation might have been that the shopkeepers of nonlocal origin were not attempting to create the same relationship with their customers, and certainly, this is a claim made several times in justification of an antipathy, especially toward Asian shopkeepers. My evidence, however, suggested otherwise. There was the same diversity within this group as historically had been the case with others. Some of the Asian shopkeepers are indeed uninterested in extending beyond a functional relationship and in at least one case could be described as rude and unpleasant. But he is a single and exceptional case. On the other hand, another Asian shopkeeper is one of the friendliest of all those working on the street and works hard to establish conversational relations with regular customers as well as being helpful in many practical ways. Yet in conversation he was as much a target of negative comments as the other Asian shopkeepers. An appraisal of this factor is complicated by the powerful presence of other negative feelings toward the grocery and newsagent section of the parades, which constitute the biggest group within the whole. A proper assessment of racism, therefore, needs to await a larger examination of attitudes to the shopping parade.

Middle-Class Ambivalence

Although the street was chosen in some ways to limit the sense of class polarization, in the end I had to acknowledge that traditional class categories remain the most authentic forms of generalization about most households on the street (see Miller et al. 1998, chapter 7), at least with respect to certain issues, including those of this chapter.

The relationship between the middle class and the local shops is complex and starts to open up the major concerns of this chapter in terms of a dialectical tension in people's identification with neighborhood. The middle-class parents' obsession with the development of their children provides the first pragmatic grounds for a set of relationships that revolve around the local shops. In many cases, they identify a clear phase in the socialization of children during which they are not allowed to go to the main shopping centers but are encouraged to use local shops. This is viewed as a kind of safe training ground for learning the skills of shopping, in particular, and of negotiating public space more generally. The children in turn focus on the local shops first as the source of sweets and various playground crazes or hobbies and later for magazines and other such goods. In addition, having young children makes it more difficult for the parents to go on longer shopping trips, makes shopping "emergencies" that much more common, and makes the corner shop a kind of minimal leisure outing from the claustrophobia of child care. A middle-class mother noted the following:

(A) I feel every area should have, you know, a few shops, really. I mean, I don't use them that much now, but at different times in your life you use shops more. So when I was at home and I worked part-time or when they were both babies and toddlers, then I would go on a more regular basis. And I think at the time there was that fruit shop down there, and I used to go and buy my fruit every other day sort of thing.

(Q) When they were young you wanted to get out?

(A) Yes, you might. That's true in the summer. Now I might take them down and buy them an ice lolly or something. Also I think it's quite important for the children in the area. They couldn't go down to Wood Green on their own. Well, I wouldn't want them to. But I think they need to. It's quite important for them to learn some kind of, I mean, they have pocket money every week and they're responsible for buying their comics, sweets, whatever, out of that money, and that's it. I don't buy those as extra and then give them pocket money.

(Q) They go alone?

(A) Yes, they can go down there.

(Q) From what age?

(A)   Well, I wouldn't let the eight year old go on his own, but he can go with other friends. So I suppose it's very hard to make hard and fast rules, for different children are ready for different things, but I suppose the older one's been going down there for the last year and he's ten.

On Owl Crescent, which is the street where the middle class have the clearest sense of an active neighborhood community, this can develop into something further:

(A)   On a Saturday what generally happens is people knock on the door about nine o'clock or some ghastly even earlier time, and everybody's got their pocket money, and a parade will go down to buy their football stickers or whatever it is, sweets, or Beano, whatever. Then they all come back together swapping their stickers or whatever, and then they go for some football practice together. So that tends to a game for the children quite often; it's a whole group activity to go off.

(Q)   To one particular newsagent?

(A)   They tend to. Our children tend to have a sort of a craze for one thing. So it's either like Premier League football stickers, or this thing I don't know if you've got it in your research, its called "pogs." The "in" craze. You have these little round cards with different little characters on. They're in packets like football stickers and you pay for a packet. It's got seven different little round little card disks, and you pile them up. And you have a plastic one in each pack, and you flick them and any ones that land upside down after you flick them your opponent is allowed to keep. And there's like a set of, altogether, fifty, so by playing this game you win them off other people. So you tick them off on your list until you have managed to win a whole set. It's another collecting thing. It's a real rip off. It's very expensive, I think they're about 99p a packet or something. That will be a craze, and one of the shops won't have any pogs in, so what they'll do then is go on a tour. They'll go down to Jay Road. It's the same for football stickers or whatever it happens to be at the time. And you go down there, and if they haven't got any they would then go on a little parade around. But only really within those Jay Road shops as far down as, you know, the one actually on the end. That's their limit. But the word goes round; somebody will come up and say, "Hey they've got some," you know, so and so have got some.

An older teenage girl expressed her own sense of the importance of the newsagents:

> Some magazine I used to always get and I was going to start ordering it, but then I didn't bother buying it for a while. But my friend upstairs, every week they go over and they get about five magazines every week. And the man keeps them for them because they're mad into this pop group Take That, so they buy every magazine in case they've got anything in them.

This topic of use associated with children was unusual because the grounds remain largely pragmatic. More generally, conversations about the use of the shops quickly become enmeshed in complex webs of ambivalence that reveal the degree to which the relationship is ideologically charged. Typical comments were:

> For newspapers as much as often, and we buy emergency eggs or taramasalata, potatoes, veg and the local hardware shop when we need it—we try and support them.

> I accept that they do have to charge more, yes. I mean, I did actually go through a phase when I did try very very hard at this corner shop down here. I would shop at the supermarkets once a month and it was a financial experiment to be honest with you, and I think I broke even really. You know, what I'm saying is that I shopped at the supermarket once a month for things that you would buy maybe four cans of beans and all that sort of stuff, but I did that only once a month and I supplemented them when I ran out of the basics and whatever. And definitely our fridge wasn't as interesting as it normally is but I didn't actually end up spending any more because I could buy one of something down there without feeling that I was being. And so I was actually quite prepared to do that, you know. Then I was spending a lot of money down there, maybe £30 a week down there.

> Well I would like to see (and I do understand it in terms of how difficult it is to operate on a small scale any more), but I would very much like to have local shops. And I do, one of the things that I do (when you talk about boycotting), I tend to in the supermarkets is not to buy. I say to the boys, we'll call into a magazine shop somewhere. I don't allow them to buy magazines or newspapers, or I won't buy flowers in the supermar-

> ket, and I won't buy (if I can possibly avoid it or if I can take
> the time) anything to do with the pharmacy or anything. I use
> it as a source of food and I buy the vegetables there. So I use
> that as a form of boycotting, really because I really do feel
> that they have taken any incentive away from anybody to open
> anything up on a smaller basis, really. So I would very much
> like to have pleasant local shop, and it would be very nice to
> see them reopen really.

(Q) Make a difference if it wasn't there?

(A) It would make a difference in two ways, I think. One is as a
> kind of emergency backup thing. It is useful having it there,
> and secondly, there is this curious feeling when you have got a
> few local shops around you, it changes the atmosphere of the
> neighborhood. It gives it a kind of center, whatever that
> means. If it was all houses all the way it would make a differ-
> ence in appearance terms, which would somehow matter.

Unlike working-class shoppers, the middle class would draw attention
to the fact that the children of the local shopkeepers went to the same primary schools as their children and that this ought to be further grounds
for patronage of the shops in question:

> Yes, I do go to them, and I tend to go to the one over the road
> for no particular reason, but in fact the child—one of the chil-
> dren in that family is in Simon's class—so I have chatted to
> the mother quite a bit. We were pregnant at the same time so I
> tend to go in there.

There were several conversations with regard to local milkmen that implied that if at all possible one would have used them or that people had
used them as long as possible, but the change from an individual who had
worked the area for many years to a succession of less familiar faces who
also came later with the milk had been grounds for finishing with this tradition. But again, the way this was said was such that it seemed as though
loyalty had merely delayed the destruction what had come to be seen as
an antiquated system.

The attitude to the shops as expressed in these quotes does not seem to
correlate particularly well with who actually uses them and here lies the
rub for local shops. At a time when they are not particularly good value for
the money or essential for supplies, there has nevertheless been an un-
wavering appeal to sentiment. In general, they are the good guys, and
the supermarkets are often seen by the middle class as the embodiments

of materialistic evil. One can find articles in the middle-class newspapers almost every week that are aimed at reflecting these sentiments; attacking the rise of supermarkets and out-of-town malls as the death of the corner shop. Yet despite the tenacity of their ideological convictions, the middle class manages to avoid much use of the very same shops that they defend. In order to account for this discrepancy, we need to examine the alternative objectification of community that exists for this class. My central argument is that the main reason they can avoid using the local shops is that they have another locality nearby that can satisfy their projected discourse of community.

The alternative that presents itself is the shopping area Ibis Pond, which is similar to many shopping areas that serve the suburbs of London. These are mainly based around the various "villages" that existed prior to their incorporation within the expansion of London proper. The ability of Ibis Pond to stand for a vague idealized sense of nature, which includes the nostalgic sense of a "natural" relationship between a community and its shops has been described in detail elsewhere (Miller et al. 1998, 123–27). One of the ironies of this objectification is that the shops in Ibis Pond are generally far more expensive than even the local corner shops. But this expense is covered by what might be called the "high production values" that lie behind Ibis Pond's performance as culture. The "olde-worlde" storefronts, the imported European clothing, means that Ibis Pond is not just an enactment of community—it does it with style.

The appeal of Ibis Pond also rests on the fact that members of the middle class can indeed walk around browsing the shop windows of Ibis Pond and not only meet people they know, but the locality (usually reached by car) has largely filtered out the working-class shoppers they would meet in the corner shops and left them with those who would be familiar with the relevant rituals of the new yuppie coffees and croissants. Despite the residential juxtaposition within Jay Road, class distinctions are already well bifurcated by the two main housing types and even more by the enormous importance given to which of the two local primary schools their children manage to gain entry into. The primary school with clear middle-class aspirations and identity is situated much closer to Ibis Pond itself, and during the ethnography it was the parents of children at that school who were most likely to meet each other while shopping in Ibis Pond.

Ibis Pond is replete with the little arts and crafts shops that emphasize gift-related sociality (cf. Sherry and McGrath 1989) and also the charity shops, which manage to construct a gloss of personalized shopping as not altogether an alien commodity form. This kind of delicatessen as neighborhood was clearly a viable alternative for the middle class who could use the supermarkets in the same area for their basic food provisioning, while keeping a sense of "neighborhood" through excluding these from their dominant image of Ibis Pond. This image consisted largely of smaller shops that evoked intimacy and sociality within what was actually quite an extensive and expensive shopping center. Ibis Pond can charge its high prices because what it is selling is itself as a mediation in the contradiction between a discourse of community and a dissatisfaction with the actual locality that ought to objectify this discourse—that is, the corner shop. This, then, becomes a prime example of the use of shops in the resolving of dialectical tensions, though rather different from that of the previous chapter.

By comparison, the rundown local shops of Jay Road that can ill afford such decorative facades simply do not look the part for playing a role as the pivot of middle-class community life. Indeed, in discussing the future of the street parade, "gentrification" was seen by these shoppers as one solution:

> I can't think that people wouldn't start shopping locally with a butcher any more, and because the butcher in Hawk Hill, for example, they've held on there and are holding on literally by the skin of their teeth because they're very badly effected by the supermarket. But they've made an effort. They now do some organic, and they do a lot of nice Greek sausages, so there's still, they're making an effort really to say to people, you will get different things here. . . . It had occurred to me like a secondhand children's supply shop. I think you would never make a lot of money out of it, but it could have worked had it been approached in the right way.

Working-Class Disassociation

Whereas the primary relationship expressed in middle-class households was one of ambivalence and a general discrepancy between discourse and practice, among working-class households there was a less ambiguous sense of disassociation. The dislike of the local grocery and newsagent shops was most palpable on the Lark Estate. The following are five typical comments:

> Shops in this road? They're too expensive, they are too expensive.

> I will often buy my newspaper just on the corner here if I haven't bought one during the day when I'm out. And I might go up to the post office and buy stamps. And that's probably

the only local shop here that I use. Everything else I either do in the supermarket or do at work.

Well, their prices are, you know, they stick it on, don't they.

Across the road, it's not a delicatessen now, it's a dirty old shop. Very sort of worried sometimes about buying things in there. I bought some whole runner beans, frozen Bird's Eye whole runner beans. I know they're frozen, right, but I didn't notice until I'd eaten them that the sell by date on them was a year old. They were perfectly OK but they shouldn't have sold them to me at the price they sold them to me at.

Try not to use it. It's really expensive. I mean just for milk and bread. I usually end up spending a fiver just for a few little bits so I try not to use it, even if I just run out of milk I just run down to Iceland because it's only down. . . . it's easier.

Even a cursory glance would demonstrate that local shops are indeed offering lesser quality at higher prices (see Piachaud and Webb [1996] for corroboration derived from a more systematic survey). In general, if one went only on the verbal evidence it would seem that poorer people do not use these shops at all. The evidence from actually shopping with people is more complex. Some do manage to avoid these shops except for very occasional emergencies, while others use them fairly regularly. In general, they use them more than the middle-class shoppers that espouse their social value. Both working-class groups, those that use and those that avoid these shops, seemed more or less equal in their vehement denial of any positive relationship with these shops. It was quite clear that most working-class people on the estates do not see the shops as constituting any kind of neighborhood with which they would identify or feel positive about. Relationships exist with individual shops, such as the betting shop, hardware shop, the launderette and—for the pensioners—also the hairdresser's (he is too expensive for younger working-class clients). As noted elsewhere (Miller et al. 1998, chapter 4), there was an interesting disparity among the elderly who tended to affirm a positive relationship to corner shops when collected in a focus group conversing within an established genre of nostalgia, but individually tended to dislike such shops and talked positively about the major supermarkets and shopping centers.

This disparity was also very evident when accompanying working-class shoppers. The general antipathy was clearest in a question I often asked about whether people would be sorry to see the local shops disappear altogether. In many cases, people noted some pragmatic grounds as to why the shops serve a function, such as emergencies when something needs to be obtained quickly, but then noted that the shops were quite likely to not stock such items anyway. A common response among the working class was "Good riddance," a term that seemed to sum up the general attitude, even though it was recognized that the demise of the corner stores would be at some cost in terms of convenience.

With regard to the social relationship between shopkeeper and customer, opinions are ambivalent about what the shops should try to do. In general, working-class shoppers came to negative conclusions:

> I mean, I used to try very hard with this local grocer down here to sort of give as much custom as possible, but they just, they don't seem—I mean, I had a shop myself in Ireland for eight years, and I think I know how it is what customers expect really. It's just friendliness, and even temperateness, you know, whereas down here you never know. Some days they're terribly friendly; other days, they're not, and he would change a twenty pound note for a penny. You know, I used to be a very good customer in that shop down there and I just now tend to think in the supermarket, or if I'm, say, perhaps without washing powder for a day, I think, fine, I'll do two lots of washing. You know, I tend to not bother, really, because they don't seem to realize, I mean, we all appreciate having a local shop, and I think they should appreciate having local customers.

(A) I think some of them try to be too friendly. Yes, I think they try too hard. I think we really just want to go in. It's nice of them to talk to people, but if you think they're naturally like that you don't mind. If you think they're just talking to you because you're a customer, then that's not right, is it.

(Q) What kind of things?

(A) Oh, they just ask you how you are when I'm sure they don't hear what you say when you.

(Q) They don't remember next time you come in?

(A) Oh no, I don't think some of them will. The one at the top is quite nice, the post office we use but apart from that I wouldn't really miss the shops round here anyway.

As I have noted, the pattern of use does not conform to the degree of disassociation, but there are exceptions, as one would expect. Two examples of these may serve (but the point remains that they are very much a minority view on the estates). The first is that of a young man:

(A) Very expensive, but convenient, just across the road. He also lets me buy things on credit, which is an attractive thing to do.

(Q) How long does he give you?

(A) Well, we haven't. I'll always try and pay it off as quickly as possible. I never really owe him money for more than two weeks.

The other opinion belongs to an elderly single male:

(Q) Do you use grocers here?

(A) Every day, twice a day. I reckon I spend 30 quid a week in those two shops between them, I only bought a paper this morning. Actually, I owe him 30 pence from this morning because I had to get some money out to pay my bill in Wood Green.

(Q) Are they chatty?

(A) Very friendly. I get on well with them.

THE MYTHS OF AUTHENTIC WORKING-CLASS SOCIALITY

Understanding this dismissal of the potential of local shops for the objectification of neighborhood and community is complex since what is most commonly represented in this space is actually constructed by the middle class and projected onto the working class. For this reason the larger history of the discourse must be understood as the context to any such representations, which returns us to the academic involvement in these constructions.

During this century up until the 1970s, more or less coincident with the ethnographic reification of the "village" and "tribe" as the primary units of fieldwork, there was an equivalent place held in sociology by "community." This was both as a topic of inquiry and also in theory where the relationship between sociality and space, especially in various urban environments, was as important in European as it was in American studies (for a survey of these studies, see Bell and Newby 1971). In Britain, this reached its apogee with the study of Bethnal Green by Young and Willmott (1962). It says something of the centrality of fashion to academic work that social science, once it had debunked "the myth of community studies" (see Allan 1996, chapter 7; Abrams 1986, 45) is today as lacking in equivalent studies as it was rich before. In contemporary British research, the closest contemporary equivalent would probably be work on youth and ethnic minorities (e.g., Back 1996). It is particularly unfortunate that just when our understanding of place as representation and ideology has become so much more critical and sophisticated, there should be so few researchers working on streets and neighborhoods to rethink the relationship back to social relations and practice.

In Britain, academic studies and representations have to be seen in the light of an extremely powerful popular ideology fixated on this same relationship. Almost invariably the starting point for its consideration is the assumption that Britain was once inhabited by close working-class neighborhoods, which have subsequently disappeared. The importance of this image to the development of a specifically British media can hardly be exaggerated. The classic British films were the Ealing comedies, within which this image of authentic working-class community is the backdrop. Later on, the scene is developed into *Coronation Street,* which remains the most important soap opera in Britain and is the program that was the most popular point of reference when discussing Jay Road with its inhabitants. *Coronation Street* is based in Salford, the same place that Engels ([1845] 1987) wrote about in his work *Conditions of the Working Class* and that later Robert Roberts called *The Classic Slum* (1973). Its rival soap opera, *East-Enders,* is a locality that is redolent with the ideals of cockney authenticity, the "heart" of true Londoners. The third current major TV soap, *Brookside,* is set in Liverpool, which resonates just as strongly with an ideal of the working class as authentic culture (from the Liverpool poets to the Beatles). Imported soap opera has never been able to overcome this triumvirate of local soaps based on the three quintessential images of authentic working-class life. The constant dialogue about these soaps that pervades the real street of Jay Road thereby keeps the ideology of working-class neighborhoods as central to the consciousness of contemporary British society.

Just as these soaps have become more nuanced in their contemporary versions, so also the academic research results were always more ambiguous than had been apparent during the height of community studies. The classic research by Young and Willmott (1962) comes closest to the popular image, but even here the primary unit of sociality was female kinship. And although there was a strong sense of neighborhood relations, it did not extend very often to people coming into each other's homes. In the face of the drive toward respectability and against gossip, it was a fragile cohesion that did not survive displacement of location. Other studies have tended to be much less inclined to give credence to such a phenomenon. Summarizing his own and other studies, Allan (1996, 86–89) comes closest to my findings for Jay Road. He argued for a clear class disparity in the forms of friendship. Working-class friendships remain largely within the context within which they are formed, for example, in the workplace. Willmott (1987, 96), however, argues that Allan exaggerates this difference and that both classes have the same limited friendships within their residential locality but that the middle class simply have more extensive friendships that transcend residential area. The most scholarly and conclusive research on this topic has just arrived in the form of a historical account by McKibbin (1998, 179–98). Overall, this suggests that the media image of friendly neighbors popping into each other's houses was a myth. Circumspection was the order of the day, and to the degree to which friendship was more than kinship, this fragile development was hard hit by the rise of the housing estates. The crowded conditions of working-class life certainly meant that people were out on the street a great deal, and this created the conditions for the extensive use of public space for the (still largely circumspect) sociality, which can be found today transposed to the public space of shopping in supermarkets and in the high street. Overall, Allan's point (and my ethnographic observations) about the different modes of class friendship seems well supported.

Despite its increasing prominence as a topic of study, household consumption and shopping has not yet emerged as a central player in discussions of these issues. Sociologists such as Warde (1990) and Saunders considered the topic almost entirely in relation to the consumption of services. The attempt to develop a new form of locality studies in geography also tended to bypass this issue. This is surprising since there has probably been no country where shopping played a greater role for a longer time in the community than this "nation of shopkeepers" (see Glennie and Thrift's 1996 examination of Pepys in the seventeenth century and onward). Clammer (1997) has recently argued with respect to Japan a much more active role for shops and shopping in the construction of urban sociality. He argues that "much consumption is actually collectivism masquerading as individualism" (48) and that in the sprawling suburbs of Tokyo it is largely consumption-based activities such as intensive browsing in shops or the use of consumer cooperatives that forge networks among females, especially housewives, based around the exchange of information on prices, goods, and styles, which is essential given the profusion of choice and the desire to create normative order out of what otherwise could be chaotic activity. Indeed, he suggests that the rapid changes in fashion mean that no one can rest assured with prior knowledge, and this makes consumption a process that demands constant social interaction for the mutual benefit of all.

The curious situation in Britain is that a role for shops and shopping is absent in the academic research on sociality and neighborhood, and yet it is more or less assumed every time the role of the corner or local shop is raised in journalistic accounts. It is also the foundation for the ubiquitous critique of the rise of the large out-of-town hypermarkets and malls, to such a degree that even the Conservative government was forced by media pressure to backtrack on the expansion of these sites and impose restrictions on planning permission. There is, then, an extremely powerful discourse about working-class neighborhoods and its objectification in local shops, but what is suggested by this ethnography is that this is primarily an ideological construct, in the strict sense (e.g., Larrain 1979) of a discourse created by the dominant class and projected onto the dominated class. The British media that created the popular image of working-class life itself began as an almost entirely middle-class fiefdom. Many of the middle class inhabitants of this area belong to the "caring professions" or espouse their ethos and are left-wing in orientation. When discussing with me the decline of their local shops and the rise of the supermarket, it was not their own traditions of sociality that they claimed would be destroyed but a tradition of street life and shopping that they associate first and foremost with the working class. They tended to single out the elderly and impoverished, the very same group who are most likely to echo the phrase "Good riddance" (at least in private) to the idea that these shops might disappear, although they will dutifully support local shops when gathered together in a formal focus group (see Miller et al. 1998).

The myth of the working-class neighborhood thereby underlies almost all discussion of both local shops and the street itself. It is hard to articulate the kinds of quantitative sociological survey data with my highly qualitative ethnography, but one of Willmott's (1987) findings seems to correspond well. He notes that while 26 percent of the middle class define their whole street as "neighbors," only 1 percent of the working class do this (32). This seems to imply a vast difference in the degree to which each class employs a discourse of street as community. It may be significant that it is the more ethnographic studies that replicate my findings. Indeed, Mogey's (1956, 83–94) study in Oxford provides the most extreme example of working-class antipathy to neighbors, with the overwhelming expectation that people should "keep themselves to themselves." A factor noted in my study and even more in Clarke's work (1998, forthcoming a), that is, the centrality of women, especially housewives with young children, to the development of neighborhood sociality, is also born out in other research (e.g., Bell and Ribbens 1994).

This academic and ideological background is important since within the ethnography any dissociation of the working-class households from the corner shops cannot then be understood in isolation from a more general distancing from neighbors within the working class. Neighborhood shops are being treated much in the same way as neighbors. Many working-class householders would not dream of going into the home of their neighbors even when living next door for several decades. The contemporary force of this point was made evident during the ethnography. Despite my prior sensitivity to this issue I was still unable to prevent my own middle-class projection of values from interfering in the ethnographic encounter. To take a typical example of disassociation, a woman using the betting shop responds to my question, "Is the betting shop friendly?" with, "Yes, it's all right, but I mean I never hang around. I usually go in have a bet and come out again, I don't hang about in there all day." As will be evident from the direct quotations of questions that appear in this chapter, I was constantly asking about which establishments were "friendly" based on my desire to elicit the extent of community. It was only toward the end of the research that I realized that the question was almost always heard as something that implied gossip and being nosy. That is, the term "friendly," which I had taken to be positive in its connotations was generally read as implying something deeply negative. This meant that my initial premise was being rejected within the conversations through which I had hoped to research local sociality. There simply was no aspiration toward the kind of "community" whose presence I was trying to elicit. The evidence of this distancing was equally clear when it came to the actual relationship between neighbors. People are well aware of the discourse of community that is objectified in soap opera, but they react to it as observers in a manner much closer to the middle-class rather than recognizing themselves in the television representations. They constantly stressed how the areas were not like any of the soap operas. Again, there are some very noticeable exceptions—individuals who are viewed by others as "heart of gold" with a strong local and social involvement, and some neighborhood "activists" who are prominent in any venture that demands grassroots political presence. But just as two "community" shops cannot hide the lack of a community relation with nearly all the others, so also these community-minded individuals are conspicuous as much by the absence of others as by their own prominence.

The implication of the previous two sections is certainly not to suggest that the middle class are more sociable or given to the construction of neighborhood and the community than the working class. As documented elsewhere (Miller et al. 1998) what needs to be acknowledged is the framed and normative nature of sociality. Many of the working-class inhabitants in this area have themselves worked in retail and note the degree to which working people tend to empathize with and associate themselves with shop workers and especially shop assistants. This is clearly contrasted with the middle-class shoppers who commonly treat shop workers with some disdain as merely aspects of the retail process, without even a nod of recognition of their common humanity. In effect, then, the working class do not practice social relations under the umbrella of manifesting a discourse of community. Instead, they simply make dyadic friendships among fellow workers currently engaged as retail assistants within what might seem to be forbidding and anonymous supermarkets or chain stores in major high streets. There is a general friendliness between people who have a common experience of working as retail assistance that leads to particular friendships. While the middle class entertains within their homes, in the public sphere their disdainful distance from workers is opposed to the friendliness and friendships of the working class.

Just as the middle class projects a relationship between the working class and the corner shops that is the very opposite of the general antagonism that is found, so also they assume that vast supermarkets must be anonymous and friendless. But as noted in Miller et al. (1998, 123–27) working-class people simply do not have the same "problem" with large supermarkets and shopping centers that the middle-class discourse supposes they should have. Elderly people do not in practice look to the nostalgic local shops. After all, they were young during the peak period of modernism and the belief in progress. In private, they look positively to what they see as the bright lights and clean modernity of the largest shops. A factor that has made a considerable difference is the availability of free public transport for the elderly in London. As a result, one could hear, for example, a conversation between two elderly women, one of whom clearly shops regularly in the West End, while the other swears by the local major shopping center. But both assume horizons that are entirely distant from the mere street shops around the corner from where they live.

In general, poorer households also preferred the larger shops and, to a surprising degree, felt their relationship with the large shops could be relatively personable. They were the people who had tended to work at least at some stage in retail and who knew shop assistants in the area, or else were able to create a relationship with particular checkout counter clerks or security guards that defied the apparent anonymity of the large store. Take as an example this blind Asian man discussing his shopping:

(Q)   Which shop do you go to?

(A)   Tesco. Small shop I can't go, because it's too congestion, you know, yes, too small for walking is problem.

(Q)   You can tell where in the shop you are?

(A)   Oh yes, she tell me where we are going in vegetable and frozen food and dairy department, drink department.

(Q)   People there are helpful?

(A)   Yes, because I take stick, it is good. People is very good to help, you know, very good, if I somebody's help me if I'm going down stairs, somebody helps, if I'm crossing road or something like that.

He may be an extreme case but he symbolizes the discrepancy between the left-wing discourse of the middle class of the area, for whom major supermarkets "ought" to emanate anonymity and materialism especially to the elderly, poor, disabled, and to ethnic minorities, and the actual experience of those individuals who fit each of these labels and for whom these locations do not impinge at all as symbols of alienation. On the contrary, they are favored sites for meeting people and creating a public sphere. Finally, it is the elderly, poor, and minority groups that are far more likely to acknowledge the vast improvement in quality represented by supermarkets over what the elderly can recall as often low-quality, sometimes rotten, and disheveled food products that were all that was available in local food suppliers in their childhood and in the face of a squeeze on margins are becoming the norm of local shops once again.

The working class does not, therefore, need an alternative location that evokes an ideal of community as in Ibis Pond. To conclude, one of the common responses to questions about community was the precise phrase, "It's not like *Coronation Street* here, you know." In the light of the argument of this section, I do not think this should be taken as an expression of nostalgic regret for lost neighborhood that I might have assumed at first. Rather, I have come to understand that this was essentially an almost educational point that informants felt a clearly middle-class researcher really ought to understand from the outset, if he was really going to embark upon that process of empathetic understanding he constantly claimed!

Bob

The implication of the previous sections is that the local shops are caught between various contradictions. The shops are subject to the general antipathy of the working class, which are based, above all, on their relative high price and low quality. They suffer from what might be called the unrequited ideological desires of the middle class, as well as from a nearly ubiquitous racism. So these general discussions of ideology and representation in both classes must now be rethought in terms of their consequence for the local shops themselves. The relative significance of the factors uncovered is best examined through the case study of Bob. This chapter began with an examination of the hairdresser, one of the two shops that has a clear integrative role in the street. The shop that most often comes up in general conversation as embodying the ideal of a community shop is, however, not the hairdresser, but the local DIY (do-it-yourself) shop run by Bob. Today more than anyone else in the street, Bob represents the current approximation to the nostalgic image people have of the neighborhood retailer. Four brief examples provide a sense of the way Bob is viewed, and in this case with no particular class distinction:

> Yeah. He's great, he's really great, have you come across him? Bob—we call him, Do-It-All-Bob. No matter what you want, you go in, and you want a light bulb and he says "Oh, 60p to you," and he's always. I don't know how he does things quite as cheap as he does, and I don't quite want to know, but he is a really nice guy. Everybody in the neighborhood likes him, too. I sort of felt like, if I was ever locked out or something, he'd probably come round and try and help me open my door. He's that sort of person.

> Well, my sink was blocked up once, and I went in to him and he advised me what stuff to buy and we talked about having to keep a torch handy in case the lights go or something. But he's so very handy for things like that. He put the battery in for me and a new bulb and so forth. He's very nice, yes.

> The corner hardware store is excellent. He never charges you what's on the label. It's always cheaper. He's completely nice, like one day my cheque card was coming in the mail and I needed to cash a cheque and I couldn't get to town, blah, blah, blah. I said, "Bob, can I cash a cheque with you?" And he was like, "Oh no, I don't do cheques without cheque cards, but I'll loan you some money. What do you need?" I said, "Gosh, I re-

ally need 20 quid. I'll give it back to you tomorrow." And he's like, "OK." He's that sort of person. He knows everyone. James goes in and he talks fishing with him, and he's so nice and he really is great. Everybody knows Bob. He's your local character, so I definitely shop with him.

Oh, everybody knows him. We were talking about him at the group recently, in fact. Other people know him more than I do. I always say hello to him. He's just one of those people who seem to be standing around outside the shop who's very nice so I tend to say hello to him. I haven't been in there for ages, but again other people are chatting recently and lots of people do go in there. We have been in there in the past, I can't think what for, but we have been in there.

Although there is no doubt that in the context of this particular parade, these views are "coloured" by Bob's colour as the other English shop-keeper, here is clearly someone who does all he can to fit the local bill. But does this create the basis for long-term viability? Below, by way of contrast, are extracts from an interview with Bob's shop assistant. One of the reasons for Bob's popularity is that he never seems to charge the full price for anything that he sells. In most transactions he ignores the label and simply quotes a special price, which at the same time becomes a token that between him and the customer there exists a relationship that goes beyond that of the single transaction. This is also the way the bargain is read by the customer. By right this ought to make for a loyal and devoted clientele and in turn a shop that comes to profit in turnover what it sacrifices in margins. Unfortunately, there are two negative sides to the constant chatting in the street about Bob and his shop.

The first negative side to the hardware store that Bob runs is the sheer disbelief that a shopkeeper can create these bargains and be legitimate in his business. One of the four examples of positive approbation given earlier included the phrase, "I don't know how he does things quite as cheap as he does, and I don't quite want to know." This idea that Bob must in some way be on the fiddle was a constant feature of the conversations about him. Several people were convinced he was a drug dealer. Others were influenced by the fact that he did a side line in used cars to brand him as clearly part of a criminal fraternity. In particular, one had a sense of the middle-class householder unwilling to accept that a local shop could compete with the high street, since it contradicted their own generalizations. They therefore developed a set of explanations all based upon some "dark" side to this shop, none of which was based on the slightest evidence. People simply could not believe that the shop's prices really could be cheaper than those from the high street. Refusing to accept the evidence of their own encounters, they merely assumed that while this was a reduction of the usual corner shop pricing, it still could not really be cheaper.

The assistant noted the following:

> He's very good to local people. You know, if the local people go in there and, like, you saw me serving people, he'd automatically give them like a 10 percent discount. He'll give them a 10 percent discount on that, and that's why he's got such a good reputation. But that goes against you. There's a lady I used to work with. I thought, well, I've got to go past where she lives, I may as well go and tell her, "Do you want to go to a talk on garden design?" and that, and I had a chat with her, and she goes to me, "I saw you in Bob's the other day." I said I do a bit of work in there occasionally or just help him out if he needs to go somewhere, and she says, "Is it true is that just a cover for drugs?" I said what I said, "Don't you ever let Bob hear you say that," I said. "That is one of the biggest things that he is against." She said, "Well, how does he make money? because he's always knocking money off of things for people." I said, "He does that as a service to local people." I said "He's not making any money." People can't go into Safeways and say, "I want 10 percent off that." The price is the price as is on the thing. If you want it you want it, if you don't you don't. People have been duped into thinking they go to these big places and they're getting a bargain and maybe sometimes they are, sometimes they aren't, but Bob had some four-foot fans standing up, you know, and he was selling them at £29.50. And I didn't know the price, he hadn't priced them, and I tried to get through to him. This woman wanted one, she lives up in Ibis Pond and she wanted this, and Bob wasn't in at home so I couldn't get in touch with him, and I looked through the Argos catalogue and they were £44.50, and I said to her, "Well, they're £44.50 in Argos catalogue." So she goes, "They'll be a bit dearer in here then." So I said, "No, I'm sure that they weren't that dear here." She said, "Look, I'll leave you my card, can you get in touch when you get the price. I definitely want one. Do you want me to leave a deposit?" I said, "No, because that would just confuse the issue," I said, "if I'm not

here." So I phone her up and said, "They're £29.50." "Oh, I
bought one in Argos." And I said, "Well you just spent 15
quid, exactly the same, exactly the same thing.[2]

The importance of Bob, then, is that two of the key factors in the failure
of local shops to objectify community can be dispensed with. Unlike most
of the shopkeepers, he is both white and English, and unlike most of the
shops he is good, if not better, value for money than the high street. Despite this, I would predict that in the end this shop will fold, or if it sur-
vives it is only because the sociality it represents is viewed just as
positively by the shopkeeper as the shoppers. For him, too, this is the kind
of social life and role that he enjoys immensely, and he savors his role in
the community. But given the choice he would not, of course, do this at
the expense of being able to earn a living, which is very close to what is being asked of him in practice. The irony is that at the very same time there
is an ever growing ideological concern to construct images of a socially active neighborhood community among those with the highest disposable
incomes, there is a growing inability to nurture a local shop that could
serve admirably as the potential objectification of this idea. In practice,
householders find it impossible to attach this ideal to their own local practice. Once again the nature of the dialectical tension as overwhelming
other considerations comes to the fore. An individual shop simply cannot
throw off the larger determination within which it has become axiomatic
that local shops cannot resolve the contradiction between the discourse of
community and the potential objectification of that discourse. The exception here merely "proves" the rule, since as an anomaly it is explained
away as based on crime or some other devious force. The community, for
all their affection for Bob, will not allow him to dislodge their prejudices
about the relationship between shops and community. So far from abstract sentiment being the saving of the corner shop, as journalists and
others presume, it is likely to spell their doom.

CONCLUSION: CORNER SHOPS AS LANDSCAPE

If this chapter had followed along the lines of the anthropology of landscape and place (discussed in the appendix to this chapter) that have de-

2. Thanks to Alison Clarke for this interview with the shop assistant.

veloped in recent years, it would have had a very different feel—a more literary style and attention to the sensual relation of individuals with both the specific shop interiors and their goods. But as suggested in the appendix, there is plenty of ethnographic material, for example, the analysis of Australian aboriginal societies, which conforms with the findings of this chapter. The relationship to the physical environment of local shops is mediated by a fundamental ideological commitment to an imagination of sociality. Just as many anthropologists might have a preference for a sense of the unmediated and the authentic in experience so also do the households being studied; but paradoxically, their drive to immediacy, their own, as it were, phenomenological conceit leads them away rather than toward their own physical surroundings. The ironic result could be seen in the case of Bob. Such is the intellectual desire for a phenomenology of place that people cannot accept the evidence of their senses and experience.

Shops and shopping may have a rather more central role in British consciousness of themselves than in many other areas. London is, after all, one of the regions where the modern shop first arose (McKendrick 1983; Carrier 1995), and we are well aware of our reputation as the nation of shopkeepers. Much of the employment in the area is based on retail. But the dominant image of the shop that is found in soap operas and popular culture is one whose importance lies not in the things that can be bought there but in their primary role, alongside the pub, as the center of the public sphere. In our imagination, this is the place where people meet and talk. For various reasons both the home and the workplace are seen as relatively constrained sites for sociality. But the lesson from the ethnography is close to that of Myers (1986) working among the Australian Pintupi. The ethnographer has to resist the kind of romantic imagination of landscape, of ancestral wanderings, and evident physical features within an otherwise barren environment that most visitors emphasize in their accounts of aboriginal life. The ethnographer comes to see these through—not the eyes—but the ideologies of his informants. That the Pintupi, and indeed, most of the aboriginal peoples of Australia are a highly intellectual society, with complex ideas of kinship and law. Their ideals about the proper forms of sociality are crucial as signs of their ultimate relationship to transcendent worlds. These moral and religious ideologies are prior to merely everyday experience.

So in this chapter I have started and ended with attempts to evoke the depth of the relationship households achieved with Bob and the hairdresser but, finally, to show that they are never able to understand these experiences as a challenge to a powerful ideology that forbids them to generalize from those experiences. The people in the street mainly remain instead wedded to a view of the world in which local shops are no longer able to objectify their ideals of what a local shop should be. Some shops and shop assistants can mediate between such universalizing ideals and the particularity of everyday encounter, but these tend to be the shops of Ibis Pond for the middle class and the shop assistants of Wood Green for the working class. In short, it is ideology rather than experience that seems to determine how people learn from the particular shops they encounter.

In Ibis Pond it makes sense to describe the encounter in phenomenological terms since both the facade and the contents of the shops speak to the striving for authenticity and sensuality. Ibis Pond exists to objectify the "dream time" of middle-class North London. This is a nostalgic image consisting of vaguely rural ancestors who populated the landscape with sepia shopfronts (a product of the fact that early photos of the shopping center are all in sepia!) and the smell of "yuppie" coffee. In acts of self-objectification one can now buy posters and tea towels of Ibis Pond and books showing how it looked at the turn of the century, but then, one can also buy (at a much higher price) the art works in which Aboriginal society represent their own dream time. Ibis Pond may be a "dream" (time) product, but its authenticity is evident in its consumption, which is highly successful and produces about the only experience of sociality in the public domain that the middle-class practice today. So shopping can create community. As a middle-class Londoner I can attest to this attraction, since Ibis Pond is precisely the kind of area in which I enjoy shopping and meeting friends, and where I would expect to encounter other left-leaning academically trained middle-class shoppers driven by ambivalent but powerful ideals of sociality. Indeed, at the extreme end, partly as a result of having read phenomenologically influenced texts in their youth some of these shoppers create a holistic dwelling for the senses based around the smells of aromatherapy, the sound of whales calling in the deep, the taste of organic vegetables, the feel of alternative massage and the pain of natural childbirth. The fact that this is mediated does not render it unauthentic, unless one wants to suggest that the aboriginal Pintupi are also too "intellectual" to be granted authenticity to their experience of the landscape, which would be a rather daft presumption. My conclusion accords with Gell's (1995) critique of Weiner (1991), which is not to oppose phenomenology but to discriminate between those contexts where it is more or less appropriate, which in this context means to appropriate it for Ibis Pond but not for Jay Road. In North London one becomes an authentic insider through altering the landscape to fit the imagined ideal of community. The middle class has the power to patronize, and thereby create, an Ibis Pond in the image of their authentic sociality, an example of what can be called "virtualism" (Miller 1998b). To conclude: what emerges most forcefully from the ethnography are the contradictions between a discourse of locality and the local shops that were supposed to objectify this discourse but find that in practice they cannot.

Appendix

THE ANTHROPOLOGY OF PLACE

The following consists of a brief attempt to relate the material presented in chapter 3 to a general consideration of anthropological writings on landscape, place, and community. The literature on the anthropology of place and landscape has grown apace in recent years, sometimes eclipsing earlier "community" studies that focused more on social relations with only a sparse connection to the physical environment inhabited by communities. The particular focus of recent work has been on the nature of experience and it is explicitly influenced by a variety of versions of phenomenology, dominated by the work of Heidegger, on the one hand, and Merleau-Ponty, on the other. Examples of the importance of these approaches within contemporary anthropology can be found both in collections such as Feld and Basso (1996) but also in monographs based in regions from East Africa (Weiss 1996) to Melanesia (Weiner 1991). It would be easy to conflate a phenomenological approach with a dialectical perspective since the former is historically derived from the latter. Phenomenology also concerned itself with acknowledging the distance created by the objectified world, but the emphasis shifted to the manner in which people transcended any opposition between subjective experience and objectified environments. As Tilley (1994, 11–14) notes, the Heideggerian version stresses experience in relation to dwelling in the world, while those influenced by Merleau-Ponty tend to privilege a bodily orientation (or intentionality) of praxis in relation to the world. The building blocks of this approach as it applies to anthropology are described by Casey (1996), who advocates moving from the issue of creating order out of space to that of being created by the experience of place.

The best of this work has a certain sensual and humanistic quality that is undeniably attractive, but it tends to downplay the intellectual engagement people construct with the materiality of their worlds and the social and institutional forms that mediate their encounter. This is not to say that phenomenology cannot be a useful perspective, but anthropologists need to turn it from the universalist claims of philosophy to the contextual claims of particular cultural conditions. This point is made clearly by Gell (1995) in his critique of Weiner (1991). Gell notes that, ironically, many of the claims made by Merleau-Ponty work very well for the Umeda of New Guinea, whose language possesses a high degree of phonological iconism and whose relation to the environment is as much based on soundscape as landscape. But he suggests that while this applies readily to those like the Umeda or Foi who live in thickly forested environments, it may be quite inappropriate for the French people Merleau-Ponty originally had in mind.

While an English population may also have a sensitive relationship to soundscapes comparable to New Guinea, which can emerge from careful ethnography (see Tacchi 1998), an overemphasis upon the sensual relationship to the world as prior to our understanding of social and ideological orders. may not be very helpful in understanding the ethnographic evidence presented in chapter 3. Experience is certainly habituated in Bourdieu's sense. For example, one encounters the extraordinary phenomenon of elderly working-class women who live in neighboring flats on an estate on Jay Road who are friendly and kindly, but who have never stepped into each others' flats, since they inhabit a longstanding working-class culture in which such action is held to lead to breach the law of neighbors "minding one's own business," which can then lead to a loss of respectability. But this and the particular modes by which the sense of the local is objectified owe next to nothing to any kind of "bodily intentionality" beloved of phenomenology. Of course there is an obvious response to this observation, which one can certainly imagine as consistent with Weiner's work (1991), that phenomenology is mapping a relationship of authenticity for humanity that can still be found in New Guinea but is lost in the capitalist and industrial West, which is made up of precisely cultures of inauthenticity.

For this reason, it is important to make a comparison between the North London evidence and a region that has often been used as a positive example of the benefits of phenomenological approaches (e.g., Tilley 1994, 37–54), that is, the Australian Aboriginal landscape. Immediately one recognizes that this is not a homogeneous region. Myers (1986), for example, notes that the Pintupi he worked among do not seem to have the same penchant for intellectually objectified order that Munn found among the Walbiri. Munn presents us with what is, in effect, an indigenous theory of objectification (Miller 1987) in which the Walbiri recognize that there is a prior historical/mythic experience to which they must relate intellectually through the political control of knowledge. Munn noted that, "In sum ancestral transformation involves a free, untrammeled creativity and 'self-objectification' inherent in the nature of the subject" (Munn 1971, 145). But this contrasts with humans who must always submit to this previously objectified world—a distance that cannot be reconciled by mere experience. In this case, humans don't need to be phenomenological largely because the ancestors were. Instead, people use mediations such as myth and kinship in an attempt to live through such contradictions. As Morphy (1995) notes, what seems to matter most in creating the link between the symbolic order that is in the landscape and the people that presently inhabit it, is ritual, that is, action that manifests the objectified understanding of the people as a religious community.

Myers (1986) presents an excellent ethnography of this condition. The Pintupi's primary concern was with the practical problems of living in accordance with a philosophy that they understand as law, both as individuals and as a community. The "Pintupi explain about The Dreaming that it is not a product of human subjectivity or will. It is, rather an order to which all are subordinated: 'it's not our idea,' men told me. 'It's a big Law. We have to sit alongside that Law like all the dead people who went before us'" (53). The concern with the experience of the phenomenal world is a sign of the nature of that more important transcendent world that can never be directly experienced (except though dreams). Parallel with the Western idea of a codified and abstract map, the Aboriginal landscape has clear spatial coordinates, based on ancestral tracks that extend well beyond the territory experienced directly by the group in question. Similarly, they have highly sophisticated and controlled ideas of property and rights, but these are based around exclusivity of access to knowledge first, and based on land, only second. Kinship has also been developed as a system of baffling classificatory complexity, equivalent in abstraction though not in material representation to objectified culture within capitalism. For phenomenologists, Aboriginal society ought to be "rooted" through experience, in opposition to North Londoners who change houses and thus often locality about once every four years. But what matters more in both cases is the problematic of an objectified discourse about transcendent values that is not holistic but often based on the balancing of contradiction (Myers 1986, 166). Overall, then, if there is an extreme opposite to Aboriginal culture it would not be North Londoners but probably the kind of Melanesian religion that Keesing (1982) described, or in one sense failed to describe, because the relative lack of more abstracted and objectified discourses and their objectification made any description tentative and, in a sense, presumptuous.

So when the conclusions of this chapter draw attention to the various ideological constructions that seem to mediate North Londoners' experience of their street, factors such as class and ideals of sociality, I do not take this as evidence for the comparative lack of authenticity, but rather see it as analogous with what is found in other societies that tend to objectify highly abstract models through which they experience the world, such as many of the Aboriginal societies of Australia. In both cases also the relationship to landscape is mediated first and foremost by ideals of sociality. For the Pintupi as for North Londoners, happiness is supposed to reside in the close cooperation of a group (Myers 1986, 111). In the Pintupi case, this should consist of kin. In North London, while it is often the case that close sociality is still largely dominated by kin, the ideal especially for the middle class is of a community where locality should be itself an important factor in engendering sociality. What has been explicated in chapter 3 for North London are discourses of community that create a burden in that they do not arise from the experience or practice of sociality, but rather, they relate first to ideals of sociality that transcend any such experience. This, then, poses the problem of finding a suitable vehicle for the objectification of such ideals so that at least some semblance of community can be envisaged.

If there is a recent literature that accords with the ethnography of Jay Road, it is not that inspired by phenomenology but rather that which pervades the contents of Bender's (1993) collection on landscape studies where the focus is on the politics of contestation and contradiction. Bender (1993, 3–10), in her analysis of Naipaul's *Enigma of Arrival* (1987) and in her work on Stonehenge (1998), emphasizes the disparity between landscape as the objectification of a romantic vision, and its pragmatic use. She explores a politics that goes beyond simply the expression of multivocality in that she is always aware that different "voices" reflect different degrees of power and consequence. So in the North London case, the commitment to an imagination of sociality of one class is the oppression of the vision held both by the local shopkeepers and, more generally, by retail workers. Here, as also in Tarlo's recent study of a gentrified shopping area in Delhi (1996, 284–317), the focus needs to be on the invidious consequences of these projected discourses upon those who become potential objectifications by which discourse is given meaning. My stress on contradiction between discourse and practice also has resonance with Hirsch (1995) in his focus on the tension between the foreground of the here and now pragmatic world and the background of a transcendent image of ideal sociality; especially in that Hirsch wishes to use the comparative study of landscape in his edited volume (Hirsch and O'Hanlon 1995) to advance beyond a common distinction that had developed in such studies between "authentic" insiders who live the land and the outsiders who objectify and then change the land according to their imagined idyll.

THE DIALECTICS
OF ETHICS AND IDENTITY

Chapter 2 considered shopping in relation to the conceptualization and practice of kinship and the family. Chapter 3 moved outward to the consideration of the street, and in this chapter this movement is continued to examine how shopping is used to conceptualize and act toward the wider world. Two points of articulation will be considered. The first is concerned with identity, and the second, with morality. In both cases shopping is used to reveal the manner in which people become invested in a stance taken toward the world, which may or may not also include a sense of responsibility. In this book these topics have been placed at a level equivalent to civil society or citizenship that occupies a position midway between the issue of community that was discussed in the previous chapter and the working of political economy, which will be discussed in the following chapter. As will become evident, there are problems with such a positioning, but nevertheless, the issues raised here are in some ways the grounded and everyday equivalents of debates about civil society and the public sphere. In this chapter, they will be examined as they arose from the ethnography, while in chapter 6 their implications for such debates will be made more explicit.

Once again, the emphasis will be on the contradictions that are manifested through these issues of ethics and identity and on whether shopping is used to express, mediate, or resolve these contradictions. In the first example, the focus will be on the relationship between locality expressed in the symbolism or origin of commodities and identity expressed in ethnicity, nationality, and other socio-spatial representations. In the second example, the question of ethics will be addressed largely through the issue of "Green," that is, environmental concerns and any evidence for altruistic behavior by the shoppers. In both cases, the form of shopping to be considered will be narrowed down from the entire gamut of formal shopping considered in the preceding two chapters to the specific arena of shopping for food. The choice of food is heuristic, in that this was the genre of goods through which issues of ethics and identity were constantly raised, while such issues were virtually absent from other genres such as clothing or household goods. It is not presumed that this is because of some intrinsic property of food as opposed to other goods. Work on clothing in other regions, such as South Asia (Bayly 1986; Bean 1989; Cohn 1989; Tarlo 1996) would reveal just as rich a debate about political identity and moral values through that medium as happens to have developed through food in this North London context.

One of the properties of foods that may be central, but equally may be irrelevant, to their selection by a shopper is knowledge of the food item's origin and other ways in which foods evoke the sense of place from where they have come or peoples who produced them (Leslie and Riemer 1999). In many cases, the two are elided in what becomes an attribution of ethnicity or nationality to the foods in question. This can on occasion also implicate "Red" (as against the more familiar "Green") ethics if it implies a concern with the social consequences of purchases upon the welfare of those involved in production. This would be true, for example, in the case of some consumer boycotts. In other studies, the locality of food has been demonstrated to be central to a variety of strategies of identity creation. Wilk (1993) provides an example from Belize. Here local people have a wide range of potential identities that might be expressed through the associations of food, including that of being American, Belizian, and Indian. By observing the dynamics of food consumption in recent years and in particular, the rise of what he calls "visceral" or "embodied" nationalism, Wilk demonstrates the central role of food within the development of contemporary identity (and more general) politics in Belize. Foster has pointed to the more general role of commodity localities in the formation of regional and national identities in Papua New Guinea (Foster 1995). Within Britain there are a whole series of recent books on the relationship of food and identity (e.g., Bell and Valentine 1997; Caplan et al. 1998), mainly a result of the government funding a major program of research under the generic title of The Nation's Diet (Murcott 1998). These suggest that in certain circumstances the issue may become explicit and important. One case study examined how food was recategorized as part of a dynamic relationship between local identity and tourist identity in Wales (Williams 1997).

By way of contrast, in commerce the purported origins of food may be little more than as a means of legitimating a new variety of flavors in some particular food product. Lien (1997) provides a well-documented case of this alternative attenuated relationship within her ethnography of food marketing in Norway. Working in a situation in which the national food of Norway has become a local frozen pizza with the potential to be viewed as a "folkepizzaen," the marketing company is deciding whether other varieties might be better marketed to Norwegian consumers as Italian or American where this becomes little more than the designation of a "flavor"—what a nation should taste of and smell of (Lien 1997, 168–81). This contrast is important to bear in mind. A rise in food "ethnicity" or in "cosmopolitan" foods may signify a larger shift in social and cultural relations, but equally, it may be simply a result of fashions in food marketing. This is one of the reasons why it is important to study the ethnography of food consumption and not just assume the significance of food semiotics. Equally common—as I have argued in more detail through the case study of the drinks industry in Trinidad—there may be complex symbolic trends operating within both commerce and consumption, respectively, with relatively weak points of articulation between them (Miller 1997a, chapter 4). Another of the problems with some of the literature on food and identity is that it tends to remain relatively parochial when drawing its consequences, assuming that these are important only to the extent that they are "political." A perspective from anthropology should help us to delve more deeply into the forms of value, morality, and cosmological principles that underlie the degree to which people identify with the attribution of origins to goods.

SHOPPING FOR ONE'S ORIGINS

A survey of first languages of those attending the local primary school confirms the immediate impression that this part of North London is extremely cosmopolitan. Many of the households within the study have origins outside of the U.K. Not surprisingly, shopping often became an important area for expressing some identification with the place of family origin as against current residence. But equally for shoppers of local origin, commodities may represent a powerful embodiment and representation of a vast range of other localities that may bear upon their sense of identity. In the disciplines of geography and sociology there has been some discussion recently as to whether a cosmopolitanism in terms of taste is relevant to a cosmopolitanism expressed in tolerant or positive attitudes to peoples of varied or plural origin (see Cheah and Robbins 1998 for more general "cosmopolitics"). As Cook and Crang (1996) and Cook, Crang, and Thorpe (1999) note, this is not just a question of specific localities. There is also the general use of cuisine, in particular, as a symbol of the "multicultural" or "cosmopolitan." There are a whole slew of forms that these "multicultural imaginaries," as they call them, can take. The academic debate has largely been between those who attack such sentiments as vicarious "feel good" experiences that deny the problematic nature of any actual encounter with otherness, as against those who see the diverse forms of pluralism objectified in food as having a positive mediating factor in the broadening of personal identity and attitudes to people of different origins.

One of the reasons that the origin of the shopper often became a pertinent factor in the ethnography of shopping was that in so many cases this was not shared by the household as a whole. This was often true of partners. It might be that their country of origin was different. On this street there also seemed to be many couples where one partner was Jewish, but hardly any where both were Jewish. It seemed such couples identified with a location that was itself on the fringe of major Jewish settlements in North London. There were also many cases in which a generational issue arose between children born in Britain and their immigrant parents. Even if the child shows very little concern with this distinction, it may become deeply embroiled in the inevitable ambivalence that is central to parent-child relationships (Miller 1997b; Parker 1995).

An example of this last point is a South American housewife who deliberately makes occasional forays to a shop outside of her main area of provisioning precisely in order to buy the fruits and vegetables that she associates with her homeland to which she may or may not return one day with her family. But during the same expedition she bought Easter eggs, a tradition that has no bearing on her own experience; she feels it is important that the children come to know about this peculiar "English" ritual. Sometimes these kinds of actions work in the opposite direction. Most English parents assume the same "naturalness" of identification with taste in their children that they associate with themselves. They ex-

THE DIALECTICS OF ETHICS AND IDENTITY · 115

pect their children to prefer the bland tastes associated with most tradi-tional English foods, while a taste for "foreign" food will be only be ac-quired with growing knowledge and maturity. So an English mother was astonished and rather put out that her child loved the taste of tara-masalata, given that the child was extremely fussy and fastidious about other food. Such a "foreign" food should not in her opinion have formed part of the basic conservative repertoire that most such children seem to develop often in defiance of adult desire for them to "try" other foods.

Place of birth could rarely be isolated from other factors when deter-mining the justification of a particular purchase. For example, there is a Spanish housewife whose home contains many objects that relate to Spain and whose cooking is marked by a Spanish influence. But the inter-pretation of these preferences is complex. She sees herself as simply look-ing for good quality rather than expressing any kind of general national sentiment in her choice. In several areas of food, but also in household goods such as ceramics, she simply asserts that the Spanish examples are better quality and since she travels frequently to Spain she has access to them. At one point she notes how much better the Spanish bouillon cubes are compared with the "awful" English variety, but she actually buys a brand of German cubes that are available locally and to her way of think-ing are similar to the Spanish ones. Often she cooks Spanish food because she says her husband (who is English-Jewish) loves the cuisine, or there may be an item such as Spanish omelets, which simply pairs well with the likes of fish fingers as within the range of easy and acceptable foods for her children. So for her, Spanish is often a taken-for-granted standard of qual-ity. If asked explicitly about what she buys out of sentiment rather than quality, she would say it was English things. She sees her Spanish pur-chases as functional and convenience purchases, while for her it is the En-glish purchases that are experienced as expressive—exactly the opposite of my initial interpretation of her actions.

Quite often nationality becomes a kind of token presence, one of a repertoire of gestures that is used by one partner to acknowledge the indi-viduality of the other. For example, in a relationship in which the hus-band does very little domestic work, there is an expectation that he will at least buy that which pertains to his particular tastes. As the wife puts it, "He will go to Flamingo Lanes to the Turkish shops and get certain Turkish things that he likes. So that's his little forte. He trots off there because I can't be bothered to go to Flamingo Lanes just for a few bits and pieces." Similarly, in the relationship between the American husband and Irish wife who were introduced in chapter 2, I observed him buying six very large bottles of Irish water. In this case the purchase was intended as a kind of routine gesture of care for his partner, in that while he was expected to buy water, the very quantity he purchased was an acknowledgment that water can be one of the heaviest ingredients in shopping expeditions. In the same way, the choice of Irish water was a token of her identity. As noted in chapter 2, his wife in turn had once gone to considerable efforts to try and cook a particular American dish (clam chowder) that he missed in the way "his mother would have cooked it," but gave up since they agreed this was simply something that, with the best intentions in the world, she could not achieve. In most such cases, the gestures are not particularly seen as significant in themselves; rather, they form part of the general sense of sensitivity or concern that are assumed to form part of successful long-term relationships. Much of the eating of traditional regional cuisine is viewed more as conservatism or habit; this would be particularly true for those of Cypriot and Asian origin. It is still relatively rare that it is reobjectified as a positive assertion of roots, though there is some evidence of this among Jews who have resided in London for long enough to go through a cycle of having forgotten and then restored their traditional cuisine.

SHOPPING FOR LOCALITY

With respect to the significance of purchases of "foreign" foods by those of English origin, the evidence that is probably most useful derives from direct participation in shopping expeditions. It is difficult to be categorical about this material, but the impression given was that the commodity has little bearing on the relationship between the identity of the consumer and others. When one analyzes the content of food trolleys a surprisingly high percentage of shopping seemed to remain within a very standard Anglo-American cuisine. By this I do not mean items that seem expressively English such as corned beef or suet pudding, which were rare. Most shopping baskets are dominated by goods such as minced beef, lamb chops, fish in batter, or breadcrumbs, peas, chips, and other such goods. Equally common is a range of brands such as Heinz and Kellogg's together with supermarket own-label brands that clearly emulate such products. Other goods were not only less common than I would have expected, but their interpretation is also problematic.

To take one example, the shopping basket of a nurse, despite being married to a husband from Southeast Asia, seemed very English in its connotations. She purchased "saver" sausages, minty lamp chops, potatoes, lettuce, tomatoes, canned peaches, jam tarts, and fish fingers. The American brand products tended to be Heinz and Kellogg's. Also present were goods that could be used to suggest an interest in or relation to other European countries such as fromage frais for France and pizza for Italy. But this would be a highly implausible interpretation. On closer inspection, the fromage frais is a variety named after the Flintstones, the pizza is the mini-cheese-and-tomato variety, which is a long way from anything one might see in Naples.

So the ethnicity of goods does not usually imply a concern with their origin. This becomes still clearer when shoppers readily buy "Greek" yogurt or "Italian" pasta or "Indian" bread, all of which are British-made and which, therefore, cannot imply any interest in the place of manufacture or the welfare of the peoples of those regions. Ethnicity is manifestly more important as a symbol related to the consumption rather than the production of goods. That is to say, shoppers are much more interested in the range of tastes of foods they can experience. Rather as in the case of the Norwegian food marketing referred to above, nationality is little more than a food flavor. The same goes for the concern with ingredients. Shoppers have expressed sufficient interest in "French" flour being used in French bread for the supermarkets to start to use flour imported from France. This again is a desire for the authenticity of the experience represented by taste. It was certainly not intended to favor the French economy. The problem with the academic discussion of "ethnic food" is the lack of attention to consumption itself as providing sufficient grounds in itself to account for the evident demand for such goods. Time and again, the main concern seemed centered on the problem of "boredom" and the desire for something new. Although the main foods used in this case are identified with populations who exist as minorities in Britain, I suspect the possible capacity of food to "spice up one's life" has nothing to do with ethnic relations.

Within the middle class, shoppers manipulate the ethnicity of food in a manner that is quite familiar to me as an anthropologist who also cooks for friends from a similar milieu. There may be considerable prestige attached to making sure one's recipe for palm oil stew is "authentically" West African and carried out to the letter, or if South Asian "curry" has become part of working-class food, then the middle-class emphasis will be on the precise distinctions between the regional cuisines of Maharashtra and Tamil Nadu. Within the working class, the purchase of "ethnic" food simply does not act as a representation of difference since it has merged with the everyday food of British cuisine to become an unmarked part of the diet. These are foods such as Italian pasta and pizza, or going out for an

"Indian" or indeed the use of curry sauce within a fish-and-chip shop. In cases like the curry sauce, these have themselves become markers of working-class taste now dispensed with by the middle class who, having been emulated, keep their distance by moving on to these newer refinements. Vindaloo, the pop song that topped the charts as an expression of highly nationalist English football supporters traveling to France in 1998 for the football World Cup was named after the bucket of vindaloo (a particularly hot version of curry) they were carrying with them. It is worth noting, however, that this may also be a reflection of the general extent to which North London has become more cosmopolitan in its taste than much of the rest of the country. Martens and Warde (1998) have found that for much of the rest of the country, even these well-established Chinese, Indian, and Italian foods have remained sufficiently exotic as to still represent middle-class cosmopolitanism.

A much better guide to the interest in more cosmopolitan foods would come from Bourdieu's (1984) work *Distinction* in as much as these choices seem saturated with class. Indeed this is one of the few areas where "stereotypes" traded in popular discourse seemed to be close to the mark. The people who buy ciabatta bread, unusual cheeses, and exotic fruits and cook regional Indian cuisines are clearly differentiated from people whose shopping contains none of these things on the basis of many other evident signs of "class" difference. There seems little reason to try and improve upon Bourdieu's conclusion that cosmopolitan taste is used as the basis of class discrimination. It seems very likely that in contemporary Britain the concept of "refined" taste as being superior to "common" taste that dominated class discourse of the first half of this century (e.g., Hebdige 1981) is increasingly being replaced by the concept of "cosmopolitan" taste as against "parochial" taste. So if our concern is the ethical import of such choices, then the implication, following Bourdieu, is that the purchase of exotic foods from different parts of the world is a better sign of new strategies of social exclusion than any evidence of empathetic social inclusion.

THE ABSENCE OF "RED" SHOPPING

Compared with many other topics, the moral issues involved in shopping seem at first quite accessible to research. During the North London fieldwork there was hardly a middle-class household that did not respond immediately to a question about boycotting shops or goods with memories of boycotting South African goods during apartheid. Support for other boycotts, such as that of Nestle over the promotion of powdered milk as against breastfeeding, were less common. But these were always provided as remembered rather than present actions; indeed, they were brought up to consciousness often with clear expressions of nostalgia and sentimentality. This was one of those topics where people would classify themselves in respect to the dominant character of decades as in "sixties," "seventies," and "eighties" people. But ethical boycotts were decidedly not "nineties." There were a very few examples of potential contemporary boycotts. One was the desire to boycott Benetton as a protest against unethical and exploitative advertising, another to reject certain foods on behalf of people paid low wages for canning fruit. But active participation in contemporary boycotts was not suggested by conversation and was not evident during the observation of actual shopping.

As already noted, charity shops and catalogs were part of the research agenda of Alison Clarke, my coethnographer, but they are clearly relevant to this topic. When people can be observed using such facilities there are two possibilities in reading their intentions. A shopper who seemed to show an interest in the origin of the goods being purchased might be concerned that their money should help a good cause, or they may simply be trying for a bargain. In practice, it was usually clear that the issue was not an altruistic interest in the welfare of producers. Shoppers were primarily concerned with questions of the origins of goods when they saw this as signifying "better quality," "better tasting," "more authentic," and other such attributes. Geographers (Gregson et al. forthcoming) working on charity shops specifically have come to the conclusion that the motivation for their use is almost entirely the idea of gaining a bargain and, in practice, hardly at all a sense of altruism. Indeed, one could go further and suggest that, in effect, altruism provides moral legitimacy for self-interest in such cases. There seemed to be a general consensus among my informants that Christmas was a time when one was more likely to use an ethical catalog such as the Oxfam or the World Wildlife Fund's catalogs, since Christmas was itself a time to be more self-reflective about moral concerns. Though again, authenticity and the quality of gifts were at least as important. There is some evidence that the catalog producers are themselves aware of the ambiguities of the ethics involved in their use and collude with the consumer in trying to overcome them (see Carrier 1990; Hendrickson 1996). Overall, the evidence from my work and from others is that pure "Red" shopping based on the selection of goods primarily in consideration of benefiting others is extremely rare. This may seem to lead to a conclusion that the people being studied lacked empathy and altruism and were hypocritical. None of these implications actually follow from this material, but the reasons for rejecting them will be discussed after the evidence for the parallel case of Green shopping is presented.

DOING ONE'S BIT — GREEN SHOPPING IN CONTEXT

Issues of locality and potential "Red" shopping cropped up much less frequently than issues that could be generalized as those of "Green" shopping, which is where the bulk of explicit moral concerns seem to be currently located. I recognize that anthropology might contribute to many other aspects of environmental issues than the narrow one being considered here. Already anthropology is involved in concerns that range from work on indigenous conceptualization of the environment to environmental aspects of development projects; these are well exemplified in other texts (e.g., Davis 1993; Kempton, Boster, and Hartley 1996; Milton 1996; Stevens and De Lacy 1997). What follows is not intended as a contribution to such works but rather tries to fathom the contradictions of environmentalism as an aspect of shopping. As in chapter 2, it may be helpful to start from the point of view of an individual shopper.

Peggy is a clearly moral shopper: almost every shopping decision she makes seems to run up against the various, often conflicting, constraints imposed by the moral implications of the decision to be made. But it is by no means straightforward to specify the nature of those moral issues and isolate them as contributory factors to her shopping. In considering the food in her local supermarket, a wide range of factors impinge. Her husband, Joseph, is Jewish and is concerned to follow some of the religious laws that forbid certain foods. Although she is not herself Jewish, Peggy feels responsible for mediating the route from the store shelf to his plate, so that even when there is a product he has become quite fond of, she feels she must inform him when one day she notices that it (Muller Light Yoghurt) includes gelatin, which is forbidden by the dietary restrictions that they have agreed to follow. She herself has recently become a vegetarian, although Joseph has not. Again, however, there is a question of how fastidious she should be in observing such a categorization. In her case, she would probably consume some sweets whose only nonvegetarian additive was gelatin, and similarly, she does not buy vegetarian cheese or inspect goods for the label of the vegetarian society. Rather, she simply avoids the eating of foods that look like forms of meat. When protecting Joseph's concerns, however, Peggy takes on his more precise "religious" interpretation of food avoidance.

She is equally concerned about what her child Robin ingests. At one point, she notes:

> There are some things like we have a real dilemma about. Whether to buy sugar in things or sugar-free because you know like every other parent who's worried about sugar we sort of thought that maybe the sugar-free stuff is good and then we saw some stuff on the fact that they use more saccharin or whatever and [Joseph] feels more strongly than me that he'd rather just have proper sugar for Robin and him and not kind of go for the sugar-free things.

It is clear that discussion about the ethics of foods and other household goods is a common topic not only within her household but also in her wider social life. For example, when talking about her group of mothers and infants, Peggy notes:

> We buy that Tesco's Green, or whatever it's called. That's a subject of some discussion among the women I know. Whenever we have this conversation we end up in hysterics. Because it's exactly what we complain about in the advertising—showing women talking about their washing products. But actually we have occasionally, and there is a kind of consensus that the ecological stuff actually isn't that good as a washing powder.

As one listens to the description of such conversations, it becomes clear that much of this discussion (as in the quote just given) is about justifying a decision to end ethical shopping in practice. When she ate meat, Peggy used to make a special effort to buy organic meat at a butcher in a shopping center other than where she now shops, but then she gave up the effort. When it comes to organic vegetables, she complains.

> The price of them—I maybe am a bit sensitive to price when it comes to them. I do occasionally buy them. I sometimes wonder if I should buy more.

She also talks in detail about all the food she buys and allows to rot in the fridge and which then has to be thrown away, as well as the problem of whether to eat foods that are past their expiration date. She doesn't give them to her daughter—but allows Joseph to eat them instead! She also feels she should make more homemade food instead of buying prepared foods whose ingredients she has no control over. Not surprisingly, there is a parallel discussion about her "good" intention to eat less fattening foods and her actual tendency to consume rather more alcohol than she feels is good for her.

During the year of fieldwork, I was engaged in countless such discussions about the ethics and morality of shopping and, in particular, the issues surrounding various foodstuffs. One of the most obvious problems in analyzing this material is that it does not fall easily into discrete categories where the relationship between action and intention can be confidently asserted. The reasons for avoiding a high-fat diet relates to a public discourse on health, which all these informants could recite backward, but there are many times in the conversation when it becomes clear that the main issue of concern is their physical appearance. One can listen for some time to a conversation that appears to demonstrate a concern with the environment and that is evidence for the altruism of the speaker, before it becomes quite clear that almost all the incentive for spending the extra money or searching out the pure ingredient is coming from a fear of the harm the food will do to the speaker and their family if some polluting substance is ingested. The way people who do not show such "Green" concerns are talked about also make it clear that, at least in this North London context, the topic is full of allusions to class. The vulgarity of the "common" person who does not control their weight is extended to their supposed immorality when it comes to their lack of concern for the environment. Finally, the constant turning of such discussions back to issues to do with parental attempts to keep their children "pure" may have a great deal more to do with particular aspects of the narcissistic relationship that is central to middle-class parental projections onto their infants (for an analysis of this, see Miller 1997b), which again suggests that any apparent altruism may be misleading.

One of the reasons for this complexity is that the categories of "nature" and the "natural" is doing an extraordinary amount of work within contemporary discourses. In Miller et al. (1998, chapter 6), this is made evident in terms of attitudes to retail. Spending vast sums on opening up shopping malls to "natural light" is clearly not the same as the way shoppers define as "natural" the English reticence of shop assistants against obtrusive "American" style shop assistance. There is also the "natural" that forms part of the ideal of authenticity of Ibis Pond. The term "natural" seems vital to the legitimization of new ideologies, but mainly at the expense of any semantic consistency.

There has clearly been a tremendous rise in the importance of Green issues as part of public discourse. People commonly referred to them both within the home and in public. Although these concerns vary with gender, class, age, and ethnicity (Caplan et al. 1997), almost everyone is far more cognizant of the relevant criteria. Associated with this is the extraordinary capacity for guilt and anxiety that women, in particular, have developed and that is directed at many aspects of basic provisioning. For example, Suzie notes:

> We do have more stuff at the end of the week than we should have, that's gone off. Mushrooms, chicken—this week that was an awful waste—it got shoved to the back of the fridge and forgotten about, which I feel really guilty about. But I won't eat it if it's gone past the sell by date, whereas my partner probably would. Mainly vegetables, I suppose, mainly they go soggy in the salad drawer.

Often when there are two alternative forms of action, both will condemned as in the discussion of sugar above, in which both sugar and sugar substitutes are viewed as bad. The main product of such discussion of food choice and food waste is guilt itself.

These problems of ambivalence are wrapped up in the sheer complexity of ethical dialogues. Ethics have become extremely diffused across many different issues. As a result, the various strands of altruism, taste, self-interest, and so forth are so deeply interwoven within the same sentence. As a result, the other side to the coin of a general feeling of guilt is a general goal that takes the form of being "good" and of "doing one's bit." What I am suggesting is that most people simply don't try, in practice, to consider whether their concerns come from discrete issues of, on the one hand, the environment or, on the other hand, whether they will look too fat. In all such matters, they perceive a moral dimension so that they know generally what is "good" and what is "bad," and it really doesn't matter in practice how the various implications of the various moralities involved coalesce or contradict each other. So following a religious rule may become seamlessly integrated into a worry about pesticides and making sure that your child has the work discipline considered appropriate to the better class of primary school. It is all part of being "good" and "doing one's bit." Below is a typical example of a concern for organic foods turning into a preference for vegetarianism and, finally, into the choice of "tradition" as though these were equivalent.

(Q) Do you buy organic?

(A) Yeah, well, not organic, I suppose; we don't eat much red meat at all, really. I buy sausages, that's the nearest to red meat we get. I look for the ones that are the traditional, sort of handmade sort of thing.

As well as leading to a proliferation of discussion of issues at least within the middle classes, Green concerns have led to a confrontation with the potential of some increasingly standard practices. Dominant topics included the purchase of Green "ecological" cleaning materials, the preference for organic fruit and vegetables, the recycling of paper, bottles, and often also clothing, the purchase of free-range eggs (and less often, chickens), and a concern over meat, such as beef with BSE, or "mad cow disease." But these issues are reflected in a number of lesser concerns, often extended to become a movement toward vegetarianism, especially among the children. Also associated is a general tendency to prefer "traditional" foods such as sausages or beer made according to some local or regional recipe, and a common use of the health food shops to purchase a wide range of related goods such as homeopathic medicines and special foods such as rice cakes for infants. Related to all these aspirations is a general antipathy to certain shops that are seen as an anathema to such values, of which MacDonald's (and similar burger outlets) and the toy shop Toys "R" Us would have pride of place in the demonization of retail. Indeed, Wilk (1997) has argued that in defining themselves as "positions" people are often much clearer about what they are against than what they are for, and Green issues can often turn into diatribes against pet hates. But all of this emerges from the discussion of Green concerns. Before reaching any conclusion about this Green discourse, another form of evidence needs to be taken into account—that is, direct observation.

THE EVIDENCE FROM SHOPPING

Teaching within material culture studies, I am familiar with huge discrepancies between what people say and what they do. Rarely though have I encountered an example as striking as that which emerged when I set out to complement the evidence just discussed with that taken from a systematic reading through of fifty recordings out of my accompanied shopping expeditions involving thirty different households. I examined these for evidence of ethical concerns demonstrated in shopping. During these fifty shopping expeditions only on one occasion did a shopper actually take materials back for recycling as part of that trip. I concede that I failed to record consistently whether people bought free-range eggs, so I am having to leave this out of the evidence. But with respect to other purchases, there were only two occasions within the fifty shopping trips when a shopper could be seen to clearly purchase "ethical goods." Although I had obviously been present during the shopping, this result contrasted markedly with my own expectations and "memories." I would have sworn this was a more prevalent behavior during my accompanied shopping. Part of the reason for this is that there were a number of these shopping expeditions that included discussions about buying Green or organic goods. But even where these discourses continue right inside the shops themselves, they hardly ever generated actual ethical purchases. The discrepancy was between what people are saying and what they are doing while they are in the act of shopping.

Even those who in discussion were known to be vegetarian and have wide environmental concerns did not make particular purchases that are ethically "marked." The only two shoppers that were observed to do so were individuals where these issues were so heavily scored into their personal lives as to render them at the "extreme" end of the spectrum of concerned individuals. In both cases, quite a number of their purchases were undertaken with ethical issues in mind. Cynthia, for example, bought a wide range of organic vegetables, and purchased two kinds of vegetarian cheese. She specifically sought out Greenland halibut while telling me about new research that has shown how the waters around Greenland are now the cleanest in the world. Cynthia strongly considered a snack food with a logo about money to be given to the World Wildlife Trust on the packet, though in the event she purchased the cheaper Tesco equivalent, and she then followed the supermarket shop with a visit to a health food shop. Cynthia was clearly an individual who would have been identified by others as having Green concerns emblematic of her "lifestyle."

So in direct contrast to the conclusions from interviews and discussion the evidence of shopping suggests that Green and similar issues have faded away to become largely inconsequential for the vast majority of shoppers and have instead become a niche of specialist shopping for a subgenre of dedicated activists entirely within the middle class. Furthermore, this concern was almost wholly related to the topic of food purchase (and cleaning materials), since at no time during the year's fieldwork were any other purchases such as clothing or furnishing implicated in any suggestion of ethical concern.

When I consider my own presence as an ethnographer on these shopping trips and the degree to which this might have made shoppers self-conscious and "defensive" about their actual purchases, together with the evidence from discussions and interviews that most people are well aware of the nature of the ethical debates and their implications, then I would certainly have expected people to make ethical purchases in my presence that they might not have made without me being there. I can see no logic at all that would account for the opposite phenomenon. The lack of altruism is still more evident when one turns from action to cause. As already noted for the use of charity shops, there are essentially two potential, though related, reasons shoppers might have for being engaged in purchasing most of the goods that would constitute "ethical" concerns. The first reason would indeed be ethical in that the purchases are based on an altruistic concern and empathy with other people. The second reason would be any advantage to the self-interest of the consumer, which in this case includes the idea that the goods in question are healthier. The evidence from the shopping is that the main motive underlying the ethical purchase of food and cleaners (the only goods subject to ethical purchase) is the desire to avoid substances such as pollutants that are regarded as harmful when ingested; for example, that fish from Greenland is healthier for the eater. Green shopping is not in practice ethical shopping; it derives from a strong sense of self-interest based on the idea that non-Green foods will be harmful to the purchaser. If we remove this factor, then it is hardly an exaggeration to say that ethical concerns are nonexistent as a factor determining shopping choice.

This finding comes after a period when virtually every shopper has been bombarded with media programs and other pressures to be involved in environmentalism; when every child has done projects on ecology and the environment at primary school and watched Green cartoon shows such as "Captain Planet" who saves the world from the evil of science, and when, with the decline of formal religion, the question of consumer responsibility had become almost the standard substitute for ethics in general in educational and media discussion within the public domain. The discrepancy is also evident in terms of the conversations held with the very same shoppers. If one returns to my original example of Peggy, one can see that even within the discourse of shopping, ethics most often relate to a concern for the effects of the products on her family rather than any wider concern for the health of the world at large. With her and others one also had the sense that Green issues were becoming "dated" and that much of the conversation was in the past tense though the main grounds being given for the end of such practices being either price or relative ineffectiveness at, for example, cleaning. Clearly, there is considerable other objective evidence for the importance of Green issues in shopping from market research reports and other bodies that monitor them from the retail perspective. Again, it is difficult to interpret quantitative data, but sales of organic and similar goods, while much discussed at the time of my fieldwork, remained small, and in some areas were in decline. Surveys suggested that one would have expected around 4 percent of shopping expeditions would have included an ethical dimension. So despite my small sample my results are not particularly surprising when set against such sales statistics. Although the relevant shopping centers have a health food shop and the major supermarkets have health food and organic food sections, these are prominent rather than large when compared with the vast bulk of goods that have no such connotations. All of this is useful when it comes to looking again at the "discourse" of Green and ethical shopping, which often suggested a recent decline a short time in the past. Typical statements were

> Yeah, I have Ecover washing up liquid, and I would buy organic a lot more if it was a lot more easily available. And at the moment you can hardly find it, so when you do, it's outrageously expensive.

or

(Q) Do you do recycling?

(A) Bottles, my husband is quite into it, but I get so fed up with bottles everywhere that I throw them away.

(Q) Do you buy organic?

(A) We went through a phase of buying organic things but they didn't work as much, so I went back to the others but try to use less of them.

No case of actual resistance to the ideology of Green issues was found in middle-class households. In working-class households the reaction was more varied. Some would reiterate much the same discourse of being "good" and doing one's bit for the environment; many were simply less interested in these issues, which did not tend to arise accept when directly inquired into. But one also came across the sense that this is something that "other" people do. A particular instance of this was a working-class woman who had worked for a while in a health food shop and was fascinated by the behavior and attitude of the customers. She would never buy from the bulk bins at wholefood stores for herself since she had seen too many "crawly things" in goods that were not fully sealed. But what really got to her was the sheer amount of money that people would spend on, say, "two apples" because of their supposed healthier nature.

What remains true across the classes is the complexity of values and variables that form part of these choices. Although moral issues may be less explicit, they are as fully interwoven with issues of taste. For example, a working-class unemployed man waxed lyrical on the superior taste of the vegetables he produced in his own garden and thereby condemns the supermarkets goods as tasteless and offensive versions of industrialized food. In general, given the lower level of Green discussion, there was less social pressure to be defensive or anxious since there was much less discrepancy between practice and ideology.

The context for this evidence is the wider development of Green consumption as both rhetoric and practice. This is certainly not new: the first environmentally sound consumer guides were coming out in the mid-1970s, and the ideological premise that consumer sovereignty could become the basis for a new Green consumption was fully established in the late 1980s. As Simmonds (1995) has noted, this was based on a curious conjuncture between two developments. On the one hand this was the period when Reagan and Thatcher succeeded in promoting a hard line economics view that the market could of itself provide the solution to almost any problem, and at the same time the development of high-profile Green activism encouraged individual consumers to believe that the use this new power of consumers in the market could shift the overall balance of consumption in a Green direction. By the late 1980s, government, the media, and activists were pulling in the same direction, translated quickly by market researchers into new commercial moves to provide the goods to suit the growing Green demand. By 1988, nearly half of all consumers in the United Kingdom identified themselves as "Green" (151). But even at that time it was unclear how far such identification translated into practice, and by the early 1990s, a cynicism about the superficiality of both shoppers and business motives had set in. One of the most evident problems had become that of trust in the claims made by Green goods. All sorts of goods were joining a bandwagon of "Green" by appearance. Journals such as *Ethical Consumer* were known to a tiny minority, and the supermarkets, which today have achieved extraordinary levels of trust, have only now started to take on the role of environmental guardians on behalf of consumers (mainly in the United Kingdom over the issue of genetically modified foods, which took place after this fieldwork). None of the evidence for the macrocontext, however, helps explain the extraordinary discrepancy between discourse and practice that was found during the ethnography.

THREE EXPLANATIONS

The evidence from the ethnography suggests that, notwithstanding a thriving discourse, actual ethical concerns expressed in the practice of shopping are remarkably sparse. To account for these observations, I want to make three tentative interpretations, although I suspect the third is by far the most important. The first resides in the objectification of ethical consumption as a sub-cultural "lifestyle"; the second is the generic nature of legitimization expressed in "doing one's bit"; and the third is a fundamental contradiction between what I will call morality and ethics.

Explanation One: Linda Snell

The first interpretation is perhaps more an extension of the description than constituting an explanation. As already noted when shoppers comment on Green or ethical shopping with a tone that implies that these are somehow dated they often do so in terms of the character of decades as in "Green, oh dear, how terribly eighties!" (or seventies or sixties). Such characterization is equally used in relation to people who are seen as having been formed within a certain period and then somehow remained stuck in some time warp so that ever after they remind others of how they imagine that period once was. This phenomenon became most evident when for example hippies continued to "look" sixties in places such as Amsterdam for the next thirty years. Those who would wish to promote Green concerns would certainly hope that ethics is not reducible to "lifestyle," and that what would be fostered would be a gradual raising of consciousness in the population at large about issues that cannot be denied. To some degree it must surely be the case that ecological concerns have become part of a much wider public consciousness than when the Club of Rome first brought them to general attention in 1972. The discourse of Green at least, has become a ubiquitous feature of public debate. On the other hand, the evidence here suggested that part of the current lack of Green practice may well be that at least the most active version of such concerns has become narrowed down into the attribute of particular kinds of people.

An example of this phenomenon would be Linda Snell, a fictional character in the long running British radio soap opera *The Archers*. This soap opera character is a caricature of how ethical concerns might become parochially resident in a particular type of person whose identity is thoroughly bound up in a "habitus" (Bourdieu 1977) which might now be considered dated as in "eighties," "seventies," or sixties." As such, the response of such a character to all new situations is entirely predictable—they will be outraged by almost any new development that threatens what they see as the values enshrined in either the environment as status quo or tradition itself. While at times they will be effective activists articulating concerns that are more generally held and converting these concerns from mere antipathy into intervention, at other times this type of person will be seen as intensely irritating and narrow in their one-dimensional attitude and largely puritanical outlook. Indeed, the last attribute may be more relevant than usually thought as it is likely that the "alterna-tive" and "holistic" movement (in Britain) owes something to a longer tradition of nonconformity in British religious traditions[1] (Searle-Chatter-jee, 1997, personal communication).

This narrowing down of environmentalism to a particular lifestyle cer-tainly fits the ethnographic evidence. The only shoppers that showed eth-ical concerns in actual shopping managed to make virtually every item they purchased an ethical issue. There was a strong suggestion that they also used such issues as a medium of power and discipline in their rela-tionships with children and partners. This type of shopper would be viewed as highly opinionated and specific in their outlook on life by oth-ers. As such, they conform to the general sense of "lifestyle" in which cer-tain constellations of values and aesthetics are held to envelop the person. Even among the middle class who shared Green concerns, there was a sense that the customers of health food shops still included the "cranks" who were problematic because not only were they opinionated but they could suddenly launch into harangues from which fellow customers found it difficult to extricate themselves. Ethics become pigeonholed as a "type" of person or perspective, which thereby limits the involvement of the larger population who may be embarrassed at being associated with the characteristics that are thought to pertain to that particular lifestyle. This might in part account for a shift in ethical consumption from a grow-ing point of concern in at least a dominant class, if not the population as a whole, to a niche market for the expression of a particular position in the social/cultural space in the late nineties (Bourdieu 1984). In short, many of the people who espouse Green concerns are afraid of being seen as a "Green" kind of person.

Explanation Two: Doing One's Bit
The second problem may be discerned in the finer details of the ethno-graphic evidence as I have presented it here. This goes back to the difficul-ties of determining the relationship between practice, discourse, and intention when it comes to both what was said and what was done in re-lation to Green issues. As noted in the early part of this chapter, when one listens to general conversations about ethical consumption it is easy to lose the thread of the debate. The most glaring instance referred to on sev-eral occasions is a stance that seemingly expresses an altruistic concern for others but in fact masks an anxiety about one's own health. But equally

1. Thanks for this observation to Mary Searle-Chatterjee, who has been conducting research on the topic of these links.

important was the observation that in conversation what comes across is a very general sense of "doing one's bit" and being generally "good." The problem here is that people do not discriminate between a very wide range of such behaviors. As a result, something that helps a person stick to a diet or favors the appropriate behavior of a child at primary school or even adds to class exclusion through expressing cosmopolitan knowledge can be entered into a general discourse on ethics as evidence that the speaker is engaged in ethical consumption. It comes as something of a surprise to have engaged in half an hour of general discussion about Green and ethical issues only to analyze the taped conversation and realize that in the end the sense of doing good came down to avoiding high-fat foods. Going on a diet is not, in the final analysis, going to do much for the developing world! So the use of charity shops or the purchase of items that claim ethical goals may not be evidence at all for the altruistic practice of the shopper. On the contrary, my suspicion based on this evidence is that it is almost the opposite. These are facilities that are used by the shopper to engage in those activities such as thrift, in the case of the charity shop, or the appearance of altruism, in the case of many other products, in such a manner as to give the shopper the feeling that they have done their bit, but in practice at no cost to themselves. This is the problem of translating a statistic about the growth in the purchasing of organic foods and assuming it shows a growth in altruistic concerns for the environment, when it may indicate merely a fear that pesticide residues will harm the eater.

The implications of this explanation may be drawn out by considering a typical "Green" argument in *The Guardian,* a newspaper that tends to promote such concerns. One author Joanna Blythman criticizes supermarkets (7 May 1998) for not reflecting the true extent of shoppers' desire to buy free-range eggs. She notes that instead, they are using labels such as "Fresh" to gain the credit and profit of "ethical" eggs while selling "unethical" eggs. The supermarkets defend this by claiming that "fresh" eggs are simply a reflection of consumer demand. The author's cynicism with regard to the motives of business seems entirely reasonable. The large retailers are clearly happy to promote ethical-sounding labels that can command premium prices to affluent consumers, but are not likely to undertake ethical actions they deem unprofitable. There are occasions when supermarkets have proved proactive, most surprisingly when the supermarket Iceland, which is not an upmarket firm, took an early firm stand against genetically modified food that subsequently proved a very popular move, but more usually it is the upmarket firms that promote such stances as part of premium pricing. So the author's comments seem reasonable enough as a critique of the shop, but when it comes to the shoppers themselves it is the author who seems naive: while business is duplicitous and contradictory, shoppers are viewed as simple and straightforward in their ethical desires. They either want ethical goods or they don't. Furthermore, the ethical argument of the journalist is ultimately based entirely on the same factor as is the argument of business. Both claim that they represent the true desires of the consumer. In the end, they differ mainly on the evidence for what actually constitutes consumer desire. The ethnography suggests that consumers are just as contradictory and prone to collusion as is business. They feel the same pressure to act ethically, but in practice, if they can find a way to substitute the difficulties of actual ethical action by a collusion with retail that provides all the appearance of having been on the side of the angels with none of the costs, then that is the way they will act. Convenience ethics have proved just as popular as prepared foods.

There is, however, a further, more complex factor underlying this point, which is that we would be quite wrong to expect consistency between discourse and practice in the first place. Central to the more general theory of shopping I have outlined elsewhere (Miller 1998a) is the argument that shopping consists of a three-part ritual. I argue that the second part of this ritual process, that is, the practice of shopping, is a specific attempt to negate the first part which emerges from the discourse of shopping. I have argued that practice may be understood in general as a systematic attempt to negate rather than to express discourse. The discourse of consumption as wasteful and destructive is not just a "Green" development, but is found in many societies around the world including many nonindustrial countries (see Meyer [1997] for an African example and Munn [1986] for a New Guinea example). While production creates objects such as foods, consumption by its very nature destroys them. As a result, there are many cosmologies and regions of the world where consumption is seen as intrinsically evil and destructive. I have argued that much of the logic of traditional sacrifice and exchange is itself an attempt to avoid these dangerous and immoral consequence of consumption as an act that uses up resources. So the specific concerns fostered by Green consciousness have become wedded to much deeper and long-standing fears about the evils of consumption more generally. Where in other societies aspects of sacrifice and exchange are employed to prevent the realization of these imminent evils of consumption, in our society the practice of consumption is itself turned into a three-stage ritual that has the same effect of negating what is seen as its destructive nature. Specifically, this takes the form of making the discourse an explicit objectification of these evils and then making sure that the practice, that is, the act of shopping, is used to negate the discourse, usually by turning consumption from an idea of spending money into a practice that is devoted to thrift and saving money (see Miller 1998a for the details of this argument). So the discrepancy between discourse and practice with regard to ethical shopping is part of the larger discrepancy that pertains to all shopping.

Explanation Three: The Contradiction of Ethics and Morality

If the evidence could be reduced to a simple accusation of hypocrisy or lack of altruism, then the two prior explanations might be sufficient. But this is not the case. When considered within a larger compass allowed by the method of ethnographic enquiry, then many, if not most, of these same informants appeared remarkable in the degree of altruism and charity that they manifested not only in principle but also in practice. Given often low incomes and difficulties in meeting what they saw as basic needs, there was a tremendous concern with charitable causes and philanthropic activity varying from helping the elderly and the disabled with their shopping (often by doing it for them) to the general giving of money to charity, which is reflected in national statistics of charitable donations. I saw countless clear examples of generosity and altruism in activities outside of the context of shopping. So the central problem of this chapter is not that there is a discrepancy between the discourse and practice of altruism, because there wasn't. It is only that with respect to the particular activity of shopping we see such a contradiction. The question is, rather, what is it about shopping that should create this contradiction around altruism, such that notwithstanding the tremendous pressures to make shopping itself an expression of altruism, there is no altruistic shopping. The implication seems to be that there is some particular contradiction that prevents the shoppers from expressing altruism in this particular category of action. I wish to suggest this through a third explanation of the evidence.

This explanation rests upon a distinction that could be drawn between ethics and morality. This distinction follows what seemed to be the colloquial usage and connotation of these terms rather than implicating any formal academic or philosophical distinction. "Morality" is most often the term used to suggest that an activity involves general questions of good versus bad, or right versus wrong behavior by the social actor themselves. The term "ethics" seemed to imply the direct involvement of altruistic concern for others and, in particular, distant others. There is considerable evidence that shopping has become an increasingly moral activity (though it probably always was to some degree). Two of the main conclusions I come to in *A Theory of Shopping* (Miller 1998a) may be used to make this point. First, as just noted, the central ritual of shopping takes the discourse of shopping as an antisocial, hedonistic, and materialistic pursuit and turns it into a practice that consists of the dutiful attempt to save money on behalf of the household at large. By legitimating shopping practice in terms of money saved, the shopper ensures the larger sense that they are indeed carrying out a moral activity. Mere individual and hedonistic desire is relegated to the specific category of the "treat" that then become the exception that proves this general rule. This provides for a general objectification of the morality of the household, which complements the more specific objectification of kinship described in chapter 2.

Thrift expresses the larger significance of working on behalf of the household as a moral enterprise. This part of the morality of shopping has either increased or maintained its role (depending upon one's interpretation of recent history). The problem when reconsidered in relation to the current context is that it proves to be incompatible with ethical shopping. Ethical shopping is a means by which the immediate interests of the household are subsumed in the larger concern for others. These others may be the social welfare of producers or a general sense of the global environment, but they are defined as large and global in contradistinction to the parochialism of the household as a focus. The incompatibility of these two agendas is particularly clear when it comes to the question of price, since, at present, ethical shopping is almost always regarded as more expensive than ordinary shopping. If moral shopping is almost entirely defined by the act of thrift and saving money, then the expense of ethical shopping can make it regarded as a form of extravagance that betrays the underlying morality of shopping. Shopping in consideration of distant others is found to be at the expense of the moral concern to serve the interests and husband the resources of one's own household. In short, I would argue that ethical shopping is experienced as opposed to moral shopping, while moral shopping constrains any possibility of ethical shopping. What we have is a direct clash between the micro- and macro-perspective as experienced by the shopper. This, then, becomes a particular version of contradictions that are well established in political philosophy by Rawls and others between the problem of "care" and that of "justice," or more recently, between that of the consumer and that of the citizen.

This is not expressed usually as a contradiction by the shoppers although a sense of it may be gained from some things that they say. The problem for shoppers is that when they try and translate their ethical discourse into practice, contradictions that were hidden by the generalized nature of the discourse of "doing one's bit" become apparent. Shoppers constantly search for ways to resolve such contradictions. A parallel case arises from James's study of the simultaneous heavy consumption and heavy condemnation of sweets and chocolates in the United Kingdom. She notes that this is partly resolved by the degree to which these can first be presented as gifts expressing positive sociality (James 1990). In some cases, people look to mythic and ideological forms for such a resolution; in my fieldwork it emerged from the surrounding conversations that they largely look to the state.

There is some awareness that this contradiction could have been solved for the shopper if responsibility for ethics had been transferred from the domain of individual decision making to that of higher authorities. It is the British government's more recent insistence that it is the "market" as an expression of the will of the individual consumer that should determine policy that creates the contradiction I have just outlined. From the perspective of the shopper, it is the government that should take on this responsibility. Londoners here are closer to European than to U.S. sentiment in often preferring authority to be the responsibility of the state rather than of individual choice. Shoppers commonly note that with ethical shopping they either lack the relevant information or they lack the ability to determine the truth of the information they are given. They note that all sorts of goods make claims to being ethically superior, but suspect some of these are false. They note that health recommendations are often contradictory. Their view of science is that it should always provide consistent and correct advice; there is very little sense that science is itself uncertain and dynamic in its process of discovery. The overall point is that the government is seen to have vastly better resources for determining what is an ethical product and which ones should be promoted. To foist this decision upon the individual consumer who does not have these resources seems much more like an abrogation of governmental responsibility than of giving the consumer more choice.

It does not follow that consumers would be happy for the government to ban all substances regarded as harmful, since all such involvements depend upon the particular sense of risk and pleasure involved. So when beef on the bone was banned in the United Kingdom this was unpopular because most people seemed to feel that the risk was infinitesimal and not worth the aggravation. But in general the delegation of ethical decisions to government would leave the shoppers free to grumble but accept as fate the need for ethical concerns. So contrary to economic theory, it is not always in the interests of the consumers to be the sole arbiter of what is sold.

In the absence of government action, the consumers have to rely on the supermarkets themselves. After all, how else can they buy organic goods except by accepting that the stuff with a bit more dirt on it in one corner of the fruit and vegetable section of the supermarket really doesn't contain residues that are imperceptible to the eye? There is some evidence that this is what they are doing, from the increasing trust that the general public gives to large retailers at a time when trust in government and the professions are in decline. This has been suggested by surveys on trust by organizations such as the Henley Centre for forecasting.

The second relevant conclusion of *A Theory of Shopping* (Miller 1998a) is that the primary motivation of most contemporary shopping is the desire to express love implicitly through a material practice. Shopping today is used as a means to express the ideals of contemporary love, and those ideals have changed significantly over the last thirty years. Where love was once a more conventional and normative quality that could be expressed by established gestures such as taking home flowers on an appropriate occasion, today it has become judged as an expression of highly individualized sensitivity to the particular person. What are increasingly required are gestures that demonstrate careful research and knowledge of the object of one's love. Good shopping is an activity that demonstrates a high degree of sensitivity to mood, circumstance as well as the broader desires of the person shopped for. Many examples were presented in chapter 2. The relevant implication here is that this provides a basis for using the ever increasing variety of goods on sale (137–48). The more goods that one has to choose from, the more specific and "sensitive" is the eventual choice. This can be seen in the complex social meaning of particular purchases. Love today is knowing that he prefers jeans to formal trousers, but as his work prospects will be enhanced by attire less casual than jeans, buying a new variety of stay-press jeans will be a good compromise and he will respect the thought that has gone into someone else solving this problem. Love is knowing that she doesn't want to not feel inadequate among the set of other new mothers she is inviting around for the first time and that she wants to know that Thai food has the right amount of cache as new as against Indian food, without being seen as pretentious and exclusionary so she can relax knowing that this is suitable for this occasion. The point is that vast amounts of "difference" do not lead to shoppers viewing their actions as hedonistic or materialistic but quite the opposite; it increases the opportunity for them to experience choice as the expression of that most basic of moral precepts, the proper foundation of social relationships in love.

Specific refusals such as vegetarianism can, as Willetts (1997) has shown in another London-based study, create conflicts with such expressions of

THE DIALECTICS OF ETHICS AND IDENTITY · 137

family sentiments. Here again there is a conflict between the parochialism of morality and the global expression of ethics. In the ethnography, the interest in Green or organic foods and other such concerns could be experienced not as a sign of the ethical depth of the shopper but as a sign that the shopper is more concerned to express their self-indulgent "issues" and is unprepared to subsume these wider concerns within what should be their first concern for their immediate household members. This overlaps with my first explanation in that Green activists may be seen as rather self-absorbed in their ethical mission. In short, when seen from the perspective of the household, Green shopping or a concern with others may paradoxically be viewed merely as a sign of the selfishness of the individual shopper. Within the ethnography this was most commonly expressed in the way that ethical shopping is viewed by many people as a kind of "cold" attitude largely practiced by cold people (e.g., Linda Snell), which is antipathetic to "warm" shopping, which is generally an expression of love for people one feels responsible for, in collusion with their fallible natures. The activist vegetarian was often associated with unpalatable "macrobiotic" foods that were caricatured as inevitably a muddy brown. As vegetarianism has become more mainstream, the majority expresses the desire to combine their abstinence with a continued search for variety and cuisine, such that the movement has spread much more easily now that supermarkets sell vegetarian food as a form of cuisine rather than as an alternative to cuisine (see Beardswoth and Keil 1997, 239).

Finally, then, we may be coming close to the kinds of factor that would indeed account for the refusal of the mass of the population to engage in practice with an ethos that at a public level has overwhelming support and all the pressure and weight of being backed by formal ethics. We can also solve the paradox by which those who appear most generous and altruistic come to be seen as cold and inappropriately calculative by their peers.

CONTEXTS

My conclusions on Green shopping largely support those of Simmonds (1995) who argued that the key problem lay in the contradictions within which Green consumerism first arose, that it developed alongside an expression of the ideal of pure market economics in which individual consumer sovereignty alone was held to be the legitimate source of any change in the market. As Smith (1990) notes, under the rubric of consumer sovereignty the ideal of ethical consumption becomes itself an argument for the free capitalist market (3). This is notwithstanding the fact that in many areas it was the left-wing, more socially orientated consumers who tended to support environmental concerns (e.g., Lavik and Lunde 1991 for Norway). It is important to note that it need not have happened this way. The most important precedent in ethical consumption was the mass development of consumer cooperatives, which were spearheaded by Gide at the turn of the century in which the ethos was decidedly collectivist (Gide 1921; Furlough 1991), and which lies closer to the kinds of cooperative action that are found today in the powerful Japanese consumer movements (Clammer 1992; Knight 1998).

The larger philosophical questions raised by many papers in Crocker and Linden (1998) and also Goodwin, Ackerman, and Kiron (1997), which direct attention to overall levels of consumption as opposed to what is consumed, hardly appear in the ethnography. The ethnographic evidence rather accords with that of Segal (1998) and Lichtenberg (1998) reflecting upon on average consumption in the United States. They suggest that most ordinary shoppers see themselves as struggling against incomes lower than they feel they need on the basis of a normative model structured by reference to other consumers. They have no sense of "fat" that they could trim for a good cause, except for when they are discussing consumption in the abstract (or their bodies in particular!).

At a micro- and a specific level what has been identified here is symptomatic of contradictions that have been a primary concern of political and moral philosophy for centuries. It also accords with the long struggle between an asceticism that wants to define basic needs as against luxury and the relativist defense of desire as contingent (see Berry 1994; Gudeman and Rivera 1990). As various papers in de Grazia (1996, see especially Auslander 1996) make clear, these shifts in the ideology of goods and consumption are closely tied with changes in the conceptualization of gender and the domestic arena. One of the reasons the level of generality used in this chapter can be sustained within an extraordinarily diverse and cosmopolitan population is that it has developed as discourse with clear historical underpinnings and precedents (see, for example, the close relation of health and diet in Porter's [1993] study of the term "consumption"). These generalities now constitute the dominant, if not the only, discourse within which such discussions are socially acceptable, which also makes them highly repetitive.

The argument for a contradiction in "Green" shopping may also shed light on the evidence that was presented at the beginning of this chapter with respect to ethnicity and cosmopolitan foods. There is no reason why food locality should not be of potential importance in people's imagination of otherness; whether positive as in helping them become familiar with difference, or negative as in a vicarious or displaced form of too easily assimilated difference. But the evidence was that, on the whole, this was not the case. People did not relate food origin to their sense of other people. Indeed, within the British context there are three quite distinct modes of articulation present. First, there is the case of South Asians, a large immigrant population with a well-known ethnic cuisine that is intimately associated with them. Second, there are Afro-Caribbeans, a large immigrant population whose cuisine is almost unknown by the dominant society either in the form of restaurants or as foods purchased within supermarkets. Third, there are the Chinese, whose well-known ethnic cuisine is the only exposure of the Chinese themselves in society. These three cases provide the three logical outcomes of a potential relationship of food locality and ethnic minorities. The fact that all three seem to develop simultaneously should alone make us highly suspect of reading too much into these relationships. Difference is important largely because it is consumed as difference per se within regimes of cuisine rather than as a pointer to the attitudes and aspirations of the eater for their relationship with other peoples.

Taken in the light of the analysis of "Green" consumption, this evidence may be reassessed. As James (1996, 1997) has noted for contemporary British food tastes it is regional authenticity, authentic hybridity, or even a new authentic Britishness that is sought, mainly for reasons of status and class delineation. Similarly, both the ability to clearly articulate the logic of Green as discourse and to give an account of oneself in those terms, as also the ability to actually afford the practice of Green shopping, are differentiated along lines of class. The claims to morality they assert tend to become the claim to the moral superiority of the middle class. The effective privatization of health traced by Coward (1989) where it is the individual who now is given back responsibility and blame for their own health as the state tries to divest itself of such responsibilities, makes the refusal of health foods and organic foods appear as a kind of working-class irresponsibility. Similarly, the assertion of cosmopolitan taste and ethnic chic provides a facade of liberal tolerance. Illiberal attitudes to other peoples or lack of environmental concern are recast as the natural conservatism and intolerance of the working class. My argument is not, however, that power and class are the prime forces behind the contradictions that have been described but rather that the forms by which ethics are expressed immediately implicate them in the mire of social conflict and social distinction.

Just as the ethics of Green consumption were repudiated by the moral concerns for one's immediate household, so also the ethics of Red consumption were repudiated by food "ethnicity" being directed at the context of food consumption. The use of diversity in cuisine has far more to do with ideas of boredom and excitement in the relationship between partners expressed in cooking than anything extraneous to the household. Giving one's partner the spice of difference proves more exciting and immediately rewarding than using mealtimes to evoke tolerance for minorities. Once again, then, it seems that identity—as with morality and charity—begins (but sometimes also ends) at home. The conclusion from both the material and analysis presented here is *not*, however, that these people are not altruistic in motive and deed; the conclusion is that there are contradictions that explain why that altruism is not manifested at certain points where one might expect it and where it is often claimed.

CAVEATS, COMPARISONS, AND CONCLUSIONS

It is important that these observations and analytical conclusions are not reduced to any of three misleading dichotomies, between individuals and society, between what is said and what is done, and between a purely moral and a purely ethical outlook (following the use of these terms described above). It is also important that such a simplification does not lead to an easy dismissal of the ethnographic subjects as hypocritical, deluded, or lacking in reflexive insight. To prevent such misreadings requires a return to an explicit discussion of the concept of "discourse" that has been used throughout this book. As noted in chapter 1, this term is intended neither to evoke writings on "discourse analysis" nor to emulate Foucault. Following Stuart Hall, the intention is to develop the critical concept of ideology, not to abandon it (Hall 1996, 135–36). Nevertheless, it may be worthwhile at this point to turn to the positive purposes intended in using the term and rethinking it in relation to the material of this chapter.

Discourse has been used to describe and account for the normative language, practice, and conceptualization around which a set of values is manifested. The key term here is normative, which implies not only typicality but also pressure, usually moral pressure to conform. The discourse of Green, therefore, exists quite apart from the conversations that are recorded in this ethnography. The routinized nature of these conversations suggests the presence of a transcending discourse to which informants are to a greater or lesser degree attempting to conform or at least take cognizance of. Indeed, Green discourse may be said to be powerful in as much as it has become hard to imagine speech and writing about environmentalist and materialistic values that was not based on a stance toward this discourse. But just because Green issues were commonly explicit and debated does not mean that they were reflective. For some people they were; for others, they were simply highly normative debates that—as it were—tripped off the tongue. The term "discourse" provides an expectation of homogeneity and permits many of the generalizations that are contained in this account. But used in the loose fashion intended here it is also respectful of exceptions and aware of the diversity of actual expression.

It follows that the subjects of the ethnography are as much the creations of discourse as the authors of discourse, which they may be socialized into and surrounded by, often with limited access to alternative perspectives. Although I am quoting individuals, the discourse I present is not merely the accretion of their voices but rather a set of values and expectations that they tend to manifest as social actors—almost in the sense of acting out or enacting discourse. Indeed, the degree to which society recognizes people as "individuals" is itself a product of discursive forms as Strathern (1992) pointed out in some detail in a previous Morgan Lectures volume (see also Dumont 1986 on individualism as a particular expression of collectivism). This still permits an emphasis upon how subjects strategically and otherwise use discourse, rather than solely a focus upon the degree to which they are its products. So when talking about discourse it is recognized that people are often trying to reconcile themselves to something that is both part of themselves and also evidently transcends them as individuals.

Similarly, in the previous chapters the discourse of "child" or "community" already contains the individuals who embody these terms and ideals. No parent can relate to an infant other than through the social and normative discourse that describes infants as a normative category, and no parent can relate to such a discourse unaffected by their experience of their own particular infant. The philosopher Hegel was clear as to what must be avoided: "he tried to reconceived such subject-subject relation in a way that avoided any suggestions of fully formed, self-inspecting rational agents confronting each other in social space" (Pippin 1993, 79). Rather, individual informants relate both to others and equally to themselves through the mediation of the relationship between discourse and particularity. What we observe is the constant process by which they become individuals only as social and ethical beings.

Any simple identification of discourse with either language or practice

is also undermined by the evidence presented. Green discourse is power-
fully located in institutions such as education and the media and has
reached a point where almost anyone could recite its premises and implications. But its influence on action is extremely muted. By contrast, love
and care in chapter 2 are primarily a form of daily practice, and in some
English families are but rarely explicated in language. Thus, discourse in
the latter case has very little to do with language and is largely an observation of practice. As suggested in the appendix to chapter 1, language and
practice may be found equated as a single discourse in one arena, while in
another they may be opposed. By the same token, that which contradicts
discourse can be another discourse, as between the discourses of ethics
and morality. But in the case of the contradiction between kin role and
one's actual kin, it makes no sense to call the ad hoc specificity of the particular kin a "discourse" since it is neither normative nor collective.

The term "discourse" also helps us avoid any simple ascription of
hypocrisy. It should be evident that the contradictions being described
here exist in large part because individuals live within the contradictions
of their culture. In this chapter, two imperatives contradict each other, so
that the development of one becomes inimical to the other. But contradiction can be avoided if each of these remains largely within a given
frame. Inside their houses, a family may have a highly modernist bath-
room and an olde worlde living room. These do not "clash" because
rooms work as frames to keep them apart. In the same way my presence as
anthropologist sometimes may have caused discomfort when actions taking place in supermarkets were posed directly against conversations held
in kitchens. Otherwise these need not come into direct juxtaposition. The
term "frame" may also be related to what in chapter 1 became the defense
of the organization of this volume. The same people are being discussed in
each of the last three chapters, but they are framed by those chapters as
discussions of kinship, community, and identity, respectively. This reflects
in part the framing of their relationship to shopping within such semiautonomous fields. But the third explanation used in this chapter demonstrates that such autonomy is not absolute, and what has now been
encountered is precisely a clash between the imperatives created in what
otherwise might have been separate domains. Where ethical shopping is
confronted by the morality of kinship we are forced to recognize the arti-
ficial nature of this book's construction and turn to the connections between the material of different chapters. Through the use of framing,
through collusion with commerce and through the unreflective nature
of some of the discursive representations that have been described here,
people are often able to avoid contradictions. Changes in circumstance,

such as the withdrawal of the state from taking responsibility for ethical decisions about commodities, may, however, break the power of frames to keep contradictory imperatives apart, which then gives them the appearance of hypocrisy. Coward (1989) presents a similar argument with respect to the growth of the alternative health movement and the attempt by the state to put the burden of responsibility for good health onto the individual citizen under an ideology of free choice.

It was noted in the appendix to chapter 1 that the use of the term "discourse" here would differ from most other academic works in that there is less stress placed on institutional forms and powers in creating or manipulating discourse. The term will come into close correspondence with its use by theorists such as Leyshon and Thrift (1997), working on a similar topic, in the next chapter, where I argue that discourse is institutionally located in such a way that its power permeates those institutions in a genuinely constitutive form. Much of that which could be called discursive in the last three chapters has been the product of popular culture often in collusion with markets but not merely an imposition by them on the population. The evidence on food and ethnicity parallels the findings within the well-researched field of music and ethnicity where recent work from Gilroy (1993) and Back (1996) and others indicate the difficulty of any simple semiotic reading of ethnicity from music, since the creativity within music production is echoed by the creativity with which the musical product is subsequently employed in forms of identification. Discourses arise from below as well as being imposed from above.

Finally this chapter illustrates how persons themselves as against either their language or practice can become instruments for the expression of values and of discourse. One of the reasons that Green individuals are seen as cold is that they are viewed as highly calculative in their determination of what are acceptable goods and behaviors, turning rational choice into an explicit act of decision making and elucidating the precise criteria by which shopping decisions should be made. This conflicts with a morality of shopping according to which, although decisions about goods may be extraordinarily precise in, for example, matching a particular outfit to a particular person, ultimately the purchase of an outfit is intended to express a relationship through a mode (in both senses of that term) that is quite different from that of rationality and calculation. The ideal of care is one that is supposed to be founded on affective rather than rational decision. Clearly the paradox by which people who think of their values as expressing care and concern become seen by others as relatively cold and selfish demonstrates rather clearly the way discourse transcends any attempt by an individual to construct themselves as the objectification of values. It is neither the intention nor the fault of Green activists that they should be regarded as cold or calculative, instead of warm and unselfish.

In the appendix to chapter 4, this discussion of discourse is extended to a broader anthropological analysis of contradictions in religion and other ethical discourses, which indicate why a simplistic attribution of hypocrisy ignores the degree to which people live in contexts that are themselves contradictory. Instead, the final section of this chapter has tried to realign the argument with that of the two previous chapters. It has returned us to the issue of discourse and that which transcends discourse, which is the constant tension between generality and particularity that makes dialectics the foundation for all these discussions. In these three chapters, the focus has been on the ethnography, where people can be seen to both experience and attempt to resolve such contradictions. The next chapter moves upward and outward from the ethnography to situations that could not be observed within such a local compass but which have to be included in this account because they are critical to the determination of what facilities are available to the shopper in the first place.

Appendix

GILSENAN ON CONTRADICTION IN RELIGION

    The position of the moralities and ideals discussed in chapter 4 are akin to that of more formal religious beliefs as situated discourses, which then implicate contradictions between religion and practice. So although they are not examples of formal religion, some light might be shed upon them through a comparative anthropological study of religion and ideology. For example, the simultaneity of feasting and fasting, or materialism with asceticism in traditional religion at the time of Rabelais or under Calvinism (Schama 1987) just as much as within the modern holiday of Christmas (Miller 1993) depends upon much more sophisticated anthropological insights than merely some simplistic ascription of hypocrisy to those involved. I want, therefore, to turn to the work of one author whose studies illustrate both what has been argued in chapter 4 with respect to discourse and also the issue of contradiction when discourse is analyzed in context.

    Although he does not use the term, Gilsenan (1996) provides an unusually clear example of what might be meant by the term discourse. He examines the narratives through which the dominant forms of power and its associated violence are constituted within a relatively peripheral area of North Lebanon still ruled by large landowners. He presents a series of genres of narrative. For example, "This idealization of the generous, fear-inducing and fearless lord to whose palace everyone comes was typical of the hagiography of property and force"

(52). Narrative, itself a highly cultivated social practice, is complemented by other forms of representation and performance, including the many acts of violence that are referred to within such narratives. I would argue that discourse may or may not take the form of narrative. To return to the example used in chapter 1 of Seale discussing death, his work showed that psychological accounts often take a more clearly narrative form than medical accounts. For reasons discussed in considerable detail by Ricoeur (1984–88), narrative is often a particularly powerful form of discourse, but there are alternatives, and what medical accounts lack in narrative they claim in powers of efficacy.

In Gilsenan's work one can trace how discourse in the form of narrative and the violence that both stems from and provides material for narrative help reproduce the structures within which power is given meaning and retained. One of the factors that makes discourse a compulsive direction to action is its very cultural elaboration. It is the subtle relationship between play and seriousness, threat and event, honor and humiliation that makes this an endless foundation for cultivating life as the agile activity of public performance and private strategizing. The perils of performance are part of its very attraction. There are alternatives—men who refuse this cultivation of masculinity in alternative scenarios of work and livelihood and an ideal untroubled life of cultivation; but they are thereby marginalized from what makes life (and death) meaningful for most males, for whom honor is also the primary bond between males as kindred. Gilsenan recognizes the contradictions that are generated within this discourse as between the power and interests of fathers and sons, although contradictions and ambiguity are often themselves the foundation for further play and strategy. The burdensome nature of discourse is evident in the compulsion to take action simply because one has been forced to recognize in the public domain an anomaly, such as the presence of a representative of the opposing feudal group, even though there is no personal desire for such action (i.e., killing the person seen), and its consequence are clearly inimical to one's personal interests.

The situation moves still closer to the circumstances of chapter 4 when we turn to Gilsenan's previous book (1982) on the place of religion in such a society. Religion is one of the most obvious examples of a discourse that, at the very least, claims hegemony and asserts a universalistic right to determine how people should account for their actions. But in practice, religions such as Christianity, Islam, and Judaism have always existed in tension with the very diversity of the social and cultural contexts within which they are followed. Gilsenan starts his book with anecdotes about young men who respect the religiosity of the public sphere in hand kisses and formal and respectful address, but once home quickly discard these trappings and turn to pop music and other interests. Islam is not easily separated out as a field of merely public belief since it sees itself as a religion of practice, yet Gilsenan argues it is precisely at the level of practice that the diversity of ways of living and acting confront it as difference that may or may not be acknowledged. The ethnographic nature of the study soon brings out the importance of contextual features such as class and power in considering these articulations and denials, in much the same way that the rise of the Green and of the cosmopolitan as discourses are saturated with the examples of the sort of class constructions and disavowals that Bourdieu (1984) noted lie at the heart of "taste." So when Gilsenan writes of central Islamic concepts and institutions that "They are universalistic terms. There is always an inherent tension between them and such particularistic forces as a given regime's attempts to appropriate religion to itself as an instrument of power" (1982, 52), the parallel may be drawn to the contradictions of our own lives within which Green ideals are most commonly encountered through the medium of supermarkets as an instrument of profit. In both cases we may feel we can only gain access to the expression of our own universalistic beliefs through a medium that is antipathetic to those same beliefs

Gilsenan does not directly pose the relationship between the Islam he presents in 1982 and the narratives of violence and honor he describes in 1996. An analogous juxtaposition is, however, provided by Stewart (1994), who argues with respect to Christianity on the island of Naxos that honor and sanctity form two complementary "levels" of Greek ideology. He describes what often amounts to a systematic opposition or even inversion between the qualities of cunning, guile, and self-regard that foster honor among males and the values promoted by what is also a male hierarchy of the Church. The values that create honor are regarded as sins by the Church. In this case, the longevity of both has seen them arise in more direct complementarity using gender and, in turn, marriage to express a mode of life through which they may coexist. There are obviously many differences between the sentimentality of domestic love as the foundation for kinship in North London and the sentiments that surround honor and achievement among the males described by Gilsenan or Stewart. Nevertheless, it is clear from Gilsenan's account that these narratives of violence are fundamental to the relations of kinship and family and that there is, therefore, a direct conflict of values between those embodied in the more universalistic vision of religion and those that command the stance of individuals to their own familial relations. This appears close to the conclusions of chapter 4. Two sets of ideals were found, which when expressed within their semiautonomous and framed contexts do not clash: honor and sanctity in North Lebanon, ethics and morality in North London. But many devices are required to retain yet keep apart these two quite contrary systems of values, and such devices don't always work. The negative attitude uncovered here toward Green activists despite the formal approval of their values has its parallels with the ambivalence felt in religions such as Islam and Christianity to priests who embody religious ideals, but who thereby expose the contradictions between those ideals and the fallibilities, inconsistencies, and problematic claims to authority of those who represent them.

What Gilsenan's work implies when directed back to the material of chapter 4 is the reaffirmation that even though we can discern acts that appear as lies and hypocrisy we should be careful in our interpretations. He ends his 1982 book by referring back to the anecdotes with which he started, noting that "It is too glib to say that either the hand kiss or the address as *sir* was mere convention and mere show" (251). The contradictions that are displayed by informants often reflect the structural contradictions that are inherent in the dialectics of the world within which they move. A major source of contradiction lies in the need for ethical claims of a universalistic nature to be objectified in forms that themselves were already the expression of other moralities. So Islam becomes embedded in forms that are also narratives and practices of power and violence in North Lebanon, while in North London ethical ideals become objectified in forms that also express class distinctions, family love, and commercial imperatives.

THE DIALECTICS
OF POLITICAL ECONOMY

Fine and Leopold (1993) have raised the important question of the degree of articulation between consumption and production. They argue for a close relationship based on vertical lines of provisioning where, for example, the centrality of fashion to the clothing industry is closely tied to the particularities of manufacture and distribution in that industry. I have argued for more autonomy based on my research on the soft drink industry in Trinidad (Miller 1997a), which suggested limited points of articulation between two forms of practice—production and consumption—that knew remarkably little about each other and were directed inwardly to their own concerns. The study of shopping has reinforced this conclusion, since the issues expressed in shopping do not easily divide into different sectors such as shopping for underwear as opposed to shopping for cleaning materials, though sometimes, as in the last chapter, which concentrates on shopping for food, such divisions do seem appropriate.

There is unlikely to be a fixed relationship between production and consumption that holds for diverse times and places. In general, while shopping is clearly not simply a derivative from business, in most cases it is not entirely autonomous, either. At a broad level the possibilities that exist for the shopper are determined by forces that relate to commercial issues such as profitability and the placement of capital. So major changes in retail such as the rise of out-of-town hypermarkets and new malls cannot be understood from anything that is immediately evident in the actions of the shoppers themselves. The implications of this for anthropology in acknowledging the limits of ethnography were noted in chapter 1. The material presented in this chapter is mainly derived from different research methods and objectives from the rest of the volume. Its starting point and ultimate rationale does, however, lie in the ethnography of shopping.

Jay Road included a wide range of household incomes, and its inhabitants use a wide range of retail outlets. For the most impoverished households two retail chains stood out within the local high street as appropriate for their basic provisioning. One was Iceland, which concentrated on frozen foods; the other was called Kwik-Save, which appeared to be a stripped down version of the larger supermarkets directed toward this down market clientele. It was the only supermarket in the area that presented itself as a discount store, and that was certainly the way it was seen by the shoppers. Only three of the households studied used this as their primary store. One, an elderly man, went shopping there for himself, although when he was shopping for a bedridden neighbor he used Sainsbury's. He gave the impression that Kwik-Save would not really be suitable fare when purchased on behalf of another. The second was an unemployed mother with two daughters on youth training schemes, who used both Kwik-Save and a well-known market stall that tended to have particularly cheap canned goods.

The third shopper who shopped mainly at Kwik-Save was a housewife, Maureen, married to a building laborer with two children. The family positively identified with a traditional English working-class culture, and Kwik-Save reflected their unpretentious attitude. It was part of their general desire to find a bargain, which was also reflected in their involvement in car boot sales. I went shopping with her twice. One occasion was based at Iceland, the other trip at Kwik-Save. The aura of Kwik-Save is dominated by its lack of pretension, with goods put on sale while still in their original cardboard packaging. It evoked the street market as much as the supermarket. The site is full of exhortations about "Why spend more?" Goods are all brand-name except for its own value "no frills" brand. Most of what she buys are standard branded goods such as Nescafe instant coffee, Heinz spaghetti, Tate and Lyle sugar, Kellogg's Corn Flakes, but also less well-known brands such as Lord Raleigh milk. As a shopper, she pays less time considering purchases than almost any other. Shopping here is reduced to a largely mechanical operation of finding the regular goods. There seemed no expectation of either considering or buying anything that does not already form part of her regular list. She also uses the in-store concessionary butcher. The main problem noted by her and another of the regular users was, first, that Kwik-Save stock is relatively limited compared with the larger supermarkets, but also that it was less reliable in the sense of one knowing that a specific line of goods would be present on any particular occasion. The consequence of this was that one was more likely to have to include a visit to another shop than was the case with the much larger and more reliable supermarkets. Nevertheless, they had no doubt that Kwik-Save was the cheapest outlet for their regular purchases, and this was supported by my own price comparisons.

A couple of other shoppers mentioned using Kwik-Save when they were short of money, but otherwise would prefer not to. All those who used this shop lived on council estates. There was not a single case of shopping there by a person in private housing. Indeed, it was difficult to imagine a middle-class shopper in the store. Even within the working class, many negative attitudes could be found, for example, a nurse of Caribbean background noted the following:

> **I found it rotten—you know, poor quality. I'm not saying I have a considerable amount of money but I didn't like how it was laid out. I didn't like how they, you know, position their stuff. I just didn't like it, so [I went there] maybe three times and that was it.**

As would be evident from the previous chapters, it is hard to separate out thrift from a wide spectrum of shopping imperatives. Indeed, in Miller (1998a) thrift is analyzed within a quite different perspective based upon the anthropology of religion. Its relationship here, suggesting an association of the "thrift" shop with low social status, may have had repercussions for the overall structure of the retail trade, since, as Wrigley and Clarke (forthcoming) have noted, the "deep discount" section of the retail food industry seems unable to rise much above 10 percent of the grocery trade as a whole.

Even in the local primary school, many children identified Kwik-Save as the cheapest shop in the area. So while the shopper I accompanied there positively identified with the lack of pretension and the apparently clear-cut bargains, many people found it incompatible with a certain kind of respectability and avoided it. It is possible, therefore, that some shoppers simply didn't tell me about their use of this store. Clearly, however, as a source of cheap goods it was an important shop, if only as a fall back for when times were hard. According to the statistics of shoppers given in the company's annual reports and the Institute of Grocery Distribution (IGD) surveys, while Kwik-Save does attract a clientele that is more elderly, less well-off, and from larger families, this is only a matter of degree, and middle-class shoppers do shop there. Possibly my observation reflects the locality and that class and other differences in use would be much slighter in a small-town environment where there are fewer alternatives and where there is, perhaps, less of an onus on reputation than in North London. In this North London area, the sheer range of supermarkets creates conditions for class and income differences to be more clearly expressed, and individual shops occupy narrower niches.

Just as my work on this volume began, the financial papers recorded that Kwik-Save had merged with another supermarket chain, Somerfield— well, it was called a "merger." A more detailed inspection clearly showed that it was more of a takeover by Somerfield. It seemed that if I was to follow my goal of a "top down" perspective on political economy to complement the "bottom up" perspective of shopping ethnography, then the omens had provided an obvious research topic. Forces were afoot that were about to change one of the central options available to the most impoverished shoppers. I have no previous experience working on British capitalism or the retail trade, and I therefore contacted colleagues who either knew of or worked in retail for a guide as to what was going on. The story they told me seemed at first quite straightforward. British supermarket retailing is an extraordinarily dynamic sector that has been characterized over the last two decades by the rise to dominance of a few firms that have concentrated around ever larger chains and stores. These were highly competitive, and in that climate there was a general feeling that there were still too many players in the game. The weaker ones would simply have to merge if they were to survive. Kwik-Save was certainly struggling, and from the point of view of retail competition a merger with Somerfield seemed an entirely logical outcome of the present competitive situation. The advantage of this story is that it does not take us too far from the kinds of concern that have been raised through the study of shopping itself. We can see a close relationship between the styles of retailing that have been attempted, as represented in the various retail chains, and potentially relate these to changes in the desires and dictates of shopping itself. The bottom up and top down approaches need not be very far apart.

I will therefore start by giving the detailed evidence behind this story. But as my investigation proceeded, I came to believe that things were not actually quite so straightforward and that the reason Kwik-Save merged has much more to do with other factors, which could more truly be considered to be top down in orientation leading us into the more esoteric worlds of contemporary capitalism. Furthermore, the story that unfolded may be particularly revealing of the contradictions that arise from the dialectical tensions that remain at the heart of capitalism today. So after describing the history and conditions of the firms that merged, I want to turn to the other powers that seemed to be pulling the strings from behind the scenes and then to the larger implications of this case study when placed in the context of other studies of retail capital.

THE KWIK-SAVE AND SOMERFIELD MERGER

The basic history of Kwik-Save is given by Sparks (1990, 1995). It was founded under another name by Albert Gubay in 1959 with an emphasis on late store hours and easy car parking, but after a trip to the United States, Gubay emulated new ideas he discovered there. Kwik-Save became a discount grocery store that stripped back costs to provide the cheapest prices, concentrating on selling second-brand goods from cardboard boxes in unreconstructed warehouse conditions, with central distribution, avoiding the usual special offers, stamps, and other common strategies of the trade, in order to concentrate on price alone. He also streamlined the sales to around 450 lines and gained additional profit from concessions that provided for areas such as meat and fresh foods that he did not intend to deal with. After he left to develop other businesses, the management he had recruited continued with this strategy, which had solidified in the late 1960s and expanded right through the 1970s and 1980s. By 1988, Kwik-Save had a turnover of £.974 million and profits of £.55 million from 575 locations and over 8,400 employees. Growth had mainly been organic and self-funded. There were plenty of imitators of this strategy but no comparable successes. It still, however, represented only 2 percent of the British grocery trade.

At this stage there were some changes. There was a small movement upmarket, with more leading brands represented. With the introduction of new electronic technologies the stock could grow to over one thousand lines. The chain had remained independent until 1987 when a company called Dairy Farm took 25 percent of the stock. Kwik-Save continued to grow, and even as late as 1994 the outlook remained reasonably rosy, according to *The Financial Times* (11 May 1994):

> **Kwik-Save now has 838 stores, and plans 80 openings a year**
> **for up to 10 years. Mr. Bowler (the CEO) said recent research**

> had identified 800 more locations throughout the UK where
> Kwik-Save stores could trade profitably, including smaller
> towns which did not interest superstore operators.

An independent survey by the IGD in 1994 also showed surprisingly little sense of things changing from this remarkable history of sustained growth. By this stage Kwik-Save had achieved a 4.3 percent share of the market.

In fact, by late 1993 things had started to go drastically wrong. As the store announced its first fall in profits, a typical commentator noted:

> Kwik-Save is paying the price for straying from its roots. As a
> discounter of a limited range of basic branded goods, it had a
> distinct appeal. That has been blurred as the group tried to
> emulate the supermarkets by doubling its product range to
> over 4,000 lines, building larger, more expensive stores and
> introducing own-label goods. That has allowed pure discoun-
> ters such as Aldi and Netto to undercut it, while the big super-
> markets have retaliated from on high by cutting prices on the
> typical Kwik-Save shopping basket. Kwik-Save is being horri-
> bly squeezed in the middle. . . . But its management seems
> wedded to continued expansion—albeit at a slower pace—and
> is planning to spend heavily on modernizing distribution and
> computer systems. To cover that investment will require even
> higher volumes, just at a time when the group's rapidly falling
> return on capital makes new store openings harder to justify.
> A more prudent approach might be for Kwik-Save to retrench
> to being a limited range discounter, cut costs and fight the
> competition on its home ground. (*Financial Times*, 3 May
> 1996)

The situation had not been helped by an expensive buyout of the Shoprite supermarket group in Scotland, which gave it a presence in that area but no profits (Sparks 1995). It was not just that continental deep dis-count stores could undercut Kwik-Save (Burt and Sparks 1995), but the biggest U.K. stores such as Tesco had in response to this brought in a value line in 1992–93 that gave them a highly discounted range but within a much pleasanter shopping environment. The tone of the IGD report in 1996 was in marked contrast to that of two years previous. The report sus-pected that some items were being sold at a loss in the attempt to keep price differentials, and underscored the threat from what are called "deep discount" shop formats coming over from Europe. The main response by management had been to call in the help of Andersen Consulting, a management consulting firm. Their recommendations formed the basis of the "New Generation" policy that followed.

At the time of the merger there was not much sign of a respite from several years of falling profits. Over four years its shares had underperformed the sector by almost 70 percent, and the high profits of the earlier period were sinking fast year by year. Although in its last annual report there was evidence of higher profit margins, the markets responded negatively. As *The Financial Times* noted (9 May 1998), the interpretation of these results was that Kwik-Save must have been raising prices and thereby "further alienating its cash-strapped customer base." The pressure from deep discounters may have been exaggerated. In 1997, discounters had a total share of 9.3 percent of grocery retailing, of which Kwik-Save had 5.9 percent and its nearest rival Aldi had 0.9 percent (Barnes, Dadamo, and Turner 1996, 239). So it may not have been any objective rival (though this was a highly significant factor in particular regions and there were the value lines of the major supermarkets to contend with) so much as the fact that few people seemed to feel Kwik-Save had much of a clue as to the solution for its problems.

The other partner in this merger had a very different history, and according to most commentators, possibilities of a very different future. *The Financial Times* (25 May 1997) summarized the background as follows:

> As the former Gateway Group, it had been subject to one of the largest leveraged buy-outs of the 1980s by the Isosceles consortium and almost collapsed under the weight of its £.2bn debt early in the 1990s. The result was a deeply discounted float price. The shares were eventually issued at 145p, putting them on prospective price/earnings ratio of barely above five. The rating for the food retail sector was double that.

The full history is rather complex. Unlike Kwik-Save, the Somerfield fascia (which was still not attached to many of its stores) covered over a history of complex mergers. The company had traded as Linfood (1977–83), Dee (1983–88), Gateway (1988–89), Isosceles (1989–94), Somerfield Holdings (1994–96) and since 1996, as Somerfield. The group developed through a wide series of purchases of more than a dozen other supermarket chains. As a result, under Gateway it had a market share of 11.4 percent and was the third largest supermarket chain in the United Kingdom (Hallsworth 1992, 115–17). But this included a wide range of shops, from deep discounters such as Shopper's Paradise through to a number of more regional chains—a rather unwieldy combination of many different formats. In this case, the sudden change in fortune came through a highly leveraged buyout (LBO; see below for an explanation of this term) in 1989 for £.2.2 billion.[1] The result of this was that the company was owned by the Isosceles Group with a truly massive debt. Part of this arrangement included selling a raft of Gateway shops to ASDA for £.705 million (which nearly collapsed itself as a result). When recession meant that further sales were unlikely to create the resources to pay off this debt the company looked doomed. It survived through ring fencing the retail sector from the debt of the holding firm.

The key that turned survival into profit was the appointment of a new CEO, David Simons, who brought financial reorganization including cost control and better buying, as well the conversion from Gateway to the Somerfield fascia, which worked on higher margins. Also in the short term there was a policy to deliberately reposition the chain through pricing, something against the tenor of grocery trade at the time. This was generally successful as was the strategy to recreate itself as the core high-street supermarket, as opposed to the emphasis on large out-of-town hypermarkets above and discounters below. Management soon saw the strategy of creating "community" stores at a high-street level as succeeding, according to *The Financial Times* (18 June 1997). In particular, stores were showing a 14 percent increase in sales when converted to the Somerfield fascia (Somerfield Annual Report 1996–97, 5). The annual report (which may include a certain amount of wishful thinking) reveals that it took on many of the latest supermarket strategies such as loyalty cards and a premium range as well as ordinary own labels, but the "third major element in our differentiation program is to make every store a focal point and an active member of the community. This takes full advantage of our large estate of neighborhood stores with relatively high frequency of customer visits" (8). Kwik-Save found their customers rather less loyal (Barnes et al. 1996, 117).

By 1996, the company felt strong enough to go back to the market through a stock-market flotation. This had the effect of paying off all its debt to Isosceles and severing any connection. Indeed, at this stage the banks that owned Isosceles simply wrote off the part of the debt they were responsible for as a lost cause. David Simons did not go unrewarded, given the £.4 million he made from the floatation. By this time Somerfield represented six hundred stores and 45,000 person staff. The memory of its older financial problems meant that the floatation was itself nearly a fail-

---

1. In British usage, "billion" is equivalent to a million million, rather than a thousand million as in U.S. English.

ure, but the company achieved creditable results soon afterward and saw its price at floatation of 145 pence floating upward to 170 pence. These histories led to the basic and apparently straightforward story about the merger that was referred to earlier. Somerfield argued that it would save £.50 million as a result of economies that could follow from the merger. Certainly it followed a remarkable performance by David Simons turning Somerfield into a company that was outperforming the market especially with its own fascia stores, with a 1998 pretax profit of £.115 million.

The merging of these two companies made some sense, then, if one saw the future of food retailing as a competition between a few key megafirms. The new firm became the fifth largest in the U.K. grocery sector. The financial press was somewhat snooty about it, referring to the "odd couple"; but when it became clear that what at first was announced as a relatively equal merger was, in fact, largely going to be a development of the Somerfield image and strategy, the "takeover" was found to be more acceptable and more promising (e.g., compare the attitude of expressed in *The Grocer* from 21 February and 6 June 1998). Although in turn this makes it unsurprising that a survey in the 29 May issue of the journal *Supermarket* found Somerfield managers rather more sanguine about their prospects than the Kwik-Save managers. In fact, the new board had only two Kwik-Save members. By 10 July 1998 *The Guardian* was able to write about Somerfield's prospects in a fairly upbeat manner predicting more jobs and new investments. Within a short time the merger seemed to have quite disproved the skepticism of the market and was looking even more promising in expecting to generate up to £.100 million of benefits and predicting that see Kwik-Save's 3 percent margins would be increasingly replaced by Somerfield's 6–7 percent margin. As so often happens in commerce, the predictions proved false (see below). But just because from the point of view of the logic of companies competing to serve a particular market, the merger makes a great deal of sense, it doesn't follow that that is why it actually took place.

I now want to suggest quite another story with quite different players, which I would argue provide the primary reason why the shops were merged at this particular point in time. Mention has already been made of the fact that Kwik-Save lost its independence as a result of an aggressive purchase of a stake in the company by Dairy Farm, which first bought 25 percent of its shares in 1987 and later increased it to 29.4 percent. An agreement was made that Dairy Farm would not increase its share beyond 30 percent or sell this in a block, but this lapsed in 1994. As part of this agreement, however, Dairy Farm secured a presence on the board that meant, in effect, it was running the company. From that point on, Dairy

Farm appears to have taken over control from those managers who had helped build up the company so successfully. One reason why this is possible with a mere 29 percent of the shares is that other major shareholders represent large fund holders, mainly of pension funds, that remained relatively passive. In this case a fund holder Phillips & Drew Fund Management (PDFM) held substantial stakes in both the companies involved in the merger but appears to have played very little role in the running of either. Fund managers rarely take a proactive role though partly in the light a poor performance PDFM could be quite aggressive in promoting takeovers (*The Financial Times*, 15 January 1999). The press is clear that the two subsequent CEOs were both Dairy Farm appointees, as were some other board members. By 1994, the Kwik-Save chairman was Simon Keswick, the chairman of the group behind Dairy Farm. Indeed, from then on most actions seem to have been dominated by Dairy Farm, and I would suggest the merger itself was no exception. The journalists covering the merger certainly saw it this way, as in *The Grocer* (21 February 1998): "analysts believe that Dairy Farm was the prime mover in the merger. . . . by releasing its equity into the bigger business, it hopes it can eventually sell that larger stake for a better return." Indeed, within a month of this article the Dairy Farm Web site (<www.irasia.com>) was able to announce that Dairy Farm had sold off its interest in the combined company, suggesting that here we may find the root cause of what was going on. It took two to tango, and in most respects what has been termed a merger was actually a takeover of Kwik-Save. But this was aided and abetted by the victim, largely because Kwik-Save was then firmly under the control of Dairy Farm, which saw this is the ideal way to maximize the financial advantage to them of pulling out. The money they could obtain from a stake in a potentially healthy larger company was considerably more than they would have gained from pulling out of a clearly ailing firm.

Dairy Farm's bucolic name rather obfuscates a rather extraordinary firm, a firm that at this particular point in time was facing a massive dilemma. Dairy Farm is in fact the retail subdivision of a company called Jardine Matheson, the largest employer and owner of urban real estate in Hong Kong. Indeed, according to the *Far Eastern Economic Review* (9 January 1997), it is the developing world's biggest multinational company, employing 220,000 people. The problem faced by this company was summarized by *The Economist* (8 April 1995) discussing the appointment of a new managing director:

> **He seems to think, for instance, that it would be a pity if Beijing were to believe the firm is anything less than 100 percent**

committed to Hong Kong, merely because it has moved its reg-
istered office to Bermuda, delisted from the Hong Kong stock
market, and switched share trading in its main subsidiaries—
Hongkong Land, the Mandarin Oriental hotel chain and Dairy
Farm, a retailer—to Singapore. Equally, it would be a pity if
the Chinese government were to interpret Henry Keswick's celebrated description of it to a British parliamentary committee
as "a Marxist-Leninist, thuggish, oppressive regime" to be an
expression of anything other than the uttermost respect. Mr.
Keswick's family in effect controls Jardines, which derived almost 60 percent of its freshly unveiled net profit of $452m
last year from Hong Kong and China. China will be taking back
Hong Kong in barely two years' time; and Jardines, long accus-
tomed to behaving as though it owned the place itself, has
been cold-shouldered for big contracts. China refuses to approve a HK$ 12 billion ($1.6 billion) deal awarded to a Jar-
dines-led consortium to build a container terminal. The
enmity stretches back to 1840, when William Jardine, an
opium trader (and an ancestor of the Keswicks by marriage)
persuaded the British government to declare war on China and
seize Hong Kong. China has not forgotten that bit of history,
any more than Mr. Morrison has forgotten that Jardines' assets
in Shanghai were lost when the Communists cleared the city of
foreigners in the 1950s. More recently, China partly blames
Jardines—and, in particular, Sir Charles Powell, a former ad-
viser to Lady Thatcher and one of the firm's London-based di-
rectors—for the appointment of the annoyingly democratic
Chris Patten as the colony's governor.

Thereby hangs the outline of a rather extraordinary tale. To understand
the Kwik-Save sale it seems we need to understand the Opium War. Jardine
Matherson was developed essentially through the sale of Indian-grown
opium to China. Le Fevour (1968) and Cheong (1979) between them document a turbulent nineteenth-century involvement. This was the company that primarily benefited from the Opium War, since the British
government used that war, first to prevent the Chinese from curbing the
trade that was central to Jardine Matheson's profits and second, to create
in Hong Kong a space for the traders. Jardine Matheson, which was the
biggest such trader, continued to make very extensive profits following
the Opium War. From 1873 when locally grown opium finally destroyed
the trade, the company managed to gain lucrative contracts for develop-

ments in China such as the railways and loans. The reaction of the direct descendants of the firm's founder to the emerging certainty that China would finally take back Hong Kong was, therefore, not surprising. The company quickly attempted to break out of its regional base by involvement around the globe, and the Kwik-Save interest was one of several new initiatives in Europe and elsewhere at that time. Kwik-Save seemed to match its experience in food retailing in the Far East (for example, see *Reuters New Service* from 18 June 1987). It also tried to protect itself by registering and trading elsewhere.

The subsequent problem was not just that its core assets remained in Hong Kong, and were, therefore, vulnerable, but that these ventures largely failed. Dairy Farm's involvement in Kwik-Save and the appointment of its managers cannot be divorced from the turnaround from constant success to failure. The Dairy Farm appointees tended not to do too badly personally, as the *Financial Times* noted (29 November 1998): "Mr. Graeme Bowler, chief executive of Kwik-Save, received a bonus larger than Mr. Archie Norman, ASDA's chairman-designate and former CEO, last year in spite of a 28 per cent decline in his company's pre-tax profits"—and notwithstanding that this came just after announcing 1,900 job cuts! The degree of control is most apparent in that the last manager of the board at Kwik-Save was none other than Simon Keswick, a direct descendent of the family that ran Jardine Matheson from the time of the Opium War. But Dairy Farm's rather panicky ventures across the globe and, more to the point, their general lack of success were starting to have consequences at their home base quite apart from the looming takeover by China. Partly as a result of having "hundreds of millions wiped off its bottom line" and most especially a fall in 40 percent in pretax profits in the Dairy Farm retail sector (*Far Eastern Economic Review,* 5 September 1997), Jardine Matheson was starting to look vulnerable to an aggressive local takeover, in particular, from a rival magnate by the name of Li Ka-Shing, who was starting to build up a stake in the firm (*Far Eastern Economic Review,* 9 October 1997).

At this point, Dairy Farm rather hurriedly sold off not just Kwik-Save but all its other European assets including a joint research development with Nestle and, significantly, its share in a Spanish supermarket group Simago, which seems to confirm that the ultimate cause is not to be found in the local context. The result of the Somerfield merger as far as Dairy Farm was concerned was that it could report a sale on 25 March 1998 of its shares for £290 million, which given a carrying value of £209 million, made it a book profit of £80 million. As Dairy Farm noted in its Web site (<www.irasia.com>), this disposal completed its exit from Europe so that it could concentrate on Asian Pacific growth. Indeed, the main impact appears to have been the use of £209.7 million to redeem its convertible preference shares. In effect, the company could pay off debt rather than pay off interest on debt. Seen from the point of view of this story, it must be concluded that Kwik-Save was going to be sold off quite irrespective of its local performance or its relationship to other supermarket competition within the British market. At this particular point in time, Jardine Matheson had other fish to wok. Curiously, as the historians show for the nineteenth century, Jardine Matheson had an unnerving record of pretty dismal commercial ventures and frequent crises from which they somehow managed to extricate themselves at the right time, often with some profit. This is exactly what happened with Kwik-Save. They mismanaged the firm and took it from profit to loss and then, at the last moment, engineered a deal such that they could withdraw with a healthy sale, which from their point of view might well have been considered a success story. It seems that things may not have changed much in two hundred years.

As it happens, by the time this book was finished the shoppers proved to have had a role in the outcome of this story. At the time I began this research, the prediction following the merger was particularly upbeat. A year later the situation looked dire. A huge fall in profits and sales together with conflict within management pointed to the failure of the merger. David Simons had to call a halt to the conversion; 350 Kwik-Save stores would not now be turned into Somerfield (see *Retail Week,* 24 October 1999). When Kwik-Save sales were revealed to have fallen by 16 percent, and Somerfield became the worst performing stock in the FTSE 250, falling from 470 pence to 94 pence, the manager responsible for overseeing the merger resigned, and Somerfield decided to put 350 of its stores back on the market, according to a report in *The Guardian* from 12 November 1999. Most of the commentators on this reversal of fortune noted that the heart of the problem was unwillingness on the part of shoppers to move from their reliance upon Kwik-Save as a important discount store that acted as a foundation for impoverished shoppers to a Somerfield fascia that had a reputation as a neighborhood, but not particularly as a discount, supermarket. It is in the poorer areas in particular that the results were problematic (*Retail Week,* 24 September 1999). A result that from the perspective of the ethnography does not look very surprising.

A conclusion that may be drawn is that the story of a merger that arose out of the logic of the retailers, their relationship to shoppers, and their varying ability to sell had been overtrumped by a top-down story that has more to do with the potential uses of retail capital, the power of finance, and in turn, the embroilment of such powers in questions of political representation—precisely that combination of factors that might properly be called political economy. Now this might simply be the outcome of a particular story chosen as was readily admitted for quite fortuitous reasons. As it happens, however, my conclusion is remarkable similar to that which has emerged from a decade of work on British food retailing more generally by a group of scholars who together amount to the "New Retail Geography" operating in Britain, in particular, the work of Guy, Hallsworth, Marsden, and Wrigley (see especially Wrigley and Lowe 1996; Wrigley 1998c). They, too, begin with tales about particular supermarket chains and their relationship to various retail strategies but tend to conclude that the key players have more to do with the nature of retail capital and political representation.

BRITISH SUPERMARKETS AND THE NEW RETAIL GEOGRAPHY

If a group of geographers were developing some interesting and important conclusions based on the study of the recent history of the British grocery retail they had picked a topic with some pretty impressive dynamics. There has been a general concentration in retail over the last three decades with a mere thirty-nine retailers accounting for over half of all retail sales in Britain. In the grocery trade, this was particularly dramatic. In one estimate, "between 1982 and 1990, the market share of the top five grocery retailers increased from under 25 per cent to 61 per cent of national sales" (Wrigley 1993, 41; precise figures depend on the definition of the market used).Today the leading firms are vast. Tesco alone can command profits of £832 million and has a staff of 164,000 in the United Kingdom with average shop size of 24,500 square feet (up to 26,600 square feet if the new inner-city "Express" stores are left out; N. Wrigley 1999, personal communication). It is also expanding rapidly in Eastern Europe and recently purchased a chain of supermarkets in Thailand. Indeed, just as Jardine Matheson is pulling out of Europe there are rumors that Tesco is interested in investing in China.

This story of expansion and concentration can be told along several different planes. Some of the literature at least starts with the technological dimension. The rise of new scanning technologies, using electronic point of sale (EPOS) through to electronic data interchange (EDI) and the various forms of just in time (JIT) supplies. Between them these have transformed the way supermarkets can respond to the patterns of purchases.

Today many on-site supermarket storerooms have become redundant, since distribution has become far more efficient. Hallsworth (1992), for example, makes these technological innovations his starting point for an investigation of the political economy of the industry (compare Humphery 1998 for the earlier impact of self-service). Today we see these supermarkets turning to the future potential of data-mining—the vast information on individual customers that has arisen from the new loyalty cards that Tesco first introduced and have now been copied by all its rivals. Feverish speculation also concerns the use of the Internet, where Tesco again has a lead. My local Tesco at the time of writing supplies a CD-ROM and Internet connection that allows me to choose through the Internet from 20,000 items that can be delivered the next day for a small fee.

Most commentators have emphasized the shift in power from manufacturers to retailers that results from the sheer scale of the contemporary retailer and their ability in the 1980s to harness their own power as a brand. More of the costs and risks could be passed backward along the chain to suppliers who remain independent but dominated. Ogbonna and Wilkenson (1998) note the complexity of this relationship, which varies according to the type of retail under consideration. Retailers can claim discounts and impose new conditions on suppliers, because, as a typical comment in the food industry suggests, "if Tesco and Sainsbury's won't sell it, you might as well not make it." As Hughes (1996) notes more generally and Doel (1996, 54–62) with respect to the particular evidence of the rise of own-brand labels, it is the retailers who seem to be making the running today. Sainsbury's were pioneers in expanding their own-label range while Marks and Spencers can be credited with emerging as the first store to develop an exclusively own-label strategy through their chilled food selection. Although they remain one of the few that trades on 100 percent own-label, this strategy now dominates all of the biggest supermarket chains. Doel (1996, 50) notes that Sainsbury's increased its own-label portfolio from 1,500 lines in 1969 to over 8,000 in the early 1990s. It is not just that they have overcome brands with high-quality goods at a range of prices, but also that they have in effect become superbrands in their own right. This means that they can now move into new sectors, as they have recently shown with a highly successful development of their own financial services. In this they have the tremendous advantage that surveys by organizations such as the Henley Centre for Forecasting show them to be more trusted by the public than either political institutions (which may not be surprising) or professional institutions.

Notwithstanding all these development in technology and the power relations within the food industry, most of the geographers involved in this study have found their attention caught by exogamous rather than endogamous factors. The core to understanding these changes lies in the wider political economy, with an initial emphasis on the economic, and a final emphasis on the political. Wrigley has tried to put the startling growth in grocery retailing within a comparative context by contrasting it with developments in the United States, which was much slower in developing this degree of concentration (1993, 1996, 1998a). By 1991, problems arose in the United Kingdom as the expansion became itself the subject of a new economic imperative. In effect, the supermarkets had tied themselves to what Wrigley calls a "treadmill of growth" in which by the end nearly two-thirds of their annual increases in sales were being generated by the new stores that had opened within the previous twelve months, demonstrating a clear dependency upon this expansive strategy. Three chains in particular, Tesco, Sainsbury's, and Safeway, had shot ahead of the rest and as Wrigley (1994) notes, it was the CEO of the fourth—ASDA—that sounded an alarm, which led to a rapid reduction in market confidence in 1991. The main problems were that this expansion was based on the rise of out-of-town superstores, increasing competition that had pushed up the prices of suitable sites and resulted in overvalued assets accompanied by the threat of discounters and the public concern at this evident dominance based on the conversion of greenbelt sites with its concomitant threat to the viability of high streets.

One effect of this shift noted by Wrigley (1996) is that the huge investment in property that at first seemed to be a positive grounding of retail capital in assets became reassessed as negative sunk costs, a more general problem arising from the fact that it can be easier to invest and expand in many areas than to accomplish "market-exit" (117). The accounting practices of the firms had helped overvalue the investment in property while any depreciation were likely to hit pretax profits and share dividends. It was ASDA, faced with the debt created by the overpriced Gateway stores it had bought as part of Gateway's LBO, that started the process of depreciating property values. The trend leads to important questions about the contradictions between the interests of various stakeholders in commerce and the general neglect of the problem of internal contradiction in studies of commerce (see Miller 1997a for the equivalent issue in Trinidad). It also leads to some fairly esoteric questions about modeling retail capital (see Ducatel and Blomley 1990, Fine and Leopold 1993, 274–95). As a result, the academics working on retail, just as the heads of retail corporations themselves have to consider a basic tension between financial markets that are only really interested in capital itself and how productively it is performing as compared with where else it might be invested, as against the specific considerations of the retail industry. It is when assets such as property valuations seem to shift in an unrelated sequence to the ordinary questions of profit from retail sales that the larger transcendent nature of business as merely an aspect of capitalism comes to the fore. Rather as with my earlier case of Kwik-Save, we can think in terms of the dynamics of retail competition, only to find that the primary cause of events has to do with the relationship between property and capital. But even this does not really reach the levels of decontexualization that are required for us to comprehend the core links between a supermarket merger and the general nature of contemporary political economy. What the new retail geographers have revealed is an additional but critical factor: the relationship to the state and to political ideology.

Today the top three U.K. grocery chains look relatively secure, though Sainsbury's is weakening and the takeover of ASDA by Wal-Mart is a long-term threat. But their value labels and price wars have held the discounters at bay, their property depreciation is strung out over forty years, internationalization has given them a wider base, and new strategies such as loyalty cards have literally paid dividends. What has changed, however, is the political climate, with central government taking a new tough stance against out-of-town developments. Much of the background to this shift lies in what at first seem arcane studies of regulation policy, but these become vital to seeing the wider picture. Whether one turns to Hallsworth, Guy, Marsden, or Wrigley the final message is that power rests on the relationship between retail and the state. The primary growth of grocery retailing as one of the most dynamic sectors of British capitalism took place under the Thatcher regime and, as Wrigley argues, it was the much more positive stance taken by the British state that accounts for much of the contrast with developments in the United States, where the state took a much more guarded view of the implications of such expansion (Wrigley 1999).

Part of the previous tendency for the British government to look favorably on the food retail sector was a result of effective political lobbying by that sector. Anecdotes abound about how Lord Sainsbury (the head of what at that time was the largest supermarket chain) was the one person who could always command the immediate attention of Margaret Thatcher when she was prime minister. But the new retail geographers have also concentrated on the revealing question of what it was that the state gained as a result of this relationship. One of the contributory factors appears to have been the desire to delegate responsibility downward for the whole arena of health regulation in foodstuffs, a topic that has become more and more important in terms of the public perception of risk and the potential for periodic crises of confidence. Over the last twenty years the state has attempted to put the onus upon the food retailers for ensuring high quality and security from food-related illnesses. In practice, the retail sector has not always agreed to take on this responsibility; in relation to the long-term shifts over the BSE beef crisis there have been periods at which the retail sector has distanced itself from state policy as well as times when it has been its agent. Nevertheless, it is retailers who have become the key to the effective regulation of food quality (Flynn, Harrison, and Marsden 1998).

But more generally, the food retail sector has been prepared to take on a mediating role in the relationship between the state and the consumer. Marsden and Wrigley (1996) describe the relationship as follows: "Of particular importance in the retailers' attempts to sustain their competitive space and justify their broad custodial role within the food system is the way they been allowed to construct and formally represent 'the consumer interest.' Empowerment of British retail capital in the 1980s went hand in hand with the unleashing of new and revised rights to consume . . . However it was largely left to the major retailers to deliver those rights to consume. In doing so, they played a powerful role in structuring consumption around their own particular notions of the 'consumer interest,' and began increasingly to represent that 'consumer interest' in their relations with government" (43). We need to recall the general flavor of politics under Thatcher where the robust attack on existing and theoretical socialism was primarily based on the supposed inability of the latter to "deliver the goods." In direct contrast, Thatcher never failed to describe herself as the grocer's daughter who rewarded the thrift of her population—in returning to what was presented as common sense values after its flirtation with left-wing ideologies—by demonstrating that the market would deliver wealth and choice. In the language of the time, the relationship of the population to the state was being turned into that of the consumer, in which state services as much as market services were judged by the "authority of the consumer" (Keat 1994), which became more or less the only authority left in political agendas.

Given this context, the site where the population most associates itself with the everyday role of the consumer was in ordinary grocery provisioning, and it was critical that this was seen as the place where the government "delivered the goods" in an exemplary fashion. It is hard to describe in concrete terms the links between what was itself a highly charged, highly ideological gambit, but it is very likely that the perceived high quality, high choice, and good delivery of the major supermarkets was critical to the popularity of the political program itself. It is in this sense, above all, that the supermarkets could be said to have delivered the citizen as consumer to the state and the promises of the state to the consumer. If this is the primary conclusion of the work of retail geographers, it tallies extremely well with the more general theory of the political economy that may be termed "virtualism" (Miller 1998b), which allows the case study to merge with a more general reconsideration of political economy.

VIRTUALISM

Neologisms, especially ones as awkward as the term "virtualism," should not be welcomed too easily into academia. In this case, the term is itself a strategy through which to raise what seems a crucial question at the start of a new century: whether what is being analyzed here is best served by being addressed as a typical emanation of capitalism, or whether the term "capitalism" itself is now so stretched through decades of use and misuse that we need a new term in order to emphasize the distinct new elements of contemporary political economy as against the undoubted continuities with previous forms of capitalism. In an edited volume, Carrier and Miller (1998) construct an argument in favor of an emphasis upon the distinctive.

Since the time of Marx, capitalism as commercial practices based around commodities has become much more integrated within social and political orders. This became most evident in the kind of social democratic capitalism of 1960s Scandinavia, which Marx never envisaged, and in more attenuated forms of what I described as "organic capitalism" in my earlier study of Trinidad (Miller 1997a). Until the 1960s, then, the production of commodities had become increasingly relocated within new political and social structures such as social democratic governments that welded the market to social ends. Sweden in the 1960s used a successful economy with a strong market element to pay for a tightly regulated state welfare system. Capitalism also created the conditions for a formidable increase in the importance of consumption that Marx had failed to foresee, and it was through consumption that most people sought to use goods to combat the alienation they felt from the vast institutions represented by the market and the state that dominated production and distribution (Miller 1987).

For Marx, capitalism became oppressive as it fostered the increasingly autonomous interest of capital and the capitalist. In the developed world of the 1970s, however, an increasingly embedded capitalism had been tamed by social and welfare programs, at least in comparison to the previous century. In the last twenty years, however, we may have seen much of this organic capitalism overtrumped by a new phase of increased abstraction and the autonomy of institutions that thereby come to oppress us, as, for example, through a return to increasing inequality in countries such as the United States. In Miller (1998c) I argued for such a turn to virtualism on the basis of three examples that implicated a wider historical trend. The first was the increasing impact of economists over politics, something already recognized by the Frankfurt School theorists in the 1930s but found in its more triumphalist phase (see Fine 1998) much more recently. This was illustrated through the development of structural adjustment, through which countries such as Trinidad became subject to highly abstract economic models foisted upon them by bodies such as the IMF and the World Bank, often with little concern for local conditions. Economic bodies have reached a position of power where they no longer need to be much interested in tailoring their models to the actual economies being studied. They have assumed the political authority to treat any discrepancies from their models as a series of "distortions," which states are instructed to eliminate. So welfare may be regarded as a distortion of the structural adjustment model that needs to be eliminated so that the model will perform properly. This change from models that simulate the real world to models that have the power to force the real world to change in the direction of the simulation is the defining principle of virtualism and has become characteristic of the impact of economics as a discipline.

A second example was taken from the very institutions of higher education within which I teach. At least in Britain we are faced with a vast increase in auditing and management, justified in the name of the student as consumer, most of which in practice takes from instructors time and flexibility to deal with matters of education and students and turns them into endless defenders of our practices against managerial models of work. Auditing redirects our time to abstract categories of practice and takes us away from the student body whether viewed as students or consumers of educational services.

My third example was intended to demonstrate that academics as well practice this virtualizing tendency. We can see in the rise of writings of social scientists about postmodernism much the same thing as economists and auditors. The term "postmodernism" is constantly legitimated by the claim that we exist in a new period, which is, above all, a new consumer culture. But the vast flood of books on postmodernism make claims about this new consumer culture, not through any study of consumers or shoppers, but rather by endless references to key gurus such as Baudrillard and Bauman and Benjamin.

What these three examples have in common is that they produce a fetishism of the consumer, whose labor is no longer recognized but displaced by models that come to stand in their place. So the audit is legitimated because it is supposed to make the institution serve its consumers, but actually we spend time satisfying managers that stand in the place of students. Postmodernism claims to be about consumer culture, but ignores actual consumers to become merely esoteric obfuscation, which Bourdieu (1984) showed is vital in elite academic claims to cleverness, here expressed in the name of the consumer. Economists claim their models are all designed to produce goods at the lowest costs in a situation of pure competition for the ultimate benefit of consumers but in practice replace consumers with models that bear no relation to flesh and blood shoppers.

To these three examples the case study of supermarket mergers adds a further two: the rise of financial abstractions and the rise of management consultancy. In both cases we see the two trends of virtualism, that is, the fetishism of the consumer and the ability of models to supplant that which they purport to simulate. Hallsworth and Taylor (1996) provides an instructive story illustrative of the increasing power of finance. They tell the tale of ASDA, which like many of the grocery retail stores in Britain, started its retail life as a fairly sensible chain store with a regional base. Before that, as Association Dairies (thus ASDA) it was a manufacturer that moved into retail to control its downstream. Initially, its retailing operation funded its own expansion largely from its own profits. The problem arose as it moved south and came within the vision of the City of London, where such forms of expansion are seen as an anathema. By contrast, the City reflects a financier's vision in which the driving force of good industry and efficient capital reproduction is debt, based either on stock or increasingly private forms of debt. Here capital is judged more abstractly in terms of comparative investment performance, as against the particular "cultures" of commerce as, for example, the local expertise in retail ventures that would be represented by ASDA. The City thereby represents (as might be expected) the transcendent logic of capitalism. This has various consequences. Hutton (1996), for example, has argued that the stress on dividends leads to much shorter-term considerations than would otherwise be healthy for the development of the firms themselves.

Such a philosophy is characteristic of conventional capitalism. Although Leyshon and Thrift (1997) show trading in securities and risk is nothing new, while capitalism is still diverse and grounded in various important ways, what we see here are new extremes that result from the power of abstract capital. ASDA soon became sucked into a particular variety of city-led debt restructuring program, which brought it within the story of the companies that were told earlier in this chapter. To recall—in 1989, ASDA bought up sixty-one superstores from Gateway (an earlier avatar of Somerfield) at a cost of £.700 million. This deal formed a kind of side serving to the main meal, an LBO by Gateway through a company formed for the purpose called Isosceles. The LBO phenomenon is itself quite extraordinary. The financier's logic is that a company should take on the huge burden of debt incurred when it buys its own stock and thus, in effect, goes private. This debt is seen as helpful in imposing the kind of discipline upon a company that will force it to take the ruthless decisions that will lead, in turn, to the most efficient use of the capital that in City terms is all that the company ultimately represents. With the LBO the "City" logic of discipline become vastly more extreme.

It is possible to understand the LBO phenomenon in terms of the interests of the key players as in the exceptionally good journalism that produced a blow by blow account of the largest LBO ever at RJR Nabisco (Burrough and Helyar 1990). This also suggests that the fees of the mediating financial institutions are quite sufficient in themselves to account for the fashion of LBOs. Another reason may be a defense of an ailing company against a potential takeover. These interests may, in turn, explain why companies become involved in debt that historically seems to do them little good. In the event both ASDA and Gateway came close to collapse following this LBO, and the end result was that the banks had to write off most of the debt. There is also the City perspective. Brokers represented the situation to me as one in which the City came to the rescue of two ailing firms, which might have been left to go under, and it was the City that lost its funds, while the firms themselves arose again as success stories. Of course the City is not a uniform beast (see Leighton and Thrift 1997), and those who placed their bets at the time of the LBO lost out while those who came in at the time Somerfield came back to the market have gained. Nevertheless, it is hard to escape the conclusion that, quite contrary to the arguments of the City, it is when firms are allowed to operate according to their own knowledge of retailing, relatively free of the discipline of debt, that they best generate actual profitability. The rebirth of ASDA and Somerfield as relative success stories in the last few years seems to come at the moment they escape the dictates of the city financiers and concentrate again on building up their retailing skills.

So apart from personal interest, the LBO exemplifies a tension, if not a contradiction, between the structures of retail and those of finance. Finance attempts to decontexualize retail into just another form for the reproduction of capital or the payment of dividends. An LBO is a point at which a company gets sucked into the logic of finance, often to its detriment. This was not the only example: Safeway, and the Southland Corporation—which ran 7-Eleven stores—both went through LBOs in the United States (Sparks forthcoming). These contradictions work against the interests of shoppers in the same way that at the heart of high finance we find the huge sums invested by pension funds operating in ways that are invidious to the interests of actual pensioners (Marsden and Clarke 1994; see more generally Davis 1990 on Los Angeles). So as in the other cases of virtualism we find a growth in abstraction that becomes a source of oppression. A parochial concern of a discount store to serve the most impoverished shoppers turns out to depend on the need for capital to protect assets in Hong Kong.

The second example of virtualism implicated in this case study comes from the astonishingly rapid rise of management consultancy. Just before it was taken over by Somerfield, Kwik-Save had secured the services of Andersen Consulting. This company had started as a mere spin-off from accountancy operations in 1989. By 1995, it had an annual income of $4.2 billion, employed 44,000 people, and had 152 offices in forty-seven countries. The scale and speed of this growth could almost be matched by other consultancy agencies such as McKinsey and Figgie. Individual companies such as AT&T can spend half a billion dollars alone on such consultants. O'Shea and Madigan (1997; see also surveys by *The Economist* in March 1997), who describe this transformation have used instructive sources, such as the accounts of court cases where management consultants have been sued, to shed considerable doubt as to what if anything companies gain from this vast expenditure on what these authors call "dangerous company." In particular, commentators are starting to realize just how formulaic are the "cures" that such companies tend to hawk from firm to firm, rather in the manner of nineteenth-century patented medicines that will relieve all troublesome symptoms with sufficient doses of the right tonic.

These generalizations fit the particular case in question. Even the financial press was skeptical of Andersen Consulting's value to Kwik-Save. *The Financial Times* remarked (9 November 1997) on the particular program that was being recommended for Kwik-Save:

> The main recommendations of the consultants seem to have been to move it further in the direction that many had seen as the cause of its problem. They wanted a higher level range of own brand goods as opposed to the no frills range already in use. They wanted more investment in cleaner brighter stores

with more electronic facilities. They also suggested selling off some loss making stores.

Given that the profits of the company in 1997 were only £73.7 million and the company was continuing to underperform in its sector by 70 percent, it is perhaps not surprising that the company decided to pull out of its program with Andersen Consulting. As a result it paid over some £9 million instead of the £18 million originally expected to go to Andersen Consulting for its services. The relationship had lasted around two years. Actually £9 million may well be an understatement, since a feature of Andersen Consulting is that they bring in a wide range of technical consultants who then obtain additional fees. As one broker commented to me, "it is impossible to know exactly how much they ended up extracting from the company." One is tempted to suggest that so far from curing the company of its ills, the fees involved may have been the final straw that broke this camel's back. This is more likely when one considers the potential costs that would have been involved in following the consultants' advice, as suggested in the new Kwik-Save plans to close 107 stores, revamp the rest of its 872 outlets, introduce a new own-label product range, and replace 75 percent of its business systems—all within the next three years. Indeed, shares in the Kwik-Save Group fell 25 pence to 341 1/2 pence, their lowest level in eight years, after the heavy costs of such a potential restructuring became clear. So the management consultants did not do a great deal for the firm's market value.

Management consultancy often involves companies giving themselves over to formulaic and costly logics, which again deny their own expertise in favor of outsiders. A broker described the advice finally proffered by Andersen Consulting as "bloody obvious" of a type they could have obtained for free. It was also suggested that what was going on here was that Dairy Farm, for all its claimed expertise in controlling retail chains, having failed to make even a half-reasonable job of Kwik-Save, were in effect turning over management to outsiders. Several key figures in British retailing such as Archie Norman (the CEO at ASDA) had previously worked for management consultants. One of the most important causes for the astonishing rise of management consultants is that they are paid huge sums essentially to take responsibility for the failure of the management of the company they are supposed to be advising. The particular irony is that while financiers and consultants see themselves as hard line business professionals as opposed to "soft" social scientists, much of what they do in the form of LBOs or consulting formulae seem mostly generated from fads and fashions in the industry.

If management consultancy is in effect a fashion industry, then the flavor of the month as far as grocery retail is concerned is "category management." This phrase has become a mantra that almost all management consultants apply to whichever supermarket group they are made responsible for and that is supposed to almost guarantee an increase in profits to whichever line of groceries it is applied to. It is not hard to find the details of this fashion, since the Institute of Grocery Distributors provides its own handy guide to the practice (McGrath 1997). It involves the reordering of goods within supermarkets to match a new set of categories that are supposed to more clearly reflect the consumer. In practice, as Cook, Crang, and Thorpe (forthcoming) have recently argued, there are grave doubts as to whether any real benefits accrue, in large measure because, as with so many of these fashions, they are applied across the board with little concern for the local knowledge that many of the grocery firms' own employees have garnered from years of service. What is particularly apropos here, however, is that category management is merely one part of a larger argument that management consultancy uses to justify the claims to its importance for grocery retail. It forms part of a larger master plan that is called "efficient consumer response." This in turn comes from a whole jargon of key terms such as "sleepers" and "supply chain management." Throughout this exercise, then, the legitimization of management consultants has to be that somehow they represent the consumer, or the way the companies can come closer to the consumer as shopper, even though it is generally evident that the opposite would be the case. The supermarkets are probably much closer to the shopper through their everyday business than the consultants who promise to deliver the shopper to them.

So the two cases of high finance and management consultancy join the three previous examples of economics, auditing, and postmodernism as examples of the wider trend toward virtualism. They all contain the two major characteristics of virtualism. On the one hand, they create a fetishism of the consumer. Management consultants take away from grocery retailers their own genuine knowledge of the consumer and replace this with their own models, just as City financiers make retailers stand for the interests of consumers while actually forcing them away from their specific commercial interests to compete with new Internet companies or sports complexes in the simple equation of returns on capital. Also, in both cases management consultants and financiers are not just parasitic models of the work of retailers; they have the power to change the practice of firms to make them conform more closely to these models, which is what gives them their "virtual" quality.

This is particularly clear when we include the political context for these shifts over the last fifteen years. What the supermarkets were trading with the government was the replacement of actual consumers by virtual consumers. In effect, the supermarkets came to stand for and represent the British consumer for the government itself. The symbol of the success of Thatcher was not so much the happy healthy shopper as the fat, prosperous, and rapidly burgeoning supermarket, its shelves groaning with abundance, choice, and quality. The connection has by no means disappeared under the Labour government that followed. The same supermarket that swallowed Kwik-Save became the center of attention of political as against commercial journalists in October 1998 when delegates to the annual conference of the ruling Labour Party, found that the very name tags they had to wear at the conference were sponsored by Somerfield.

I am not trying to argue that supermarkets in themselves are bad for shoppers. In several respects, chapter 3 was used to counter the glib and simplistic critique made against such supermarkets as compared with corner shops. Wrigley notes that the rise of retailer brands has on the whole led to an improvement in the quality of goods and the rise of quality chilled-food cuisine compared, for example, with the U.S. market. There have also been other improvements including the low risk of shops being out of stock (1998b, 120–21), which, as noted at the start of this chapter, is much appreciated by the shoppers. The problem exposed in this chapter is not that of the supermarkets but the forces that detract from their work as retailers. This problem, then, forms part of the larger conclusion to this chapter, which is that these historical process operate through a particular slight of hand, or fetishism, in which discourses about shoppers becomes central to the development of the modern political economy.

I feel the term virtualism is justified in that quite often the push toward greater abstraction and pure finance turns out to be detrimental to actually working capitalism either in the form of efficient business or profit making. What we see is not really a ratcheting up of the logic of capitalism toward greater profits but more a contradiction within capitalism in which new forms of modeling and abstraction establish their own agenda to which preexisting capitalism is forced to conform even when against its interest to do so. Just because there are many more mergers is not evidence that mergers are good for the companies that merge. The LBO phenomenon exposes contradictions within capitalism rather than seamless instrumentality.

At this level virtualism as a theory returns us to the same issues of discourse that were applied to the ethnographic observations of the previous three chapters. In the next chapter, the emphasis will be on a comparison of the conclusions of chapters 2–5 based on terms set by Hegel in *The Phi-*

losophy of Right. The relevant conclusion of this chapter is that placed within the context of this book as a whole we find that the shoppers that I studied are crucial. Everywhere virtualism is constructed in the name of people in the same guise of shoppers that I also saw them. But just as Marx showed how the interests of labor could be ignored when value became a kind of virtual labor, so here it is not shoppers with the contradictions and projects described in the previous three chapters that are present, but rather virtual shoppers, a ghostly presence in whose name free markets, consultants, auditors, and theorists of postmodernism all construct increasingly abstract models and institutions to which we are then expected or forced to conform. Foucault's approach to discourse, which would have obfuscated the observations of the previous three chapters, is quite appropriate to the results of this chapter. At the level of the dialectics of political economy it may no longer be a seamless logic of capitalism, but rather it is discourse itself that through virtualism constructs the world of practice.

6

GET "REAL"

A RETURN TO HEGEL

The journal *The Bookseller* for 6 November 1998 published the results of the annual Diagram Group Competition for the Oddest Title of 1998. I was most gratified to find that my own book *A Theory of Shopping* made it to the top four, defeating such august titles as *Woodcarving with a Chainsaw* and *Psychoanalysis and the Bored Patient*, but ultimately losing out to *Developments in Dairy Cow Breeding and Management: And New Opportunities to Widen the Uses of Straw*. I would not expect *The Dialectics of Shopping* to do as well, since unlike *A Theory of Shopping* the title sounds as though it is supposed to be pretentious, while I take this competition to be about the unwittingly odd. However, it was instructive to note that several other books on the long list shared a single obvious attribute; these included *Come Shopping in Wymondham* and *Musculoskeletal Disorders in Supermarket Cashiers*. What is evident is that any title that takes shopping too seriously is regarded as, at the very least, odd and probably funny. I have argued elsewhere (Miller 1997c) that this may be accounted for in terms of developments in political ideology, which tries to protect one particular kind of political choice—the democratic vote—as profound and significant and denigrate other aggregate choices that might be just as important in their consequence, reducing them instead to the level of the merely trivial. There are also powerful gender asymmetries that influence this tendency to refuse to grant shopping much respect.

Not withstanding the pretentiousness of this volume's title, the previous chapters would not, I imagine, have caused too much offence, at least among academics used to the intellectual challenges of taking seriously that which otherwise is dismissed as trivial. Nevertheless, if one is to start this chapter in all honesty, then it must be granted that its claims are rather more ambitious. I want to argue that shopping (of all things!) could be a primary means for understanding the Hegelian concept of *Sittlichkeit*—an ethical society in which people are reconciled to the institutions of modernity. Much as I would like to retain the light tone I have started this chapter with, the claim will be made "in all seriousness." It is a contention of this book that the anthropologist may transfer an ability to take some particular practice of another society, such as canoe building or marital alliances, as the basis for understanding comparative cosmology and philosophy and apply the same procedure to the mundane practices of the anthropologist's own society, such as that of shopping.

This implies what might be called a double dialectical moment. On the one hand, this chapter returns us to the direct juxtaposition promised in the volume's title that is a consideration of shopping in relation to dialectical thought. But at the same time it returns to the universalism implied in the philosophical perspective. But this universalism has been reached only after having passed through four chapters of ethnographic and other substantive analysis: an immersion within the particularities of shopping and its contexts. So a return to a consideration of dialectical philosophy becomes at the same time itself a dialectical attempt to transcend the opposition between philosophical universality and ethnographic particularity. The specific perspectives of the previous chapters set out a challenge to any simple attempt to use shopping as material within philosophy, and yet the significance of those chapters is much enhanced if they can be recast as insightful and comparative generalities of relevance to philosophy.

As noted in chapter 1, my own initial attempt to rethink the nature of mass consumption arose through a vulgar version of Hegelian philosophy (Miller 1987). The concept of objectification developed there still seems to me the ideal way to transcend the dualism of the social as against the material world, although other attempts to undertake a similar task are being developed, such as actor network theory by Latour (1993), Callon (1998), and Law (1994). The concept of objectification was especially helpful when it came to the discussion of the particular relationship between commodities and persons since it provided for a much more profound understanding than, for example, found in theories of representation, of how each gained their meaningful nature in respect to the other. The process of objectification underlies the perspective of chapter 2. It was argued there that kinship cannot be understood simply as forms of social relations, since social relations are continually being constructed and reconstructed through the relationship between objects. The other side of the coin lies in the constant grounding of the material relations of commodities in the dynamics of ever-changing social relations. In other words, there are no subjects or objects per se, only a process of objectification through which relationships are developed.

So the present volume has in common with my earlier (Miller 1987) approach the desire to transcend both the relationship of subjects and objects and simultaneously that between universality and particularity. In addition, however, it presents a series of "levels" that take us from the intimate world of kinship up to the macroworld of political economy. At a vulgar level it shadows the shift in Hegel's thought from a primary concern with the philosophical logic behind dialectical thought in *The Phenomenology of Spirit* to a more contextual and political consideration of the implications of his ideas in *The Philosophy of Right,* although there is plenty of politics in his earliest work and logic in his latest. So in this study the aim is not merely to find a sequence that leads "logically" from the micro- to the macrolevel but also to create a perspective that keeps each in articulation with the other. For this reason, the current chapter will be primarily based on a consideration of *The Philosophy of Right.*

GET "REAL"

The application of this later work of Hegel to a topic such as shopping has been much assisted by the publication of two recent books, which help to clear the ground for this appropriation. The first is Wood's *Hegel's Ethical Thought* (1990), and the second is Hardimon's *Hegel's Social Philosophy* (1994). Wood provides the primary grounds for this inquiry. In his terms the problem becomes one of determining how far shopping creates the conditions for human freedom. This is not simplistic freedom, as in freedom from all constraints for the individual. That goal is derided as merely negative freedom. For Hegel the concept of such simple individual freedom is almost a contradiction in terms. Rather, modern freedom depends upon preserving the institutions and social relations within which freedom is both conceived of as a project and only within which it may to a greater or lesser degree be realized, for example, law, the family, and education (Wood 1990, chapter 2).

Within this larger ambition, more immediate help may be derived from Hardimon, who tries to tackle the precise implications for political and ethical dilemmas, building upon earlier Hegel scholarship such as that of Taylor (1975). The criteria for conducting an ethical judgement of institutions and practices is provided through the concept of the "real." Hardimon (1994, 54) gives both "reality" and "actuality" as translations of the German *Wirklichkeit*. I will place the word "real" in quotation marks to signify the Hegelian term. This subsequent distinction between real and "real" would correspond to the difference between what we confront in shopping as it happens to be in the world, and the ideal of "real" shopping that actually realized the rationality inherent in it in terms of the historical moment within which we encounter it, an idea that hopefully will become clearer through illustration. Fortuitously, I find that the colloquial demand to "get real" has a surprising amount of correspondence with the idea of "real" as I will use it here, and since it also indicates the vulgarized level at which I am appropriating Hegelian concepts, I feel that the phrase "get real" best summarized the intentions and aims of this chapter. "Get real" becomes, then, the basic criteria that will be used to judge the material and the conclusions of the preceding four chapters.

The implications of "get real" as I propose to use it may be illustrated in relation to a school. Hegel argues that humanity creates institutions and customs that express a general intention in the world which objectifies human reason. This, then, provides us with a criteria by which to analyze and judge institutions, here a school, but it might also be the type of marriage custom in one society or the nature of law in another. As an anthropologist, I have a more relativist sense as to the nature of human reason, but it should still follow that the particular form of an institution may be evidence for an interpretation of the reason behind its development specific to the society within which it has been created. For example, in a given society a consensus may arise that the amount of knowledge that is required of individuals can no longer be inculcated merely through the habits picked up within family life. As such, many different societies at different periods of history have developed specific institutions devoted to more formal learning, with professional teachers dedicated to that aim. In at least some of these instances, many of the people involved would be able to articulate the basic principles behind the creation of schools. This amounts to a normative consensus on why schools exist and the purposes they serve. In others times and places these reasons are implicit in the form of the pedagogic profession and infrastructure but rarely made explicit.

It is possible, however, that a school in a given society develops in unintended directions that clearly no longer accord with these founding principles whether explicit or implicit. Consider a case in which teaching consists largely of formulaic information learned by rote. In a society in which schooling is for the inculcation of specific esoteric knowledge, as in some religious schooling, this may be entirely appropriate. In our own society where individual critical and creative thinking is espoused as a goal, then this would be seen as a failing of the school system. Rather than educating people, schools may have become primarily instruments that separate off those who have access to this esoteric information and those who do not. Critics who have suggested that education in countries such as Britain and France sometimes become more important in reproducing class distinctions than in inculcating understanding, imply that there is at least a tendency for education to renege on what explicitly was supposed to be the furtherance of reason. Similarly in this as in many other institutions it is possible that a school might come to serve primarily the interests of its own officials to the detriment of its pupils. If either tendency developed to an extreme, it could be argued that the "reason" implicit in the institution, which is also its legitimacy and which ultimately was intended to serve the welfare of that society (defined in the terms of that society), has been undermined by historical changes that have led that institution to serve other aims. In such circumstance it is incumbent upon a philosopher such as Hegel to point out the discrepancy between the ideal of that institution as an objectification of the reason behind its inception and its present practice and consequences. In such cases schools that are obviously real could be said to no longer be "real" where the same word in quotation marks stands for the degree to which the institution continues to objectify reason as an instrument of human welfare.

In an ideal world the "real" would be represented by the real school, which lives up to its role in the manifestation of reason. We do not live in ideal worlds, however, and Hegel believed that it is an intrinsic property of all cultural forms and institutions developed by societies that they may develop an autonomous self-interest and aggrandizement such that they no longer can be said to be an expression of reason. Instead, they become forms that obfuscate rather than help clarify our understanding and goals. This tendency is especially developed within the institutions established under the auspices and values of modernity and is most famously expressed through Marx's critique of capitalism. Marx argued that capitalism began as humanity's capacity for freedom was enhanced as it

loosened the shackles of the ancien regime but was channeled into becoming instead merely the interests of a particular class. But following
Hegel, I prefer to see this as a tendency of all cultural forms rather than peculiar to capitalism. So culture consists of customs and institutions that
are always in a state of contradiction between their ability to express the
"real" and their tendency to lose this ability and become instead instruments of oppressive autonomy. The work of the philosopher (or anthropologist) is to keep culture under scrutiny and to judge it by the canons of
those ethical standards that are believed to express reason as an instrument of human welfare. I take the writings of academics such as Habermas
(e.g., 1972 and 1987) to be the exemplary instance of the contemporary
academic struggle to express in detail the implications and complexity of
both the terms used such as "reason" and their application today. My
premise is that anthropology aspires to be an ethical profession.

Applied to an institution such as shopping, this perspective leads us to
expect that shopping will always contain tendencies that lead in contrary
directions. We would also expect to be able to observe some practices that
attempt to ameliorate the negative consequences of such contradiction.
These may indicate how shopping both as institution and as normative
practice serves the interests of populations. The evidence of this volume is
that such shopping could be deemed positive not usually because it solves
problems such as the need for provisioning in simple acts of rationality
expressed as choice—though it may also do this. More important, shopping may on occasion express a form of reason that is based on attempting
to understand and then mediate the complex contradictions within
which we live, for example, in the relationship between the individual
shopper and the household, or the identification of that household with
gender and class. At the same time, both the institutions and practices of
shopping may be expected to exhibit tendencies to autonomy that lead
shops and shoppers away from this expression of reason to become instead the embodiment and instrument of oppression. For example, provisioning can become possessive and individualistic greed, relationships to
commodities can replace the use of the commodity within relationships
between people. The shop may be under constant pressure to sacrifice the
interests of consumers to that of shareholders.

The previous chapters tell us a good deal about "real" shopping as well
as providing a descriptive and interpretative account of what shopping
merely exists. First, they show the various ways shoppers constantly
engage with shopping as a medium for the potential reconciliation of
contradiction. Second, they give many instances of the failure of such
projects and the collusion between shoppers and retailers to use shops

and shopping to reproduce parochial interests and hide the oppressive consequences for others. Examples include the exploitation of the labor of women as shoppers, the constraints of poverty, and the willful disregard of the consequences of consumption for producers. In this chapter, the aim is both to locate the degree to which real shopping appears to also accord with "real" shopping and where possible also to suggest ways in which the discrepancy between these may be reduced.

The advantage of trying to consider the "real" nature of shopping through ethnography rather than philosophy is that one is not reduced to an idealism that seeks a universal form of reason or freedom and then judges all societies as stages on a track that is laid out through philosophical projection and then imposed upon the diversity of human institutions. I am not trying to do as Hegel almost did: read off what institutions such as the family and civil society ought to be as manifestations of the logic of philosophical investigation alone. Rather, ethnography can start from the grounds that the people who occupy these institutions themselves reveal (explicitly or implicitly) as reason imminent in them. In short, we are simply looking at how far shopping realizes the purposes that are implicit in the way people carry it out and talk about it. But this remains consistent with Hegel, who implies that institutions and practices do implicate their particular objectification of reason. There are grounds upon which people in all societies argue among themselves and with others the legitimacy of their institutions and practices. So my inquiry does not presume any claim to know what reason ultimately is or even to adjudicate between the various claims to embody reason. There is merely an expectation that underlying the social legitimization of the institutions within which any people live may be found implicit claims to reason, which can be made explicit, and the institution in question judged against those claims. In this volume, as an anthropologist dealing with my own society I am most comfortable with an explicitly ethical and, therefore, critical stance. Where I am presenting a study of another society, my primary concern would be the achievement of empathy and the defense of the relativism of reason. This is compatible with acknowledging the internal diversity that is implicit in the term "society."

Hegel's *The Philosophy of Right* also provides more specific criteria to employ in realizing the more general aim of "get real." Hardimon suggests that "The central aim of Hegel's social philosophy was to reconcile his contemporaries to the modern social world. Hegel sought to overcome their alienation from the central social institutions—the family, civil society and the state—and to come to 'be at home' within them" (1994, 1). Translating Haridmon's concerns to the topic of shopping would imply two related considerations: how far does shopping suggest that objective conditions have created a potential home for humanity to be reconciled with, and how far does it establish the subjective perception that would enable people to reconcile themselves to that objectivity and indeed be at home in them? These are questions that cannot be posed except in relation to the specific conditions of time and place. Furthermore, it must be translated for each of the various "levels" through which we live our lives. As various commentators on Hegel's work have suggested, in themselves these two questions may lead to a relatively conservative outlook and criteria for judging institutions in the world. It is, therefore, worthwhile proposing an additional question, which is whether these institutions represent a state in which we would want people to be at home in, in the first place? In *The Philosophy of Right* Hegel divided up his world into three such levels, namely, the family, civil society, and the state. Obviously this was itself a necessary break with the complexities of social existence, so that he had to allow for the degree to which, say, judicial concerns were both part of civil society and the state. In my case, I have taken four aspects of people's lives as illustrations of what might be taken as equivalent levels: kinship, community or neighborhood, civil society or the sense of citizenship, and political economy. These were determined heuristically through the logistics of writing up the ethnography, not through some prior logic or political philosophy. They were chosen because at this point in time they seem to occupy relatively autonomous worlds, although any individual is always constituted by their relationship to all of them—and many other domains such as the workplace besides. At each level the potential of shopping as a form of reconciliation differs, but I would still seek to defend the proposition that in every case shopping can and should be studied as praxis, that is, a material activity that is also an attempt to do philosophical work.

"REAL" KINSHIP

The ad hoc and contingent nature of shopping as praxis is particularly evident in chapter 2. Here shopping presents itself first as an everyday process usually understood as the means by which people provision their households in fulfillment of their sense of need. What becomes clear from the observation of this activity as described in chapter 2 is that social relations are also object relations, not just in the psychoanalytical sense (that we relate primarily to our internalized projections of others—see Greenberg and Mitchell 1983), but also in that it reveals the constant grounding of social relations in material relations. Any separation into discrete categories of the social and the material is false. In chapter 2 it was argued further that through kinship we relate to others both in their particularity as individual characters but also in their universality as the person/forms through which we encounter the normative structures of the discourses by which we comprehend kinship. That is to say, each of our kin is also kinship embodied. This provides the context within which shopping was found to be also an everyday attempt to resolve the contradictions that exist in our having to relate to individuals simultaneously in their particular and universal aspects.

This might be called the "peanut butter approach" to kinship, where peanut butter is the one food that discourses insist is good for one's little angel and therefore represents responsible parenting, and also that the damn infant in question will actually eat. Neither the discourse of parenting nor the particularity of the child alone constitute the basis for what we may call "real" shopping. The "real" is that reason that attempts to transcend and reconcile them in the selection of peanut butter. Our modernity lies in the growth of the contradictions addressed by activities such as shopping. We constantly generate further normative discourses that may or may not be reflexive: about the family, our partners, children, and other more complex kin formed from step- and half-relations or pseudokin such as pets. Magazines, soap operas, conversation, and gossip act to refine and develop the normative model of each category of kin. But this drive to universality is matched by an equal and opposing drive toward particularity. This is generated by the changing nature of love. Love today is practice or technology of care and intimacy in which extreme sensitivity to the particular individual object of our love is at a premium. Shopping, therefore, becomes an ad hoc and ever-changing process that is charged with the constant task of partial reconciliation of these two opposed tendencies. Kinship itself is a process rather than a category. So even though shopping may often fail to reconcile relations within what may be highly dysfunctional families, we can excavate a "real" shopping in the Hegelian sense of the reason implicated in choosing peanut butter within a practice of kinship relations. The evidence that the case here of shopping may be generalized to many other aspects of the family is made well by Gillis (1997), in whose work the dialectic of universalistic discourse (or myth) and family practice is particularly clear.

The kinship in question is predominantly that of the looser and more diverse version of the earlier "bourgeois family" that has become the normative family of the developed world. We can follow Hegel in relating the term "family" to households that are organized principally around consumption rather than production. Today, households are increasingly legitimated by sentiment, that is, love, rather than a sense of the contractual or of rights that are the preserve of civil society. We wish to act as a mother out of love, not out of obligation. The effect of this reliance upon love as a force for greater sensitivity is that we are unlikely to merely reproduce kinship as the status quo. We constantly modify our kinship discourse in the light of our experience just as our experience is, in turn, modified in the light of discourse. But however such relations change and however radical our stance to them may be, there would exist some normative structure by which we strive to be reconciled to each other both as individuals and as the embodiments of universals objectified in kinship categories. This is not a product of the bourgeois or any other particular family type. These contradictions would persist if kinship was primarily homosexual or organized in collectives. The reason for swinging the emphasis back to Hegel from Marx as argued in Miller (1987), was that Marxism created as communism the false expectation that we could create a world in which contradiction itself was eliminated—one in which we could always feel at home. Although it is right and proper to attempt to change the world for the better, at the level of family and indeed at the level of any institution such utopianism is unhelpful. Our problems reside in the constant need to create means by which we may be at home in worlds that are intrinsically contradictory. Thus, we could indeed change family relations, making them more equal and more contractual, but the fundamental contradictions between the universality and particularity of kinship would remain.

What is derided within a Hegelian approach is the idea of kinship or the family as merely some kind of constraint against which struggles an idealized free individual. On the contrary, Hegel correctly insists that freedom is only possible through social and political relations. It is kinship as an expression of universalized ideals that permits the flourishing of the particular and idiosyncratic, which is precisely why shopping is so important as the medium of articulation between these. Hegel argued that the family is the precondition for the development, rather than the suppression of (although it may indeed suppress in practice) the emotional and personal development of individuals, whose very individuality is always itself a social and ideological project (Strathern 1992). "In Hegel's view the family is the only institutional sphere within which one finds emotional acceptance of one's particularity" (Hardimon 1994, 101). This seems a more subtle understanding of family as practice than found in Bourdieu (1996), who follows a similar ideal of practice theory, but then proposes a narrower emphasis on the oppressive effects of discourse. There is no pristine subjectivity; we are all created in the tension between particularity and norms and discourses. In Hegel's view it is only through individuality that we are reconciled to the social world and only through sociality that we can become "real" individuals (Hardimon 1994, 144–73).

The implications are particular to time and place. They would be quite different for shopping in North London in the 1950s or in, say, Argentina today. Shopping as an activity may take its place in relation to many different dilemmas. This point is well made by Abelson (1989) in her study of the contradictions in shopping at the turn of the century. She focuses on the rise of the concept of "kleptomania" devised by doctors and psychiatrists and supported by luminaries such as Sir Arthur Conan Doyle (173–96). The term was used to resolve the contradiction of respectable and often wealthy women engaged in what seemed at the time to be a flood of shoplifting from the new department stores. It was impossible for either the courts, the families, or the stores to reconcile themselves to the evidence that such women (and such good customers) could be thieves. The concept of kleptomania allowed all involved to blame the unconscious and, therefore, the inability of these shoplifters to control themselves for medical reasons. This still provided for the sending to jail of poor people stealing objects they did require such as bread, which was made to seem rational and culpable by comparison (see also Pinch 1998 for a still earlier example of this tension). So while the term "kleptomania" allowed people to be reconciled to a contradiction between subjective conceptualization and objective conditions, it fails our third criteria in that they are thereby reconciled to a "home," that is, a state of affairs that increased the oppression of others.

Of course what is revealed is an imminent potential of shopping rather than a description. The shopping we observe is often not "real," but its observation helps us locate the reasons that lie imminent in its everyday practice and thus approach a delineation and understanding of the "real." The task is to determine when an activity may be considered "real" or when it is merely a failure of those ideals of reason. To illustrate this point, Hardimon (1994, 228–36) concentrates on Hegel's attitude to divorce. Hegel regards divorce as an entirely appropriate mechanism that should be granted when it is clear that the "real" basis of marriage does not exist. A marriage that is a marriage in name alone could not be seen as a "real" marriage. A similar concern with the discrepancy between the "real" and the lived may be at the heart of popular culture today. Among the most popular icons of the contemporary U.S. media are programs such as *The Simpsons, King of the Hill,* or *Roseanne.* I would argue this is because their principal effect is to reveal the "real" in family life. They all dwell on the dysfunctional aspects of family relations, but they also have a powerful ideological message which brings love and mutual sentimentality as the underlying premise against which such dysfunctional practices can be judged. They constantly dwell upon such issues as parental ambivalence about the socialization of their children, bearing up against the misfortunes of poverty or failure, and the sense of the alienation from large-scale institutionalized forces in the workplace. Even where they delight in negating mere sentiment and asserting self-interest (the basis of much of the humor in *The Simpsons* and *Roseanne*), it is within a context that shows they can afford such irony and explicit self-interest because they cannot break the deep foundations of sentiment that connects them as members of a family. Indeed, I (and I imagine many audiences) find these caricatures of the dysfunctional are a great deal "warmer" in conveying a sense of the family as a "real" institution that the cloying sentimentality of drama and sitcoms based on idealized, functional families.

The same argument may be made for the ethnography of shopping. When observed closely, shopping often reveals the points of fissure in kinship. For example, the discrepancies between an ideal of kids and partners who should be the appropriate recipients of what is purchased for them and what usually happens when they are present make it obvious that they are highly unappreciative of the labor of shopping (see DeVault 1991, in particular, for this tension). It is that sense of shoppers who don't know whether to laugh or cry at what their infants are getting up to in the middle of supermarket shopping that resonates with the poignant humor of such television programs.

What the ethnography of shopping adds to this argument is the revelation of the complex and contradictory technologies that are required to realize the "real." For example, long-term taken-for-granted provisioning, buying the same brands and basic household goods one has been buying for many years is carried out simultaneously with buying exciting new and different goods exploiting the fashion and gimmickry presented by commerce in order to show one has not become stuck in a rut. Other examples included the relationship between thrift and the treat (Miller 1998a), or the means of overcoming the dualism of person and thing when dealing with a stillbirth or the death of a loved pet. All of this reveals the manner by which the diversity of goods is used to dialectically continue kinship as a process of relating.

There is no reason to reduce this to some defense of capitalist production and the massive increase in material culture today. On the contrary, it demonstrates that the way people exploit their objective circumstance (in this case, the plethora of goods) is not dictated by the conditions that give rise to these goods in the first place. Its legitimization arises from the problems of consumption per se. The argument for the dialectic role of material culture is not specific to capitalism (Miller 1987). For example, MacKenzie (1991) analyzed the intricate details of net bag technologies in New Guinea. In her case it is the dialectical nature of gender relations, which are expressed through the way different decorative traditions in manufacturing of net bags are widened to the larger semiotics of net bags as meaningful artifacts. Women's relationship to the basic looping technology of net bag creation is complemented by men's embellishments of these same artifacts using other technologies. In that study, a relatively sparse material culture is exploited in the larger process of culture as dialectic that creates differences (of gender) precisely in order to transcend them. In North London, there may be rather more radical contradictions that have to be overcome. Consumption is pitted against a sense of alienation from vast institutionalized forces, from which shopping tries to create the conditions for relations of love and care. Buying something for a loved family relation consists of examining a mass of clothes in the stores in order to buy just the right one. To return to the first example used in chapter 2, it was a white blouse that provides the means to reconcile several conflicting family viewpoints upon what a teenage girl could or should wear. The context is a love, which may often include jealousy, ambivalence, and anger but still strives to express the "real" in kinship at whatever attenuated form it is lived. At this level, shopping seems to equate with Hegel's philosophical notion of *Sittlichkeit* as a constant process of transcendence that aims to reconcile us with our social world both by changing the objective world to one that creates a home and by facilitating the subjective perception that would allow us to feel at home in such a world.

"REAL" COMMUNITY

For me there is one great monument to perspicacity in considering the future of shopping, and this remains Emile Zola's work *The Ladies' Paradise* ([1883] 1992). If told with far greater eloquence and ability, the stories of the small shops provided in chapter 3 would vary little in implication from those Zola described for the Paris of the 1860s. One could not hope for a more carefully observed or empathetic account of the struggle between the largest and smallest shops. Yet the politics and implications of

Zola's work has been undermined by the selective manner in which his ideas have been appropriated. Both Bowlby (1985) and Williams (1982) make use of this novel, but their emphasis is on the rich detail given by Zola of retailing as male seduction of female desire, while there seems some embarrassment at the larger politics contained in the novel itself. Blomley (1996) is more nuanced but still keeps the focus on the modernity of retail as an idiom for gender, rather than the other way around.

The importance of this novel to me is that after employing the thorough research, for which he was renowned, Zola tackles the contradictions of modernity with eyes wide open. It is hard to imagine a more poignant treatment of the horrendous fate of the small shopkeepers. He forces the reader to observe in detail their fate as starvation, disability, and despair—the painful evidence of their demise through an inability to compete with their grandiose new neighbor, the department store. Certainly, Zola (who was, after all, one of the greatest writers in defense of the oppressed) spares no detail either in bringing us face to face with the death throes of the small shops or equally in his account of the inequalities of work within the department store and the wiles of the clever retailer in selling though a store that is constantly described as a monster ([1883] 1992, 66–76, 208–209).

Nevertheless, Zola is clearly impressed by the large store as a technique within the progressive potential of modernity; that it can embrace standards, provide quality and efficiency that make the previous form of selling look stupid and antiquated. As other writers have shown Zola does indeed objectify the struggle of value through the idiom of gender, but ultimately his heroine Denise succeeds. Instructively she achieves her aims not through the conservatism that would have led her to attempt to save her relatives' small shop, a possibility she constantly considers and rejects, but through her ability to seduce the seducer, to overcome the amorality of male capitalism through the feminine insistence upon welfare and humanity within the department store itself (313–18). Her historical task of transforming the labor relations of the department store is taken up in the midst of a funeral for a pallid corpse that comes to represent the tortured death of the small shop (321–45). It is this core to the book, Zola's positive outlook for a "tamed" modernity that all the recent commentators seem to wish to ignore. Yet this is typical of Zola's genius, which lay in his ability to draw readers into sharing the pain of the victims of modern business, whether coal mines *(Germinal)* or street markets (*The Fat and the Thin*). Yet he never responded by simplistic conservatism or unmediated revolution, but took on the responsibility for envisaging a taming of the forces unleashed in modernity to bend them back to the services of humanity. In the terms of this chapter, Zola sought to redirect modernity back toward the "real."

In emulation of Zola, then, a contemporary ethnography that sets itself up to consider the consequence of what it encounters has to acknowledge that any policy implication is advocated with "eyes wide open" as to the suffering and dislocation for which it may be responsible. Weber (1948) gives the grounds for emulating the role of the bureaucrat or politician (or, in this case, novelist or academic) who employs research in order to face up to responsibility. The implication is that one recognizes that just because local shops are extant, that some people can make ends meet within current conditions, does not mean one has to fight to aid and protect them, as long as one can envisage a pragmatic alternative that would be formulated to provide welfare benefits to both buyer and seller. Initially what is required is a realistic appraisal of the status quo and a consideration of the future in the light of some clear criteria. The status quo for small shops is pretty dire. Shops ranging from the specialist bakers, butchers, and fishmongers to the village corner shop continue to be in considerable decline.

Chapter 2 has been shown to exemplify the way people strive as shoppers to enact their sense of the "real." This would not work for chapter 3 partly because in chapter 2 we are dealing with shopping as a continual and ad hoc practice. In chapter 3, by contrast, we are dealing with the contradictions that emerge within the category of local shop. Although as an ideal this makes it rather easier to delineate a sense of "real," it makes it a great deal harder to see how this ideal could be realized. The role of the local shop within the larger project of a humanity seeking to be at home in the world is expressed by many of the informants. The imagined local shop would act as a practical hub in which busy people, who have difficulty maintaining their wished for links to the community and neighborhood aspire to, could in fact obtain their goods efficiently and within a nexus of gossip and communication. They would thereby also contribute directly to a local expression of civil society that would provide several roles in the formation and maintenance of community, for example, as a place where localized information is shared around a range of interests from babysitting to sports. The practical functions of the shop would reconcile the life of everyday needs of provisioning with the desire to go beyond the privatized world of the household and create some sense of community that has a resonance of neighborhood and locality. This ideal is a powerful one and one that would have appealed to a Hegelian notion of civil society in which "civility" was just as important as institutional responsibility. Such a neighborhood would provide the wider watch over children's safety, an alleviation of the isolation of the elderly on the estates, and become a meeting place within which people could retain the plurality of difference and the advantages of association.

So the "real" local shop is evident in the normative discourse that is expressed by many. It is clearly central to the relationship between households and the two shops that comes closest to its objectification, that is, Bob's and the hairdresser's. But what emerged from the ethnography are the factors that have become inimical to the survival of the shops that were present on the street itself. These include the use of alternative sites for the objectification of a discourse that feeds off this image of "real" shops but then acts to suppress them. The ethnography reveals a huge discrepancy between the ideals and practices of consumers, which has made their relationship to the local shops a highly attenuated one. These contradictions are expressed, for example, by the elderly who most need such a support but who find that the high price and low quality of most local shops combined with their own racism leads to a negative attitude to them. Indeed, the degree to which these ideals were not realized in practice was highlighted by the "good riddance" reaction of some to the idea that the local shops would disappear, although the chapter also described the diversity of experience and attitude and its relation to class.

In chapter 2, we can see shopping as an attempted reconciliation, which sometimes works and sometimes fails, but is too ad hoc and personal to suggest much in the way of positive intervention. In the case of chapter 3, we have a very different situation in which it is clear that the subjective perception that would allow people to be at home in the world of the local shop remains well developed. The consciousness that would seek to overcome alienation is there and is clearly articulated. Rather, what is missing is the objective conditions that could create a home to which people might become reconciled. Most of the local shops are simply unable to become what both an observer and the people on the street would call "real" local shops. In this case, the response of the academic can be quite different. It suggests at least the possibility of a critical engagement that seeks to intervene by envisaging how a "real" local shop might come into being and be maintained. The criteria of "real" is important here for policy making, since it implies something beyond an academic trying to sentimentalize or project their own ideal of sociality upon the shops. Rather, policy here is generated from the desire to reconcile objective conditions to the expressions of desire of the shoppers and the shopkeepers.

Since the problem is one of objective conditions, then the consequence seemed to be a practical intervention that might help change those conditions. In this case, then, my response was to produce a policy document, in the form of a plan for the future viability of the local shop. This attempts to fulfil as far as possible the aspirations that seemed imminent in the conceptualization of the local shop, including the village shop as an ideal node within a potential community. Only a glimpse of the plan can be included here. It suggests three major changes with a view to envisaging local shopping in around fifteen to twenty years time, focusing on the potential of the Internet. Local shops would become both the node for ordering goods for those who need help in using these technologies without being exploited and also become the depot centers for the distribution of the goods ordered. This would make the local shop once again a viable alternative to individual households engaged in long-haul car-based shopping. Second, it recommends the establishment of a local shop that becomes the focal point for the delivery of a wide range of government services, including legal, medical, and social security services, combining elements of the current post office and pharmacy, but adding to these the use of the Internet to link citizens and government information. This service could also become a local "cafe" or meeting point.

The third and largest component concerned food and clothing supplies. It envisages the local shops collaborating rather than competing with the major retail chains through a system of partial franchising. This would allow people access to cheap and high-quality goods, complemented by alternative goods that the major chains do not stock. For example, there would be franchised food delivered by supermarket chains complemented by homemade (for high-income) and cheaper (for low-income) alternatives. This includes temporary storage for daily or twice daily deliveries to the shops, which then take up the provision for home delivery. It also suggests a franchised clothing system based on combining catalog shopping with the use of a newly developed "body scanner," which digitizes information on body size and shape. Again, the franchised service is complemented by a nonfranchised complementary service, for example, greater exclusivity for high-income areas, marketlike services for low-income areas. An important role would be training to help people use informational technologies in viewing and ordering goods, but also to protect them from exploitation by unscrupulous commercial abuses of the Internet when used from private homes. One reason for preemptive government involvement is the prediction that such state intervention will be required anyway since the Internet creates vast new opportunities for the exploitation of vulnerable and low-income shoppers within the private sphere. A stripped-down version of the scheme could serve to replace the single village shop.

It is not expected that this will constitute all shopping in the future, but that such changes could help to bring back enough functions to make these shops viable and attempt to transcend certain key contradictions. Many of these suggestions respond directly to the privately expressed desires of elderly residents in the area and differ markedly from popular conceptions of what the elderly would or should desire. The scheme tries to reconcile the modernity the elderly seem to seek with explicit measures to contextualize each shop in its local and community context. Other aspects of the document address the particular needs of single person and single-parent households, low-income households, and also the improvements in the security and conditions of shop owners and workers. Other implications addressed include issues of transport, franchise arrangements, potential profitability, training and technical infrastructure, and why such changes might be simultaneously beneficial to government, commerce, and the citizen. The intended effect would be to put local shops back into contention as institutions that would allow shopping to again be a means of reconciling particularity and universality, often expressed as the advantages of the local and of the global.

The document was submitted to various government and nongovernmental bodies, a process that gave me some insight into the difficulty of creating an academic impact where the initiative is taken by the academic! Since the time it was written, two of the ideas contained there, the franchising of supermarket goods through village shops and the introduction of the body scanner in clothing retail, do seem to be imminent (though I am certain neither resulted from the influence of my document). Other issues such as the implication for transport congestion of Internet shopping are emerging in the media. I fully recognize that the changes suggested, if ever realized or influential, would also create dislocation, curtail certain freedoms, and prevent the realization of some alternative scenarios. This section opened with the example of Zola as illustration that a policy that advocates change must do so with eyes wide open as to any suffering that it is of itself responsible for, and that needs to be justified by the claim that the situation, if not addressed, would be even worse for shopkeepers while also failing to realize shoppers' aspirations.

"REAL" ETHICS

In the Hegelian terminology of *The Philosophy of Right,* the production of *Sittlichkeit* requires both the objective determination of a home in the world and the subjective intentionality that would make citizens desire to be at home in it. When the contents of chapter 3 were set against these criteria, the outcome was to suggest the need for changes in those objective conditions. The material described in chapter 4, by contrast, suggests something rather different, which is the need for a change in subjective intentionality. There is no simple overlap between the chapters of this volume and the levels that were designated by Hegel, but many of the issues raised by chapter 4 come close to the concerns that Hegel expressed in his imagination of the role of "civil society" and the need to develop an active relationship of citizenship. The use of the term "civil society" is certainly not intended to suggest some body that stands in opposition to the state or to the individual, which would be a misleading representation of at least Hegel's conceptualization (my reading is very different from, say, Hann [1996, 4]). Rather, Hegel saw the concept of civil society as a mediation between (which thereby included) both individuals and governance.

Hegel's primary concern was to view civil society (and within that, economic relations) as opportunities by which people could come to a more profound conception of the ultimate relationship between universalism and particularism. It is not merely a set of institutions but an opportunity for consciousness. This is what makes it entirely appropriate as a perspective on the material presented in chapter 4. The discourses of "Green" and the cosmopolitan are precisely forms by which people understand that what some would reduce to atomized economic relations are actually routes to an ethics of and identification with other peoples and the world at large. Shopping here become a point at which people come to consciousness of the nature of larger political and universalistic aspirations and responsibilities. In many ways they were found to be more an act of consciousness than of practice (i.e., they talked a great deal more about Green shopping than they did it). But through the development of these aspirations shoppers also enter into the contradictions these then pose for the reconciliation of universalistic and particularistic levels of understanding and practice—the contradictions that formed the basis for the analysis presented in chapter 4.

Hegel describes civil society in ways that must seem very odd to those who interpret this concept more narrowly. This section of *The Philosophy of Right* starts with "the system of needs" and then moves on to "the administration of justice." He begins by characterizing the vision that he wants to reject—that of needs as a purely particularistic or individual materialism. He notes, "Particularity by itself, given free rein in every direction to satisfy its needs, accidental caprices and subjective desires, destroys itself and its substantive concept in this process of gratification" (Hegel [1821] 1967, 123). This reiterates the larger point made throughout his text that the ideal of pure individual fulfillment is not only futile but based on a fantasy. A pure individual outside of society would have only the most basic and restricted needs or desires. Most of the desires we wish to cultivate and then fulfil are a product of our being socialized in the first place. A concern with Green issues is hardly an intrinsic condition. As all the proceeding chapters have indicated we cannot even think of needs except through the filter of a whole gamut of highly normative discourses. For Hegel, once we recognize the fallacy of individual needs we proceed to a higher level of understanding: "Consequently individuals can attain their ends only in so far as they themselves determine their knowing, willing and acting in a universal way and make themselves links in this chain of social connections" (124). To gain our ends we move beyond this vision of a system of individual needs and recognize that discourses such as those described in chapter 4 are primarily social judgements that are trying to express a sense of universal values and aspirations rather than some instinctual desire. We do not start with shopping and then hit up against the constraints of the discourse of Green. On the contrary, the ethnographic evidence suggests that basic discourses about materialism and moral responsibility are transcendent, that is, they are the prior systems of categories through which alone we are able to think about shopping in day-to-day life (see also Miller 1998a, 65–72).

When Hegel goes straight from the system of needs to the adjudication of justice, he is suggesting that to gain a more profound sense of the universality behind our particularistic use of discourse requires the concrete manifestation of that impulse toward the universal in the form of law. "The principle of rightness passes over in civil society into law. My individual right, whose embodiment has hitherto been immediate and abstract, now similarly becomes embodied in the existent will and knowledge of everyone, in the sense that it becomes recognized" (139). This process can thereby extend our subjective understanding of this relationship. Law not only adjudicates but also becomes the means by which we can comprehend our own desires. Gillian Rose was one of those philosophers who helps us excavate something of the original profundity of Hegel's argument. In one essay (1996) she characterizes law as that almost comic process in which we stumble through our various misunderstandings as we attempt to formulate and objectify more general understandings. In chapter 4, we can see shoppers also almost comically floundering around in their desire to espouse and to practice discourses that would bring them into a higher ethical relationship to the world around them and yet which prove elusive, contradictory, and sometimes not only superficial but just plain empty. As Rose would predict this is a place where we mourn the loss of something unattainable—that is, full mutual recognition. While on other occasions these same ethical aspirations can become a key moment in which we really do feel we have transcended the stupidity of what we think of as self-interest.

For Hegel, unlike for much modern political parlance, forms of governance that is, bodies that regulate the particular on behalf of the population, are aspects of civil society—not of the state. He used the term "state" to refer only to pure universalistic expressions of sovereignty (see Brod 1992, 92). So the adjudication of justice is an aspect of civil society that resolves issues that arise out of the satisfaction of needs. Returned to the specifics of the material of chapter 4, this argument suggests we need both to understand the sources of subjective aspiration toward more universal concerns but also that we need to reconsider the relationship between the subjective consciousness of such aspirations and the forms or laws in which they become concretized as expressions of a more universalistic will to ethics. This should lead to the development of "real" ethical identity. It also provides for a rethinking of the role of the anthropologist.

Chapter 4 was based on extracting two common discourses about shopping that clearly turned everyday food shopping into a possibility (that had either to be explicitly acknowledged or refused) for considering the wider implications of the purchase of food. The source of subjective intentionality in this case lies primarily in certain core discourses that are constantly being reinforced by material on the media, in education, and indeed, in general conversation between shoppers. But one striking discovery of the ethnography was that while the discourse on Green and environmentalist issues is relatively sophisticated and informed, when we look at the equivalent (Red) discourse about the impact of shopping on the producers of commodities, we find the discourse is generally partial and ill-informed. Shoppers may be increasingly aware of the effects of what they do on the planet, but they show very little awareness of the consequences of their shopping for other people in their role as workers and distributors.

By contrast, anthropologists (and geographers—see Leslie and Reimer 1999) are becoming increasingly aware of the direct relationship between the welfare of the various peoples among whom they work and the activities of first-world shoppers. Not long ago it was mainly the impact of cash crops and general economic development that impinged upon the anthropologist conducting fieldwork. But today it is the relationships between these changes in production and the dynamics of the market and consumption that has emerged as of enormous importance to the producers as well as to the consumers. New communication technologies have shrunk these distances, and contemporary anthropologists can often directly link the effect of, for example, replacing local crops with intensive cultivation of cut flowers in Kenya to the shops in France or Italy where these flowers are sold. Similarly, after the pioneering study of sugar by Mintz (1985) the sense of the commodity chain where consumption is linked back to production has become much more central to anthropology (e.g., Weiss 1996 for coffee; Steiner 1994 for art). The commodity chain is bidirectional, including also the issues raised by European and U.S. goods being consumed in the developing world.

For these reasons, we have to include the additional criteria noted above as a proviso in evoking Hegel, which is to ensure that when people seek to be at home in the world, it is the larger world of justice and not just a parochial world. When working in our own societies subjective intentionality itself is not merely what we encounter as the observed character of ethnographic subjects, but something we seek to change by inculcating within it the knowledge we have by virtue of the kind of work we do. We might be more circumspect in imposing our critique upon other societies, but in our own land we have a responsibility toward the raising of critical consciousness. The other implication is that anthropologists need to do far more work on commodity chains themselves to bring us to a position where we can claim authority to mediate in this relationship. The problem today is not that anthropologists have too much authority thanks to some grand narrative of rationalism, but that they have so little influence compared with, for example, economists. To conclude civil society as described by Hegel is not a context we work in but rather a description of our proper practice, a movement toward *Sittlichkeit*.

Informing people in the attempt to awake their consciousness as to the implications of their shopping is, however, only one side of this dialectical relationship. Shoppers have to care about this and have to be willing for this information to have consequences. Ideally, ethical choice should not just be objectified in the administration of justice, but also in these acts of everyday choice. Indeed, by Hegel's own criteria the latter is preferable since it is a means by which citizens come to experience and be conscious of their responsibilities to the larger world. Law is, however, the vital additional complement since it can control the primary regulation of production and distribution that ensures that the citizen is able to exercise an ethical choice in the first place.

Chapter 4 showed why neither the changing of consciousness nor the inscription of ethics in law is at all straightforward. Even where, as in the case of Green issues, shoppers are much better informed and, in addition, there is pressure from both commerce and society to avail themselves of the facilities for Green shopping, we do not find more than a token presence for environmentally concerned shopping. The explanation suggested in chapter 4 lay largely in the contradictions faced by individual shoppers. In practice they found that the desire to practice ethical shopping that demonstrated their environmental concerns came into conflict with their primary role as moral shoppers practicing thrift on behalf of the households to whom they were responsible.

The problem arises from a failure of civil society where, as Hegel argues, the administration of justice is the prerequisite for the maintenance of ethical subjective intentionality. Instead we find that decisions that previously were made by governments are being dumped onto individual shoppers with the claim that the market provides a more democratic system of choice than does democracy. The larger supermarket chains do have an important role to play as forms of civil society and are currently exploring these. They are increasingly attempting to represent themselves as the "administration of justice" that is educating as well as reflecting ways that shoppers can leave to them the burden of deciding what is environmentally sound, or ethical. Commercial involvement should not be dismissed and under proper regulatory regimes could play a vital role within civil society, but at present the larger frame for supermarkets is obviously dominated by competition for profit and has a built-in bias against wider regulation. In such a situation we see today the contradictions faced by individual shoppers between morality and ethics are merely being replaced by another set of contradictions intrinsic to the conflict between ethics and profits.

What is required in addition is something that Hegel himself was particularly concerned with and that later on became an even more central concern for Weber: the problem of how we can feel at home in a situation where a largely anonymous bureaucracy comes to represent us in the form of our universalistic aspirations. There are clear advantages in states, or even superstates such as the European Union, taking on much of this embodiment of law, since they have both the power and the access to higher levels of knowledge. Many of these individual consumers do not know, want to know, or can be sure whose presentation of knowledge to accept. When it comes to often quite technical questions of where an ingredient actually does come from and what is the current scientific consensus upon its likely harmful effects, the consumer depends upon bureaucratic and political adjudication of science. Yet delegation of responsibility to vast bureaucracies hardly appeals as the means to overcome alienation.

The problem may well reflect a much wider contradiction. British ideology here may be positioned geographically and actually between Western

Europe and the United States. In Western Europe, opinion polls seems to express a greater sense of civil society a là Hegel. Populations will espouse a social democratic consensus that collective forces as expressions of the universal will are the basis for the creation of individual freedom. By contrast, politics (but also popular culture such as Hollywood films—recently, *Antz*, or *The Truman Show*) in the United States appears to be dominated by what Hegel would probably have found the most pernicious and mistaken ideologies of freedom, represented as the choice of the desocialized individual acting against what is viewed as "the system."

In this British-based ethnography we can observe both the desire to delegate upward the responsibility for ethical choices, leaving the individual free to act morally, but at the same time a deep and growing suspicion of politics and bureaucracy. It is as though we have lost the understanding we once had of the role of bureaucracy in securing welfare and equality, or what Hegel and Weber saw as nobility in a profession that was supposed to rise above and be separate from political dispute and ensure more basic values (although see Du Gay, *In Praise of Bureaucracy* [2000]). The creation of a "real" ethical shopping, then, requires a shift in subjective intentionality, which implies informing people of the consequences of their individual acts of shopping. But it must also recognize that the formulation of subjective intentionality is dialectically conditional upon the externalization of ethics in law. Only law and bureaucracy can provide the foundation for the development of individualism and choice. Only with the requisite information and the regulations that ensure commodities are what they claim to be can the shopper finally obtain the freedom and choices to act politically and effectively through ethical shopping.

"UNREAL" POLITICAL ECONOMY

The chapter title is a pun on the colloquial phrase "get real." This, in turn, makes apposite another pun. One would hope that a student reading chapter 5 with its account of business developments and the virtualism it reveals would react with a gasp and a response, such as, "Wow, this is totally unreal." From a Hegelian perspective that would be an entirely appropriate response, because it is at the level of political economy that we leave the "real" world of reason for all sorts of claims to reason that, in effect, largely obfuscate our capacity to discern how these institutions actually relate back to human welfare in the way they ultimately claim to do. Virtualism, as communism before it, acts to sunder the relationships that would allow people either to create the objective conditions for being at home in the world or the consciousness of how to achieve that goal. Instead, human welfare becomes sacrificed to the autonomous authority of institutions we have created but that have turned against us. Following their increasingly autonomous interests, these alienating forces threaten to become ever more oppressive unless we find the means to tame them and bring them back into the service of our interests. Yet ironically much of this is legitimated in the name of people as shoppers, turning into mere virtual ghosts the householders who I have tried to humanize through empathy with their struggles and contradictions in the three preceding levels. The result in the terms of *The Philosophy of Right* is precisely a situation that can be described as "unreal."

What each preceding chapter included was an affirmation of the "real." For example, chapter 4 may have showed that a discourse about Green and ethical issues was rarely turned into practice, but it also demonstrated a latent rationality that, as with the discourse of the corner shop and the discourse of family, is a clear attempt to formulate a "real" world that could also become a real world of institutions and practices. The task of this chapter has been to consider various means of closing the gap between that rational impulse toward the "real" and that which conspired to prevent what could literally be termed its realization. Of course, political economy also makes such claims. The World Bank is formally dedicated to the elimination of poverty; few organizations have made as many speeches to this effect, even when critics suggest it is, after war and dictatorship, possibly the main cause of poverty in the developing world. Economics is formally intended to provide the consumer with the ideal choice of commodities. Yet in practice it constantly sacrifices the interests of consumers and, indeed, the study of economies and turns both into legitimizations for the development of abstract models, which treat the real world merely as a series of distortions of those models.

Economics is but one example of a whole series of virtual institutions such as management consultancy, auditing, and the theory of posmodernism that have mushroomed in the last fifteen years. In each case they involve a fetishism of the shopper as consumer. The real shopper is replaced by an auditor, consultant, mathematical formula, or academic trope that stands for them and enacts changes that ultimately act against the interests of ordinary shoppers. The point need not be reiterated at length here since it was made explicitly in chapter 5. The concept of "virtualism" as applied in that chapter was itself formulated originally through an application of these same Hegelian perspectives (see Miller 1998b).

For the purposes of the present chapter the identification of virtualist political economy as "unreal" takes its place within a conclusion addressed to all four previous substantive chapters. Each preceding level illustrates a different relationship to the "real" and to the task of developing *Sittlichkeit* or ethical society. Within the practice of kinship we see shopping as performing the "real" as a dialectic process. In considering the future of corner shops we come up against the problem of objective conditions and the need to change them. In dealing with ethical shopping we face instead the problem of changing consciousness as to the consequences of the act of shopping but also of objectifying that consciousness in institutional forms such as bureaucracy. Finally, the virtual political economy comes to exemplify the last logical outcome of the application of these criteria, that is, a situation in which the "real" is absent. These thereby equate with the three states of alienation that were identified by Hegel (Hardimon 1994, 119–22), what he termed "objective alienation," "subjective alienation," and "total alienation."

CONCLUSION

As a volume of the Morgan Lectures, the use of the term "dialectic" always had one more goal in mind—to designate an ambition for the discipline of anthropology. This chapter and this book conclude, therefore, with an attempt to draw out the implications of this project for anthropology. I believe there awaits a future role for that discipline analogous to that which Hegel proclaimed as the task of philosophy and Marx, as the role of revolution. Now I do not presume on behalf of anthropology quite the grandiose role previously ascribed to philosophy or revolution. Yet perhaps fortuitously, anthropology does have a particular role to play in the rebonding of humanity with its own creation, that is, culture. Anthropology has this capacity because it arose with two contrasting aims: one, its commitment to particularity, represented by ethnography; and the other, universality represented by comparison and theory. Lévi-Strauss links this back to what can fairly be claimed to have been the foundational imperative behind the formation of the modern discipline. He claimed that anthropology "takes man as its object of study but differs from the other sciences of man in striving to understand that object in its most diverse manifestations" (1985, 25). To put this in gender-neutral terms, it is about understanding the generality of humanity from its particularity.

An ethnography of shopping in North London may be used in this task because the cosmopolitan complexity of North London illustrates both the problems of distance and contradiction that must be addressed and the potential of anthropology in transcending these complexities. A consumer society differs radically from what has been termed simple societies because of the elaboration and scale of the institutional forms within which we live. These include global markets, through which we are largely sundered from the consciousness of production, vast bureaucracies, through which we are largely sundered from the consciousness of distribution, and the growth of privacy such that we are largely sundered from the experience of the plurality of consumption. Yet an anthropology of a consumer society must strive to reconnect these since they are all relevant to understanding our subjects. We face a world that looks simultaneously like an imploding and an exploding universe. On the one hand, society seems ever more private. Households disappear from the public domain. They may be exposed to vast global knowledge, but their point of access is increasingly through television and the Internet, consumed behind closed doors (Morley 1992, 270–89). When they present themselves to most academics in other disciplines it is through the normative discourse of legitimization, elicited in response to questionnaires and focus groups. These researchers must simply assume a congruence between their data and the life behind those doors. On the other hand, we find ever more abstract and esoteric institutional forms of economy and governance, which like financial derivatives seem to piggyback each new abstraction upon the mere aggregation of the level below to create the phenomenon of virtualism.

At this point, the task of anthropology in forcing us to acknowledge and consider the consequence of the relationship between these abstracted institutional forms and the private world of households looks remarkably similar to the foundational intentions of Hegelian philosophy—to strive to enable humanity to be at home in the world. A goal that would be achieved through reconciling the contradictions that inevitably arise from the distance between culture as human creativity expressing the universality of rationality, and culture as the particularity of individual interest that fails to see itself as both the creation of and the creator of that universality. Carrier and Miller (1999) trace the different ways in which anthropology has attempted to think the articulation between the micro- and the macrolevels at various periods in the development of economic anthropology, but the problem extends to all areas of anthropological inquiry. This distance between our private lives and the institutions that objectify our reason is by no means specific to economic activity, whose separation from the rest of life is itself one of the problems we strive to transcend.

Hegel's ideal of "get real" was also intended as the critique of any mere continuity of practice that has become stultified as routine or genre. I have no intention here of disparaging traditions of scholarship or suggesting that the grandiose is valuable in itself. But getting real (or getting a life!) means remembering why this research is being carried out and why these overbearing criteria of scholarship still matter. Hegel predicted that we would see an acceleration of the growth of both universality and particularity, and, therefore, the development of ever greater distance between new institutional abstractions and the need to subsume these within practices conducive to human welfare. He rightly foresaw how these represented the foundational contradiction of modernity and the source of both our alienation and our potential today. But if this is the case then it is anthropology, in particular, that is tailor-made to act for the healing of these dialectical rifts. This is because of anthropology's potential as what may be termed an "extremist" discipline. We see today an extreme of globalism and homogeneity matched by an extreme of localism and particularity. Our problem is to keep these in articulation. What is significant in anthropology is that it retains its grounding in empathetic ethnography based on the profound experience of the minutia and particular in everyday life along with an insistence on the continued authenticity of difference, and yet at the same time it is committed to analysis, to theory, and to contexualizing the particular in the comparative study of humanity as a whole.

Hegel's own chosen field of philosophy has never had this kind of experiential grounding, and some other disciplines have sunk into a kind of middle terrain, using an inappropriate naturalist epistemology to make little hypotheses with little tests but avoiding both the extremes of deep and sustained involvement and the ambition of grand theory and generality. This book has been an attempt to demonstrate the continued possibility of extremist anthropology; that the involvement in the nuances of the relationship of an aunt and her niece can and should be within the same volume as an attempt to tackle the political economy; that these are united by theory as well as by their being connected as aspects of the same people's lives. A new approach to kinship and to political economy need to be developed together. Most academic texts rest secure in the relatively small compass of linkages within either a parochial descriptive monograph or an abstracted theoretical argument. The challenge of anthropology is to stay onboard a wild roller coaster that plunges theory back into the muddy waters of everyday life and then lunges upward again to gain the perspective of philosophical generalities. This may leave other more "disciplined" academics feeling distinctly queasy, but it is an ambition

204 · CHAPTER SIX

toward the reconciliation of these opposites that anthropology should not relinquish.

There is rarely a simple flow between the microscale of everyday life that we can observe and the macroscale of global institutions whose effects we must account for. The organization of this volume has implied a series of levels that, while not discrete, contain a degree of autonomy. The same people, present here by the mere circumstance of being informants for an ethnography, are represented in successive discussions of the private worlds of kinship, the public sphere of civil society, and as customers subjected to and facilitated by the political economy of retail. The legacy of Hegel is not one that speaks to a simple humanism in which such people are best treated as biographical accounts encased in the expression of their subjectivity. Rather, his humanism lay in the consciousness that both individuals and interests are themselves constructed through processes of socialization and immersion in a gamut of normative and other discourses, some of which speak to larger projects of rationality. While at the same time there are other practices and institutions that have become sundered from any such humanism and merely follow their own internal logics, often with oppressive consequences.

I would argue that good ethnography tends to exemplify the Hegelian concept of the "real." It starts with the problem of empathy; to communicate the experience of living as a member of a particular social time and space. But while this might satisfy a television documentary, anthropology goes beyond this task. The text attempts to make sense of that larger context that is otherwise likely to remain fragmented within everyday experience. As Marcus notes, "estrangement or defamiliarization remains the distinctive trigger of ethnographic work" (1998, 16), and this is all the more important when working with the insidiously familiar, a topic such as shopping with its tendency to refuse to be analyzed beyond the most superficial appeal of "common sense."

In shopping, as I have described it, we are faced with an ever more intimate world of people consuming in highly private lives that are not revealed by focus groups or questionnaires. Anthropology remains invasive, insisting on becoming intimate with our intimacy and knowing the private lives of peoples and commodities. But equally, shopping is enveloped in vast issues of retail capital, derivatives, and consultancies. If these impinge on us as shoppers, then anthropologists need to be investigating such highly esoteric and weird "customs" as leveraged buyouts, which may determine the objective possibilities open to us as shoppers. Such studies remain in opposition to the clones of economist Gary Becker (Radnitzky and Bernolz 1987; Tommasi and Ierulli 1995), who believe they can reduce all behavior to economic models. Instead, we expose the more profound humanist sense of reason that is implicit in social action and that includes rather than denies the contradictions of culture.

The problem with totalizing narratives about Melanesian and Amazonian tribes is that now they are no longer totalizing enough, especially where, as recent accounts have argued (e.g., Foster 1995, 1996–1997; Gewertz and Errington 1999 for Melanesia) they exclude the larger forces that increasingly impinge upon the peoples in question. A study of such an utterly cosmopolitan place such as North London, which is in no sense a community, helps us to develop new approaches that strive to reintegrate such far-flung factors within our analyses in a way that might then be attempted in regions such as contemporary Melanesia and Amazonia. This agenda may stand whether the topic is the impact of a new crop in the Sudan, the subculture of truck drivers in India, medical and problem solving resources in Thailand, or shopping in North London.

Finally, this volume has tried to demonstrate that "vulgar" dialectics are not some dry philosophical logic. Rather, I take the dialectic to be the passion of humanity struggling to bring that intrinsically contradictory process we call culture back into the service of our self-creation, and this can be observed equally in the struggle of a shopper reconciling discourse and particularity in the act of shopping or in the struggle of the discipline of anthropology seeking a new role in reconciling through understanding the vast and fragmented nature of modernity.

 **BIBLIOGRAPHY**

Abelson, E. 1989. *When Ladies Go A-Thieving: Middle-Class Shoplifters in the Victorian Department Store.* New York: Oxford University Press.

Abrams, P. 1986. *Neighbours: The Work of Philip Abrams,* edited by M. Bulmer. Cambridge: Cambridge University Press.

Allan, G. 1996. *Kinship and Friendship in Modern Britain.* Oxford: Oxford University Press.

Allen, R. 1998. *The Moving Pageant: A Literary Sourcebook on London Street-Life, 1700–1914.* London: Routledge.

Auslander, L. 1996. The Gendering of Consumer Practices in Nineteenth-Century France. In *The Sex of Things: Gender and Consumption in Historical Perspective,* edited by Victoria De Grazia. Berkeley: University of California Press, 79–112.

Back, L. 1996. *New Ethnicities and Urban Culture: Racisms and Multiculture in Young Lives.* New York : St. Martin's Press.

Barnes, S., S. Dadamo, and D. Turner. 1996. *Grocery Retailing 1996: The Market Review.* Watford: Institute of Grocery Distribution.

Barrett, M., and M. McIntosh. 1982. *The Anti-Social Family.* London: New Left Books.

Bateson, G. 1936. *Naven: A Survey of the Problems Suggested by a Composite Picture of the Culture of a New Guinea Tribe Drawn from Three Points of View.* Cambridge: Cambridge University Press.

Bayly, C. 1986. The Origins of Swadeshi (Home Industry): Cloth and Indian Society, 1700–1930. In *The Social Life of Things: Commodities in Cultural Perspective,* edited by A. Appadurai. Cambridge: Cambridge University Press, 285–321.

Bean, S. 1989. Gandhi and Khadi, the Fabric of Indian independence. In *Cloth and Human Experience.* Washington: London Smithsonian Institution, 355–376.

Beardsworth, A., and T. Keil. 1997. *Sociology on the Menu: An Invitation to the Study of Food and Society.* London: Routledge.

Beck, U., and E. G. Beck-Gernsheim. 1995. *The Normal Chaos of Love.* Cambridge, U.K.: Polity Press.

Bell, C., and H. Newby. 1971. *Community Studies: An Introduction to the Sociology of the Local Community.* London: Allen and Unwin

Bell, D., and G. Valentine. 1997. *Consuming Geographies: We Are What We Eat.* London: Routledge.

Bell, L., and J. Ribbens. 1994. Isolated Housewives and Complex Maternal Worlds. *Sociological Review* 42: 227–262.

Bender, B. 1998. *Stonehenge: Making Space.* Oxford: Berg.

Bender, B., ed. 1993 *Landscape: Politics and Perspectives.* Providence: Berg.

Berry, C. 1994. *The Idea of Luxury: A Conceptual and Historical Investigation.* Cambridge: Cambridge University Press.

Blomley, N. 1996. 'I'd Like to Dress Her All Over': Masculinity, Power and Retail Space. In *Retailing, Consumption and Capital: Towards the New Retail Geography,* edited by N. Wrigley and M. Lowe. Harlow: Longman Group.

Bourdieu, P. 1977. *Outline of a Theory of Practice.* Cambridge: Cambridge University Press.

———. 1984. *Distinction: A Social Critique of the Judgement of Taste.* London: Routledge and Kegan Paul.

———. 1996. On the Family as a Realized Category. *Theory, Culture and Society* 13(3): 19–26.

Bowlby, R. 1985. *Just Looking: Consumer Culture in Dreiser, Gissing and Zola.* New York: Methuen.

Brod, H. 1992. *Hegel's Philosophy of Politics: Idealism, Identity, and Modernity.* Boulder: Westview Press.

Burman, E., and I. Parker. 1993. *Discourse Analytic Research: Repertoires and Readings of Texts in Action.* London: Routledge.

Burrough, B., and J. Helyar. 1990. *Barbarians at the Gate: The Fall of RJR Nabisco.* London: Arrow.

Burt, S., and L. Sparks. 1995. Understanding the Arrival of Limited Line Discount Stores in Britain. *European Management Journal* 13: 110–119.

Callon, M., ed. 1998. *The Laws of the Markets.* Oxford: Blackwell.

Caplan, P., ed. 1997. *Food, Health, and Identity.* London: Routledge.

Caplan, P., A. Keane, A. Willetts, and J. Williams. 1998. Studying Food Choice in its Social and Cultural Contexts: Approaches from a Social Anthropological Perspective. In *The Nation's Diet: The Social Science of Food Choice,* edited by A. Murcott. London: Longman, 168–182.

Carrier, J. 1990. The Symbolism of Possession in Commodity Advertising. *Man* 25: 693–705.

———. 1995. *Gift and Commodities: Exchange and Western Capitalism since 1700.* London: Routledge.

Carrier, J., and J. Heyman. 1997. Consumption and Political Economy. *Journal of the Royal Anthropological Institute* 3: 355–373.

Carrier, J., and D. Miller. 1999. From Private Virtue to Public Vice. In *Anthropological Theory Today,* edited by H. Moore. Cambridge, U.K.: Polity Press, 24–47.

Carrier, J., and D. Miller, eds. 1998. *Virtualism: A New Political Economy.* Oxford: Berg.

Casey, E. 1996. How to Get from Space to Place in a Fairly Short Stretch of Time: Phenomenological Prolegomena. In *Senses of Place,* edited by S. Feld and K. Basso. Sante Fe: School of American Research Press, 13–52.

Cheah, P., and B. Robbins, eds. 1998. *Cosmopolitics: Thinking and Feeling beyond the Nation*. Minneapolis: University of Minesota Press.

Cheong, W. E. 1979. *Mandarins and Merchants: Jardine, Matheson, & Co., a China Agency of the Early Nnineteenth Century*. London: Curzon Press.

Clammer, J. 1992. Aesthetics of the Self: Shopping and Social Being in Contemporary Urban Japan. In *Lifestyle Shopping: The Subject of Consumption*, edited by R. Shields. London: Routledge.

Clammer, J. R. 1997. *Contemporary Urban Japan: A Sociology of Consumption*. Oxford: Blackwell.

Clarke, A. 1998. Window Shopping at Home: Classifieds, Catalogues and New Consumer Skills. In *Material Cultures: Why Some Things Matter*, edited by D. Miller. London: UCL Press.

Clarke, A. 1999. *Tupperware: The Promise of Plastic in 1950s America*. Washington, D.C.: Smithsonian Institution Press.

Clarke, A. Forthcoming a. Mother Swapping: The Trafficking in Nearly New Children's Wear. In *Culture and Commerce*, edited by P. Jackson, M. Lowe, D. Miller, and F. Mort. Oxford: Berg.

———. Forthcoming b. Setting Up Actual and Ideal Homes in North London. In *Material Culture and the Home*, edited by D. Miller.

Clifford, J. 1997. *Routes: Travel and Translation in the Late Twentieth Century*. Berkeley: University of California Press.

Cohn, B. 1989. Cloth, Clothes, and Colonialism: India in the Nineteenth Century. In *Cloth and Human Experience*, edited by A. Weiner and J. Schneider. Washington: London Smithsonian Institution, 303–353.

Collier, J., M. Rosaldo, and S. Yanagisako. 1992. Is There a Family? New Anthropological Views. In *Rethinking the Family: Some Feminist Questions*, edited by B. Thorne and M. Yaom. Revised edition. Boston: Northeastern Univeristy Press, 31–48.

Cook, I., and P. Crang. 1996. The World of a Plate. *Journal of Material Culture* 1: 131–153.

Cook, I., P. Crang, and M. Thorpe. 1999. Eating into Britishness: Mulitcultural Imaginaries and the Identity Politics of Food. In *Practising Identities: Power and Resistance*, edited by S. Roseneil and J. Seymour. Baskingstoke: Macmillan Press.

———. Forthcoming. Category Management and Circuits of Knowledge in the UK Food Business. In *Knowledge, Space, Economy*, edited by P. Daniels, N. Henry, and J. Pollard. London: Routledge.

Coward, R. 1989. *The Whole Truth: The Myth of Alternative Health*. London: Faber and Faber.

Crocker, D., and T. Linden, eds. 1998. *Ethics of Consumption: The Good Life, Justice, and Global Stewardship*. Lanham, Md.: Rowman & Littlefield.

David, K. 1983. Until Marriage Do Us Part: A Cultural Account of Jaffna Tamil Categories for Kinsmen. *Man* 8: 521–535.

Davis, M. 1990. *City of Quartz: Excavating the Future in Los Angeles*. London: Verso.

Davis, S., ed. 1993. *Indigenous Views of Land and the Environment.* World Bank Discussion Papers, 188. Washington: The World Bank.

De Grazia, V., ed. 1996. *The Sex of Things: Gender and Consumption in Historical Perspective.* Berkeley: University of California Press.

DeVault, M. L. 1991 *Feeding the Family: The Social Organization of Caring as Gendered Work.* Chicago: University of Chicago Press.

Doel, C. 1996. Market Development and Organizational Change: The Case of the Food Industry. In *Retailing Consumption and Capital: Towards the New Retail Geography,* edited by N. Wrigley and M. Lowe. Harlow: Longman Group.

Donzelot, J. 1980. *The Policing of Families.* London: Hutchinson.

Du Gay, P. 2000. *In Praise of Bureaucracy: Weber, Organization and Ethics.* London: Sage Publications.

Ducatel, K., and N. Blomley. 1990. Rethinking Retail Capital. *International Journal of Urban and Regional Research* 14: 207–227.

Dumont, L. 1983. *Affinity as a Value: Marriage Alliance in South India, with Comparative Essays on Australia.* Chicago: University of Chicago Press.

———. 1986. *Essays on Individualism: Modern Ideology in Anthrological Perspective.* Chicago: University of Chicago Press.

Engels, F. [1845] 1987. *The Condition of the Working Class in England.* Harmondsworth: Penguin Books.

Falk, P., and C. Campbell, eds. 1997. *The Shopping Experience.* London: Sage Publications.

Feld, S., and K. Basso, eds. 1996. *Senses of Place.* Santa Fe: School of American Research Press.

Finch, J. 1989. *Family Obligations and Social Change.* Cambridge, U.K.: Polity Press.

———. 1997. Individuality and Adapatability in English Kinship. In *Family and Kinship in Europe,* edited by M. Gullestad and M. Segalen. London: Pinter, 129–145.

Fine, B. 1998. The Triumph of Economics, or, 'Rationality' Can Be Dangerous to Your Reasoning. In *Virtualism: A New Political Economy,* edited by J. Carrier and D. Miller. Oxford: Berg, 49–74.

Fine, B., and E. Leopold. 1993. *The World of Consumption.* London: Routledge.

Finnegan, R. H. 1998. *Tales of the City: A Study of Narrative and Urban Life.* Cambridge: Cambridge University Press.

Firth, R., J. Hubert, and A. Forge. 1969. *Families and Their Relatives: Kinship in a Middle-Class Sector of London: An Anthropological Study.* London: Routledge & Kegan Paul.

Flynn, A., M. Harrison, and T. Marsden. 1998. Regulation Rights and the Structuring of Food Choices. In *The Nation's Diet: The Social Science of Food Choice,* edited by A. Murcott. London: Longman, 152–167.

Foster, R. 1995. Nation Making and Print Advertisements in Metropolitan Papua New Guinea. In *Nation Making: Emergent Identities in Postcolonial Melanesia,* edited by R. Foster. Ann Arbor: University of Michigan Press.

———. 1996–1997. Commercial Mass Media in Papua New Guinea: Notes on
Agency Bodies and Commodity Consumption. In *Visual Anthropology
Review* 12: 1–16.

Fournier, S. 1998. Consumers and Their Brands: Developing Relationship Theory in Consumer Research. *Journal of Consumer Research* 24: 343–373.

Freud, S. 1984. The Ego and the Super-Ego (Ego Ideal). In *On Metapsychology:
The Theory of Psychoanalysis: 'Beyond the Pleasure Principle,' 'The Ego and the
Id' and Other Works*. Harmondsworth: Penguin, 367–379.

Furlough, E. 1991. *Consumer Cooperation in France: The Politics of Consumption,
1834–1930*. Ithaca: Cornell University Press.

Furman, F. 1997. *Facing the Mirror: Older Women and Beauty Shop Culture*. New
York: Routledge.

Gell, A. 1995. The Language of the Forest: Landscape and Phonological Iconism
in Umeda. In *The Anthropology of Landscape: Perspectives on Place and Space*,
edited by E. Hirsch and M. O'Hanlon. Oxford: Clarendon Press, 232–254.

Gewertz, D. B., and F. K. Errington. 1999. *Emerging Class in Papua New Guinea:
The Telling of Difference*. Cambridge: Cambridge University Press.

Giddens, A. 1991. *Modernity and Self-Identity: Self and Society in the Late Modern
Age*. Cambridge, U.K.: Polity Press.

———. 1992. *The Transformation of Intimacy: Sexuality, Love and Eroticism in
Modern Societies*. Cambridge, U.K.: Polity Press.

Gide, C. 1921. *Consumers' Co-Operative Societies*. New York: Haskell House.

Gillis, J. R. 1997. *A World of Their Own Making: A History of Myth and Ritual in
Family Life*. Oxford: University of Oxford Press.

Gilroy, P. 1993. *The Black Atlantic: Modernity and Double Consciousness*. London:
Verso.

Gilsenan, M. 1982. *Recognizing Islam: An Anthropologist's Instroduction*. London:
Croom Helm.

———. 1996. *Lords of the Lebanese Marches: Violence and Narrative in an Arab Society*. London: I. B. Tauriss.

Glennie, P., and N. Thrift. 1996. Consumers, Identities and Consumption
Spaces in Early Modern England. *Environment and Planning A* 28: 25–45.

Goodwin, N. R., F. Ackerman, and D. Kiron, eds. 1997. *The Consumer Society*.
Washington: Island Press.

Greenberg, J. R., and S. A. Mitchell. 1983. *Object Relations in Psychoanalytical
Theory*. Cambridge: Harvard University Press.

Gregson, N., L. Crewe, and K. Brooks. Forthcoming. *Second Hand Worlds*. London: Routledge.

Gudeman, S., and A. Rivera. 1990. *Conversations in Colombia: The Domestic Economy in Life and Text*. Cambridge: Cambridge University Press.

Gullestad, N., and M. Segalen, eds. 1997. *Family and Kinship in Europe*. London:
Pinter.

Gupta, A., and J. Ferguson. 1997. Discipline and Practice: The "Field" as Site,
Method and Location in Anthropology. In *Anthropological Locations:*

Boundaries and Grounds of a Field Science. Berkeley: University of California Press.

Habermas, J. 1972. *Knowledge and Human Interests.* London: Heinemann Educational.

———. 1987. *The Philosophical Discourse of Modernity: Twelve Lectures.* Cambridge, Mass.: MIT Press.

Hall, S. 1996. On Postmodernism and Articulation: An Interview with Stuart Hall. In *Stuart Hall: Critical Dialogues in Cultural Studies,* edited by D. Morley and K.-H. Chen. London: Routledge.

Hallsworth, A. G. 1992. *The New Geography of Consumer Spending: A Political Economy Approach.* London: Bellhaven Press.

Hallsworth, A. G., and M. Taylor. 1996. Buying Power: Interpreting Retail Change in a Circuits of Power Framework. *Environment and Planning A* 28: 2125–2137.

Hann, C. 1996. Introduction to *Civil Society: Challenging Western Models,* edited by C. M. Hann and E. Dunn. London: Routledge.

Hardimon, M. 1994. *Hegel's Social Philosophy: The Project of Reconciliation.* Cambridge: Cambridge University Press.

Hebdige, D. 1981. Towards a Cartography of Taste, 1935–1962. *Block* 4: 39–56.

Hegel, G. W. F. [1821] 1967. *Philosophy of Right,* tranlsated by T. M. Knox. London: Oxford University Press.

Hendrickson, C. 1996. Selling Guatemala: Maya Export Products in U.S. Mail-Order Catalogues. In *Cross-Cultural Consumption: Global Markets, Local Realities,* edited by D. Howes. London: Routledge.

Hirsch, E. 1995. Landscape, between Space and Place. In *The Anthropology of Landscape: Perspectives on Place and Space,* edited by E. Hirsch and M. O'Hanlon. Oxford: Clarendon Press, 1–30.

Hirsch, E., and M. O'Hanlon, eds. 1995. *The Anthropology of Landscape: Perspectives on Place and Space.* Oxford: Clarendon Press.

Holt, D. 1998. Does Cultural Capital Structure American Consumption? *Journal of Consumer Research* 25: 1–25.

Hughes, A. 1996. Forging New Cultures of Retailer-Manufacturer Relations? In *Retailing Consumption and Capital: Towards the New Retail Geography,* edited by N. Wrigley and M. Lowe. Harlow: Longman Group, 90–115.

Humphery, K. 1998. *Shelf Life: Supermarkets and the Changing Cultures of Consumption.* Cambridge, U.K.: Cambridge Univeristy Press.

Hutton, W. 1996. *The State We're In.* Revised edition. London: Vintage.

James, A. 1990. The Good, the Bad, and the Delicious: The Role of Confectionery in British Society. *Sociological Review* 38: 666–688.

———. 1996. Cooking the Books: Global or Local Identities in Contemporary British Food Cultures. In *Cross-Cultural Consumption: Global Markets, Local Realities,* edited by D. Howes. London: Routledge, 93–105.

———. 1997. How British Is British Food? In *Food, Health, and Identity,* edited by P. Caplan. London: Routledge.

Keane, W. 1997. *Signs of Recognition: Powers and Hazards of Representation in an Indonesian Society.* Berkeley: University of California Press.

Keat, R. 1994. Scepticism, Authority and the Market. In *The Authority of the Consumer,* edited by R. Keat, N. Whiteley, and N. Abercrombie. London: Routledge.

Keesing, R. M. 1982. *Kwaio Religion: The Living and the Dead in a Solomon Island Society.* New York: Columbia University Press.

Kempton, W., J. S. Boster, and J. A. Hartley. 1996. *Environmental Values in American Culture.* Cambridge, Mass.: MIT Press.

Klein, M. 1975. *Envy and Gratitude and Other Works, 1946–1963.* [New York]: Delacorte Press.

Knight, J. 1998. Selling Mother's Love? *Journal of Material Culture* 3: 153–173.

Kuechler, S. 1988. Malangan: Objects, Sacrifice and the Production of Memory. *American Ethnologist* 15(4): 625–637.

Larrain, J. 1979. *The Concept of Ideology.* London: Hutchinson.

Latour, B. 1993. We *Have Never Been Modern.* New York: Harvester Wheatsheaf.

Lavik, R., and T. Lunde. 1991. *The Freedom to Choose When Choice Is Difficult.* Lysaker: Norwegian National Institute for Consumer Research.

Law, J. 1994. *Organising Modernity.* Oxford: Blackwell.

Layne, L. 1999a. 'I Remember the Day I Shopped for Your Layette': Goods, Fetuses and Feminism in the Context of Pregnancy Loss. In *The Fetal Imperative: Feminist Practices,* edited by L. Morgan and M. Michaels. Philadelphia: University of Pennsylvania Press.

Layne, L. 1999b. 'He Was a Real Baby with Baby Things': A Material Culture Analysis of Personhood, Parenthood and Pregnancy Loss. In *Ideologies and Technologies of Motherhood,* edited by H. Ragone and W. Twine. New York: Routledge.

Layne, L., ed. 1999. *Transformative Motherhood: On Giving and Getting in a Consumer Culture.* New York: New York University Press.

Leach, E. 1954. *Political Systems of Highland Burma.* London: Athlone Press.

Le Fevour, E. 1969. *Western Enterprise in Late Chi'ing China.* Cambridge: Harvard University Press.

Lehrer, A. 1983. *Wine and Conversation.* Bloomington: Indiana University Press.

Leslie, D., and S. Reimer. 1999. Spatializing Commodity Chains. *Progress in Human Geography* 23: 401–420.

Lévi-Strauss, C. 1985. *The View from Afar,* translated by J. Neugroschel and R. Hoss. Chicago: University of Chicago Press.

Leyshon, A., and N. Thrift. 1997. *Money/Space: Geographies of Monetary Transformation.* London: Routledge.

Lichtenberg, J. 1998. Consuming Because Others Consume. In *Ethics of Consumption: The Good Life, Justice, and Global Stewardship.* Lanham: Rowman & Littlefield. 155–175.

Lien, M. E. 1997. *Marketing and Modernity.* Oxford: Berg.

Lindsey, L. 1997. *Gender Roles: A Sociological Perspective*. Third edition. Upper Saddle River, N.J.: Prentice Hall.

Löfgren, O. 1993. The Great Christmas Quarrel and Other Swedish Traditions. In *Unwrapping Christmas*, edited by D. Miller. Oxford: Clarendon Press.

McGrath, M. 1997. *A Guide to Category Managment*. Watford: IGD Business Publications.

McKendrick, N. 1983. Commercialisation and the Economy. In *The Birth of a Consumer Society: The Commercialization of Eighteenth-Century England*, edited by N. McKendrick, J. Brewer, and J. Plumb. London: Hutchinson.

MacKenzie, M. A. 1991. *Androgynous Objects: String Bags and Gender in Central New Guinea* . Chur: Harwood Academic Publishers.

McKibbin, Ross. 1998. *Classes and Cultures: England, 1918–1951*. Oxford: Oxford University Press.

Marcus, G. E. 1998. *Ethnography through Thick and Thin*. Princeton: Princeton University Press.

Marsden, P., and G. L. Clarke. 1994. The Pension Fund Economy: The Evolving Regulatory Framework in Australia. In *Money, Power, and Space,* edited by S. Corbridge, R. Martin, and N. Thrift. Oxford: Blackwell, 189–217.

Marsden, T., M. Harrison, and A. Flynn. 1998. Creating Competititve Advantage. *Environment and Planning A* 30: 481–498.

Marsden, T., and N. Wrigley. 1996. Retailing, the Food Stystem and Organizational Change: The Case of the Food Industry. In *Retailing Consumption and Capital: Towards the New Retail Geography,* edited by N. Wrigley and M. Lowe. Harlow: Longman Group, 33–47.

Martens, L., and A. Warde. 1998. The Social and Symbolic Significance of Ethnic Cuisine in England: New Cosmopolitanism and Old Xenophobia. *Sosiologisk Arbok* 1998: 111–146.

Mauss, M. 1954. *The Gift: Forms and Functions of Exchange in Archaic Societies*. London: Cohen & West.

Meyer, B. 1997. *Commodities and the Power of Prayer*. Working Papers in Globalization and the Construction of Communal Identities. Amsterdam: WOTRO.

Miller, D. 1987. *Material Culture and Mass Consumption*. Oxford: Blackwell.

———. 1988. Appropriating the state on the council estate. *Man* 23: 353–372.

———. 1994. *Modernity: An Ethnographic Approach*. Oxford: Berg.

———. 1997a. *Capitalism: An Ethnographic Approach*. Berg: Oxford.

———. 1997b. How Infants Grow Mothers in North London. *Theory, Culture and Society* 14: 66–88.

———. 1997c. Could Shopping Ever Really Matter? In *The Shopping Experience*. edited by P. Falk and C. Campbell. London: Sage Publications.

———. 1998a. *A Theory of Shopping*. Cambridge, U.K.: Polity Press.

———. 1998b. A Theory of Virtualism. In *Virtualism: A New Political Economy,* edited by J. Carrier and D. Miller. Oxford: Berg.

Miller, D., ed. 1993. *Unwrapping Christmas*. Oxford: Clarendon Press.

Miller, D., B. Jackson, B. Holbrook, N. Thrift, and M. Rowlands. 1998. *Shopping, Place, and Identity.* New York: Routledge.

Milton, K., ed. 1996. *Environmentalism and Cultural Theory: Exploring the Role of Anthropology in Environmental Discourse* London: Routledge.

Mintz, S. W. 1985. *Sweetness and Power: The Place of Sugar in Modern History.* New York: Viking.

Mogey, J. M. 1956. *Family and Neighbourhood: Two Studies in Oxford.* [London]: Oxford University Press.

Morley, D. 1992. *Television, Audiences, and Cultural Studies.* London: Routledge.

Morphy, H. 1995. Landscape and the Reproduction of the Ancestral Past. In *The Anthropology of Landscape: Perspectives on Place and Space,* edited by E. Hirsch and M. O'Hanlon. Oxford: Clarendon Press.

Mort, F. 1996. *Cultures of Consumption: Masculinities and Social Space in Late Twentieth-Century Britian.* London: Routledge.

Munn, N. D. 1971. The Transformation of Subjects into Objects in Walbiri and Pitjantjatjara Myth. In *Australian Aboriginal Anthropology,* edited by R. Berndt. Bedlands: University of Western Australia Press, 141–163,

Munn, N. D. 1986. *The Fame of Gawa: A Symbolic Study of Value Transformation in a Massim (Papua New Guinea) Society.* Cambridge: Cambridge University Press.

Murcott, A., ed. 1998. *The Nation's Diet: The Social Science of Food Choice.* London: Longman.

Myers, F. R. 1986. *Pintupi Country, Pintupi Self: Sentiment, Place and Politics among Western Desert Aborigines.* Washington: Smithsonian Institute Press.

Naipual, V. S. 1987. *The Engima of Arrival: A Novel in Five Sections.* London: Viking.

Neale, B., and C. Smart. 1997. 'Good' and 'Bad' Lawyers? Struggling in the Shadow of the New Law. *Journal of Social Welfare and Family Law* 19 (4): 377–402.

O'Hanlon, M. 1989. *Reading the Skin: Adornment, Display and Society among the Wahgi.* London: British Museum Publications.

O'Shea, J., and C. Madigan. 1997. *Dangerous Company: The Consulting Power-houses and the Businesses They Save and Ruin.* New York: Times Business.

Ogbonna, E., and M. Wilkenson. 1998. Power Relations in the U.K. Grocery Supply Trade. *Journal of Retailing and Consumer Services* 5: 77–86.

Parker, R. 1995. *Torn in Two: The Experience of Maternal Ambivalence.* London: Virago.

Peletz, M. 1995. Kinship Studies in Late Twentieth-Century Anthropology. *Annual Review of Anthropology* 24: 343–372.

Piachaud, D., and J. Webb. 1996. *The Price of Food: Missing Out on Mass Consumption.* London: STICERD.

Pinch, A. 1998. Stealing Happiness: Shoplifting in Early Nineteenth-Century England. In.*Border Fetishisms: Material Objects in Unstable Spaces,* edited by P. Spyer. New York: Routledge, 122–149.

Pippin, R. 1993. You Can't Get There from Here: Transition Problems in Hegel's *Phenomenology of Spirit*. In *The Cambridge Companion to Hegel*, edited by F. Beiser. Cambridge: Cambridge University Press, 52–85.

Porter, R. 1993. Consumption: Disease of the Consumer Society. In *Consumption and the World of Goods*, edited by J. Brewer and R. Porter. London: Routledge.

Radnitzky, G., and P. Bernholz, eds. 1987. *Economic Imperialism: The Economic Approach Applied outside the Field of Economic*. New York: Paragon House Publishers.

Ricoeur, P. 1984–1988. *Time and Narrative*. 3 volumes. Chicago: University of Chicago Press.

Roberts, R. 1973. *The Classic Slum: Salford Life in the First Quarter of the Century*. Harmondsworth: Penguin.

Rose, G. 1996. The Comedy of Hegel and the *Trauerspiel* of Modern Philosophy. In G. Rose, *Mourning Becomes the Law: Philosophy and Representation*. Cambridge: Cambridge University Press.

Schama, S. 1987. *The Embarrassment of Riches: An Interpretation of Dutch Culture in the Golden Age*. London: Collins.

Schneider, D. 1968. *American Kinship: A Cultural Account*. Englewood Cliffs, N.J.: Prentice-Hall.

Seale, C. 1998. *Constructing Death: The Sociology of Dying and Bereavement*. Cambridge: Cambridge University Press

Segal, J. 1998. Consumer Expenditures and the Growth of Need-Required Income. In *Ethics of Consumption: The Good Life, Justice, and Global Stewardship*. Lanham, Md.: Rowman & Littlefield,176–197.

Shachtman, T. 1997. *Around the Block: The Business of a Neighborhood*. New York: Harcourt Brace and Company.

Sherry, J., and M. McGrath. 1989. Unpacking the Holiday Prescence: A Comparative Ethnography of Two Midwestern American Gift Stores. In *Interpretive Consumer Research*, edited by E. Hirschman. Provo, Utah: Association for Consumer Research, 148–167.

Simmonds, P. 1995. Green Consumerism: Blurring the Boundary between Public and Private. In *Debating the Future of the Public Sphere: Transforming the Public and Private Domains in Free Market Societies*, edited by S. Edgell, S. Walklate, and G. Williams. Adlershot: Avebury, 147–161.

Simpson, B. 1997. On Gifts, Payments and Disputes: Divorce and Changing Family Structures in Contemporary Britain. *The Journal of the Royal Anthropological Institute* 3: 731–745.

Smith, N. C. 1990. *Morality and the Market: Consumer Pressure for Corporate Accountability*. London: Routledge.

Sparks, L. 1990. Spatial Structural Relations in the Retail Corporate Sector. *Service Industries Journal* 10: 25–84.

———. 1995. Challenge and Change: Shoprite and the Restructuring of Grocery Retailing in Scotland. *Environment and Planning A* 28: 261–284.

———. Forthcoming. Seven-Eleven, Japan and the Southland Corporation: A Marriage of Convenience. *International Marketing Review.*

Steiner, C. 1994. *African Art in Transit.* Cambridge: Cambridge University Press.

Stevens, S. and T. De Lacy. 1997. *Conservation through Cultural Survival: Indigenous Peoples and Protected Areas.* Washington: Island Press.

Stewart, C. 1994. Honour and Sanctity: Two Levels of Ideology in Greece. *Social Anthropology* 2: 205–228.

Strathern, M. 1979. The Self in Self-Decoration. *Oceania* 44: 241–257.

———. 1981. *Kinship at the Core: An Anthropology of Elmdon, a Village in Northwest Essex in the Nineteen-Sixties.* Cambridge: Cambridge University Press.

———. 1988. *The Gender of the Gift: Problems with Women and Problems with Society in Melanesia.* Berkeley: University of California Press.

———. 1992. *After Nature: English Kinship in the Late Twentieth Century.* Cambridge: Cambridge University Press.

Tacchi, J. 1998. Radio Texture: Between Self and Others. In *Material Cultures: Why Some Things Matter,* edited by D. Miller. Chicago: University of Chicago Press, 25–45.

Tarlo, E. 1996. *Clothing Matters: Dress and Identity in India.* London: Hurst and Company.

Taylor, C. 1975. *Hegel.* Cambridge: Cambridge University Press.

Thrift, N. J. 1996. *Spatial Formations.* London: Sage Publications.

Tilley, C. Y. 1994. *The Phenomenology of Landscape: Places, Paths, and Monuments.* Oxford: Berg.

Tommasi, M., and K. Ierulli, eds. 1995. *The New Economics of Human Behavior.* Cambridge: Cambridge University Press.

Trawick, M. 1990. *Notes on Love in a Tamil Family.* Berkeley: University of California Press.

Warde, A. 1990. Production, Consumption and Social Change: Reservations concerning Peter Saunders's Sociology of Consumption. *International Journal of Urban and Regional Research* 14: 228–248.

Weber, M. 1948. Politics as a Vocation. In *From Max Weber: Essays in Sociology,* edited by H. H. Gerth and C. W. Mills. London: Routledge & Kegan Paul.

Weiner, J. F. 1991. *The Empty Place: Poetry, Space, and Being among the Foi of Papua New Guinea.* Bloomington: Indiana University Press.

Weiss, B. 1996. Coffee Breaks and Coffee Connections: The Lived Experience of a Commodity in Tanzanian and European Worlds. In *Cross-Cultural Consumption: Global Markets, Local Realities,* edited by D. Howes. London: Routledge.

Weiss, B. 1996. *The Making and Unmaking of the Haya Lived World.* Durham: Duke University Press.

Wikan, U. 1990. *Managing Turbulent Hearts: A Balinese Formula for Living.* Chicago: University of Chicago Press.

Wilk, R. 1993. Beauty and the Feast: Official and Visceral Nationalism in Belize. *Ethnos* 58: 294–316.

———. 1997. A Critique of Desire: Distaste and Dislike in Consumer Behaviour. *Consumption Markets and Culture* 1: 175–196.

Willetts, A. 1997. Bacon Sandwiches Got the Better of Me. In *Food, Health, and Identity,* edited by P. Caplan. London: Routledge, 111–130.

Williams, J. 1997. We Never Eat Like This at Home: Food on Holiday in South-West Wales. In *Food, Health, and Identity* edited by P. Caplan. London: Routledge.

Williams, R. 1982. *Dream Worlds: Mass Consumption in Late Nineteenth-Century France.* Berkeley: University of California Press.

Willmott, P. 1987. *Friendship, Networks and Social Support.* London: Policy Studies Institute.

Winnicott, D. 1971. *Playing and Reality.* London: Tavistock Publications.

Wood, A. 1990. *Hegel's Ethical Thought.* Cambridge: Cambridge University Press.

Wrigley, N. 1993. Retail Concentration and the Internationalization of British Grocery Retailing. In *Retail Change,* edited by R. Bromley and G. Thomas. London: UCL Press, 41–68.

———. 1994. After the Store Wars; Towards a New Era of Competition in UK Food Retailing. *Journal of Retailing and Consumer Services* 1: 5–20.

———. 1996. Sunk Costs and Corporate Restructuring: British Food Retailing and the Property Crisis. In *Retailing Consumption and Capital: Towards the New Retail Geography,* edited by N. Wrigley and M. Lowe. Harlow: Longman Group, 116–136.

———. 1998a. Understanding Store Development Programmes in Post-Property-Crisis UK Food Retailing. *Environment and Planning* A 30: 15–35.

———. 1998b. How British Retailers Have Shaped Food Choice. In *The Nation's Diet: The Social Science of Food Choice,* edited by A. Murcott. London: Longman 112–128.

———. 1999. Market Rules and Spatial Outcomes: Insights from the Corporate Restructuring of U.S. Food Retailing. *Geographical Analysis* 31: 288–309.

Wrigley, N., ed. 1998c. Theme Issue: Retail Development. *Environment and Planning* A 30: 13–66.

Wrigley, N., and G. Clarke. Forthcoming. Discount Shake-Out: The Transformation of UK Discount Retailing, 1993–98. *International Review of Retail, Distribution and Consumer Research.*

Wrigley, N. and M. Lowe, eds. 1996. *Retailing Consumption and Capital: Towards the New Retail.* Harlow: Longman Group.

Yanagisako, S., and C. Delaney, eds. 1995. *Naturalizing Power: Essays in Feminist Cultural Analysis.* New York: Routledge.

Young, M., and P. Willmott. 1962. *Family and Kinship in East London.* Harmondsworth: Penguin Books.

———. 1973. *The Symmetrical Family: A Study of Work and Leisure in the London Region.* London: Routledge and Kegan Paul.

Zola, E. [1883]1992. *The Ladies' Paradise.* Berkeley: University of California Press.

 INDEX